Fashion Brands

THIRD EDITION

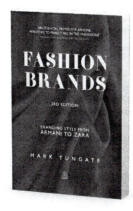

Fashion Brands
Branding style from Armani to Zara

Mark Tungate

KoganPage

LONDON PHILADELPHIA NEW DELHI

Publisher's note

Every possible effort has been made to ensure that the information contained in this book is accurate at the time of going to press, and the publishers and author cannot accept responsibility for any errors or omissions, however caused. No responsibility for loss or damage occasioned to any person acting, or refraining from action, as a result of the material in this publication can be accepted by the editor, the publisher or the author.

First published in Great Britain and the United States in 2005 by Kogan Page Limited
Second edition 2008
Third edition 2012

120 Pentonville Road	1518 Walnut Street, Suite 1100	4737/23 Ansari Road
London N1 9JN	Philadelphia PA 19102	Daryaganj
United Kingdom	USA	New Delhi 110002
www.koganpage.com		India

ISBN   978 0 7494 6446 2
E-ISBN   978 0 7494 6447 9

British Library Cataloguing-in-Publication Data

A CIP record for this book is available from the British Library.

Library of Congress Cataloging-in-Publication Data

Tungate, Mark, 1967-
    Fashion brands : branding style from Armani to Zara / Mark Tungate. – 3rd ed.
       p. cm.
    Includes bibliographical references and index.
    ISBN 978-0-7494-6446-2 – ISBN 978-0-7494-6447-9   1. Fashion merchandising.   2. Branding (Marketing)   3. Advertising–Fashion.   I. Title.
    HD9940.A2T86 2012
    746.9'20688–dc23

                                                                                              2012020099

Typeset by Graphicraft Limited, Hong Kong
Print production managed by Jellyfish
Printed and bound by CPI Group (UK) Ltd, Croydon, CR0 4YY

For my sister, whose fashion icons are
Audrey Hepburn and The Ramones –
and who somehow manages to combine the two.

CONTENTS

PREFACE TO
THE THIRD EDITION

The writer, the book and the wardrobe.

I never expected *Fashion Brands* to reach three editions.

For me, it was a piece of journalism, a snapshot of an industry at a certain period. It was also an exploration of a business I knew very little about at the time. The original idea was to plunge into Paris – my new home, a city I was overjoyed to find myself living in but only just starting to discover – and find out why it considered itself 'the capital of fashion'.

Little did I know that my quest would take me to Milan, New York, Hong Kong – and back to London. Nor did I know that I would be asked to revisit the text, not once, but twice.

I won't pretend that I found it easy. Writing a book is a long, stressful, exhausting business. The hero of Stephen King's *Misery* always lights a cigarette when he's finished a manuscript. Personally, I always feel like closing the blinds and sleeping for about a week.

You may think me pretentious for comparing myself to an author of fiction. But I can't help thinking of my books as stories, with descriptions, intriguing characters and a sort of narrative. In a conventional story, the central character emerges from his experiences changed in some way. When I write my books, that person is usually me.

The first edition of *Fashion Brands* was a success in its own modest way, and it changed my life. It led to freelance work with WGSN, the trend forecasting company. Brands sought me out for advice and copywriting jobs. Students wrote to me asking for help with their theses. I was invited to speak at conferences and universities.

And of course it led to four subsequent books. My career since my early 30s has been shaped in part by *Fashion Brands*. Which is why it always feels odd to go back to it. For one thing there's the tone of the book: tentative, slightly naïve, somewhat apologetic. Today I'm almost part of the fashion business – or at least, I have more legitimacy in the field than I did back then. No doubt I'd adopt a more knowing posture now. Which would be a shame, because I think the reason students enjoy this book so much is that I sound a lot like them.

But there you have it: the book is still popular and the editor wants an update. You don't update novels; you can't update journalism; but apparently it's ok to update a book about fashion.

So how to go about the task? Some of you may feel that I should have simply rewritten the whole book. But then it wouldn't be *this* book, it would be another one. There were practical considerations, too: the leading names in fashion are hardly the most accessible beings on earth; I couldn't see myself calling all of them to ask if I could re-interview them. So my favourite quotes are still here, intact and largely unedited.

I also found that, despite the book's very last sentence, many aspects of fashion branding remained unchanged. Its need to create fantasy worlds, its reliance on celebrities, its ability to stimulate demand by manufacturing trends, even its preference for glossy magazines over alternative media.

There were new matters to address, however. At the time of the first edition there was no Facebook, or Twitter – or iPhone or iPad. I also wanted to talk about the increasing importance of children's fashion, something I've grown acutely aware of since becoming a father a year ago. In the end, I came up with what seemed to be the ideal approach. I decided to treat the book like a wardrobe.

I threw out certain items that were far too moth-eaten or out of date to be seen again. I kept what I considered to be timeless pieces, or those that had aged reasonably well. And I went out and replenished the whole with a few sprightly new additions.

I'll admit the result is something of a patchwork: more of an eccentric, curated collection than a work of sleek modernity. But I like to think that it is still relevant. And what's more, it's still the original book, the one I finished with a sigh very late one night, wondering if it would be of any help to anyone.

Turned out, it was. I hope it still is.

Introduction

You don't buy clothes – you buy an identity.

The model struts towards the battery of cameras, profile held slightly aloft, walking with the curious avian gait that has evolved to flatter the lines of her dress. She does not spare a glance for us mere mortals in the wings; her attention is utterly focused on the arsenal of lenses at the end of the catwalk, which will whirl her image into the global maelstrom of the media barely an instant after she has turned away.

She pauses at the end of her purposeful march, a thigh thrust forward, a hand on a jutting hip, smiling at last as the flashes crackle around her like summer lightning. When she has given her audience what they came for, she swivels imperiously, flinging a contemptuous vestige of inaccessibility in their direction, before marching just as determinedly back to the oxygen-starved planet where only models, fashion designers and billionaires live.

For many consumers, the model's short stroll is the first image that springs to mind at the mention of the word 'fashion'. The runway show – with its combination of creativity, glamour and artifice – is one of the elements that drive us, again and again, to buy clothes we don't really need. It's difficult to think of an industry that does not have recourse to marketing in one form or another, but only fashion has such an overbearing reliance on it. When clothes leave the factories where they are made, they are merely 'garments' or 'apparel'. Only when the marketers get hold of them do they magically become 'fashion'.

There is nothing trivial about fashion. Although there is little consensus on the figure, it is estimated that the amount spent on clothing, footwear and accessories around the world tops US$1 trillion a year. According to Bain & Company, the global luxury goods market is currently worth US$240 billion. Fashion and leather goods account for a large proportion of the sector, alongside perfumes and cosmetics sold under the licensed names of fashion designers. Watches and jewellery take care of the rest. This vast, resilient industry is driven by a number of highly sophisticated marketing and branding techniques, which are well worth dissecting.

And it would be foolish of us to underestimate the importance of fashion in society. Clothes and accessories are expressions of how we feel, how we see ourselves – and how we wish to be treated by others. During my interview with the fashion photographer Vincent Peters (who has taken pictures of some of the most gorgeous people in the world, wearing some of the most expensive clothes), he said, 'Fashion is too prevalent to be considered trivial. Even when you say you're not interested in fashion, you've been forced to confront it. Fashion is everywhere. What you choose to wear or not to wear has become a political statement. You don't buy clothes – you buy an identity.'

This identity is linked to brand values that have been communicated via marketing. Are you elegant, flighty, debonair, streetwise, intellectual, sexy ... or all of the above, depending on your mood? Don't worry: we've got the outfit to match.

But it's not only the outfit that is on offer. Over the past decade or so, fashion has stolen into every corner of the urban landscape. Our mobile phones, our cars, our kitchens, our choice of media and the places where we meet our friends – these, too, have become subject to the vagaries of fashion. It's not enough to wear the clothes; you have to don the lifestyle, too. Fashion brands have encouraged this development by adding their names to a wide range of objects, fulfilling every imaginable function, and selling them in stores that resemble theme parks.

People will go to extreme lengths to consume fashion. Not so long ago, there was a clutch of articles about kids being mugged – even killed – for their sports shoes. While I was researching this book, an uncharacteristically sensationalist article in the French newspaper *Le Figaro* suggested that teenage girls were selling their bodies to raise enough cash to satisfy their addiction to fashion. On a less dramatic scale, few teenagers are unaware of the importance of the right brand, in the right colour, worn in the right way. And, as we're all teenagers these days, adults are becoming just as obsessive. The caprices of fashion are both exasperating and alluring. Its alchemy is mysterious. Most people, even if they refuse to be seduced by it, are intrigued by fashion.

A different view

When I started working on this project, I could make no claims to being an expert. I was just your average trade hack, writing about complex but faintly geeky subjects such as marketing and the media.

My non-fashion background proved advantageous. I could ask naïve questions that a fashion journalist might not have dared to pose for fear of undermining their credibility. I was not in the pay of the industry I was analysing (unlike glossy magazine journalists, who are in thrall to their advertisers), so I could afford to be objective. My distance from the subject enabled me to regard it with a certain irony. I admit to the occasional smirk.

This was not an easy book to research. The fashion industry, as you might expect, can be haughty and insular, and suspicious of outsiders. It was unlikely to open its arms to a journalist who wanted to deconstruct its marketing strategies. The luxury brands, particularly, are built like chateaux, their elegant façades masking impressive battlements. At first I thought the public relations people working at brands such as Chanel and Louis Vuitton were merely dismissive. I was wrong – they were being tactical. Their inaccessibility is part and parcel of their image.

One thing is certain: fashion, even at the top end of the scale, is increasingly about big business. Designers are admirably creative people, but they work for an ever-shrinking number of global conglomerates. Under-performing brands are sold without a hint of remorse, no matter how talented and artistic the people behind them might be. The clothes a designer sends out on to the runway are worthless unless they increase sales of handbags, sunglasses and perfume. Thus, marketing has taken on a crucial significance, and no designer can afford to neglect it.

The designers are not always at ease with this situation. Lanvin designer Alber Elbaz – a man as softly spoken as he is sharply witty – relates an interesting anecdote. Elbaz learnt his craft working for the legendary American designer Geoffrey Beene. One day, Beene asked the young Alber what he thought of a particular dress. 'It's very commercial,' Elbaz opined. Beene took him gently aside and said, 'Alber, you must *never* say a dress is commercial. You must say it is *desirable*.'

Until recently, I considered myself almost immune to brands and their influence. I was certainly suspicious of designer brands that charged a fortune for their labels. I was convinced that their clothes were no better than those of any chain store. I scoffed when a well-known fashion journalist told me during the Paris collections, 'I have two jackets with me, one from Zara and one from Martin Margiela. The Margiela jacket was probably five times the price of the Zara one – but I don't mind, because I like what Margiela stands for.'

Working on this book enhanced my respect for fashion designers, past and present. There cannot be many creative professions in which you are expected to prove your talent with a large body of work at least every six months. In addition, many designers are involved not only with their own collections but also with those of other brands. Certainly, they have large design teams working alongside them – to imagine otherwise would be absurd – but they are the ones who take the flack if the press reception is chilly.

For those outside the industry, it's probably easier to be cynical about fashion than it is to be admiring. As my research progressed, I found that I bounced like a pinball from one mindset to the other. I was surprised that many of the people involved in fashion marketing – the photographers, the art directors, the event organizers – retained a sense of humour about it. Yet they enjoyed grappling with an increasingly intellectual challenge. Apart from the stores they are sold in – and the bags we carry them home in – clothes have no packaging. They just sit on shelves, waiting mutely to be judged on their own appearance. All the packaging has to be done externally; otherwise, how would we know that this particular shirt represents a whole range of emotions and messages that we are supposed to be buying into?

Fashion branding may be an ephemeral business, but it is a complex and endlessly fascinating one. How does one turn a mere 'garment' into an object with seemingly mystical transformative powers? Well, let's hear it from the experts.

Author's Note: This book was originally written in 2005, with new editions in 2008 and 2012. The statistics and job titles quoted date from the period when the interviews and research were conducted. All quotes were taken from original interviews or conferences, unless otherwise stated in the text.

A history of seduction

01

Fashion is a factory that manufactures desire.

Everything began in Paris. Later we'll turn to New York and Milan, to London and Tokyo, but most experts agree that fashion, as we know it today, was born in the French capital.

From the days when the couturier Worth designed dresses for Empress Eugénie, the wife of Napoleon III, to the final episode of *Sex and the City* – surely the most fashion-conscious television series of recent times – Paris has been a byword for style. As Bruno Remaury, social anthropologist and lecturer at the Institut Français de la Mode, the leading French fashion school, points out, 'The very word "fashion" comes from the French: *façon* means to work in a certain manner, and *travaux à façon* is the traditional French term for dressmaking.'

Paris still perspires fashion. On the Right Bank, historically the commercial heart of the city, the fashion zone opens like a jewelled fan from the fulcrum of the Musée de la Mode, housed in a wing of the Louvre. It takes in the glittering boutiques along the Rue du Faubourg Saint Honoré (also home to the French edition of *Vogue*), the über-hip designer outlet Colette, the department stores of Printemps and Galeries Lafayette, and several branches of the hyper-successful retail chains H&M and Zara – not to mention acres of billboard space promoting lingerie, perfume, bags or sunglasses, depending on the season. And this is by no means all: outside that better-known fashion zone, there are many other significant style hotspots, including the Avenue Montaigne, Saint Germain and Le Marais.

In all of these places you'll find queues in front of fitting rooms and people drooling over window displays, branded handbags slung over their arms. Those who work in the fashion industry will tell you it's in crisis, but on the streets there is little evidence to back up this claim. The activity during the sales season in Paris is like a cross-breed of rugby and boxing, without the nice manners. At the beginning of the 21st century, it's terribly trendy to be fashionable.

The question is – why?

Style addicts

Fashion brands employ many techniques to persuade us to part with our hard-earned cash in return for the transient thrill of wearing something new. In our hearts we know it's all smoke and mirrors – most of us have plenty to wear, and none of it is going to fall apart for a while yet. So why do we keep buying clothes? Can it really all be about marketing?

As fashion scholar Bruno Remaury points out, 'Traditional marketing is based on need. You take a product that corresponds to an existing demand, and attempt to prove that your product is the best in its category. But fashion is based on creating a need where, in reality, there is none. Fashion is a factory that manufactures desire.'

Many of those who work in the fashion business seem surprised – or at least mildly amused – by consumers' willingness to be seduced. Fashion consultant Jean-Jacques Picart, who has worked with brands such as Christian Lacroix and Louis Vuitton, comments as follows: 'For the people who are genuinely obsessed with fashion, it's a sort of drug. This is a personal theory, but I believe it's because they equate exterior change with interior change. They feel that, if they've changed their "look" they've also evolved emotionally.'

He hints that a preoccupation with fashion reveals a level of insecurity. 'The most extreme fashionistas have a vulnerable quality about them. It's as if they are worried about being judged. They live in a state of perpetual anxiety about their appearance.'

With disarming frankness, Picart describes his job as 'a little cynical, a little perverse'. 'The métier of fashion has a sole objective: to create brand appeal, in the same way that one might try to create sex appeal. Everything we do is designed to make people fall in love with our brand. All the trimmings of our industry – the shows, the advertising, the celebrities, the media coverage – all of these things work together so that, if we've done our job well, somebody will push open the door of a shop.'

It all sounds fiendishly modern. But of course, although the bait has grown in sophistication, fashion branding has been around almost as long as the Venus flytrap.

The first fashion brand

For our purposes, fashion originated in Paris at the end of the 19th century. That was when the first designer label was created. Although its main market was France, its founder was English.

Charles Frederick Worth changed the rules of the game. Before he came along, dressmakers did not create styles or dictate fashion; they were mere suppliers, who ran up copies of gowns that their wealthy clients had seen in illustrated journals or admired at society gatherings. The clients themselves chose the fabrics and colours, and dresses were constructed around them, rather like scaffolding. Worth was the first couturier to impose his own taste on women – in effect, he was the prototype celebrity fashion designer.

Worth was born in the town of Bourne, Lincolnshire on 13 October 1826. Like many of history's most imaginative designers – from Saint Laurent to Gaultier – he came from a relatively humble background. (Indeed, the desire to escape a humdrum existence via sumptuous dresses and beautiful women is a thread running through the history of fashion.) He was the son of a local solicitor, William Worth, who appears to have run into financial difficulties when Charles was just a boy. Assuming that it was now up to him to put bread on the family table, Charles headed for London, where he became an apprentice and later a bookkeeper at a drapery firm called Swan and Edgar in Piccadilly. It was here that he developed an eye for sumptuous fabrics and showed the prodigious flair for salesmanship that was to serve him so well. At the age of 20, and by now burning with ambition, he left for Paris.

Worth got a job at the drapery house of Gagelin and Opigez at 83 Rue Richelieu. When he was not busy attending to the needs of his clients, he designed dresses for his new French bride, Marie Vernet, who also worked in the store. Soon, customers began to notice these elegant creations, which, although adhering to the bottom-heavy style of the day, seemed to have an extra dash of cut and colour. Worth was given a small department at the back of the establishment in which to display his designs. These could be made to measure for customers who admired them.

Gagelin and Opigez were unwilling to let Worth expand his business, so, with the backing of a wealthy young Swedish draper called Otto Bobergh, he branched out on his own. Worth & Bobergh was established at 7 Rue de la Paix in 1858. Although Worth had a number of influential clients, his big break came when he designed a gown for Princess Metternich, wife of the Austrian ambassador to Paris. Empress Eugénie spotted the dress at a ball in the Tuileries Palace, and summoned its designer.

Worth was soon dressing the world's most glamorous women. Unlike his predecessors, he was not a fawning servant, forced to make imitations of gowns his clients had seen elsewhere. As far as he was concerned, he had a better idea of how to enhance their looks than they did. Slowly but surely, he did away with bonnets and crinolines and began cutting dresses closer to the body. Hoop skirts were replaced by the infinitely more seductive 'sheath' dress – albeit garnished with bustles and trains that required cascades of expensive fabric.

More to the point, Worth was a marketing genius. Previously, dress designs had been displayed on wooden busts. (Scaled-down versions were sewn minutely on to dolls, which were sent out to potential clients as promotional devices.) Worth was the first couturier to sit his clients down and give them a little show – having first dressed a series of attractive young women he called *sosies*, or 'doubles', in his creations – thus inventing the concept of the fashion model. He would also identify fashionable women on whom he could place his dresses, knowing they would create a buzz as they mingled in high society. In private, he contemptuously referred to them as 'jockeys'.

In addition, Worth looked and acted like a proper fashion designer. Dapper and moustachioed, dressed from head to toe in velvet, a beret perched on his head, a cigar between his ostentatiously be-ringed fingers, he would greet clients while reclining on a divan. He had a capricious temper, too – there are reports of him furiously ripping half-finished garments to pieces because they were not exactly as he had envisaged them. Potential clients could be turned down, existing customers banished.

Here, already, we have many of the ingredients of contemporary fashion marketing: runway shows, celebrity models, elitism and, of course, a charismatic brand spokesman. Dictatorial and flamboyant, this was a man who rose from obscurity to become deified by the fabulously rich – by the time he died, on 10 March 1885, Worth had established a pattern for all other designers to follow. Certainly, he exhibited a high level of artistry, but of all the dressmakers of that period he was the first to wrap his own name in a fairy tale and resell it at a profit.

Poiret raises the stakes

The one constant of fashion is constant change. Although Worth left his business in the capable hands of his two sons, Gaston and Jean-Philippe, his brand could not remain at the forefront of style for ever. This is not to say that it didn't have a pretty good run. A stand at the Paris Exposition of 1900 did a roaring trade, and the Worth name continued to resonate up to and beyond the 1920s (with a branded Worth perfume being launched as late as 1925). By then, though, the torch had been passed on not once, but twice.

The young designer Paul Poiret, recruited to Maison Worth by Jean-Philippe, soon began to challenge the restrictive styles of his masters. The son of a fabric merchant, Poiret had started out as an apprentice umbrella maker. In his spare time he had begun using umbrella silk to dress dolls in experimental designs. Poiret wanted to free women from the over-complicated structures that encumbered the upper body. Eventually he would banish the corset altogether, revolutionizing the way women dressed.

As is often the case, Poiret's employers weren't ready to embrace his radical ideas, and in 1904 he opened his own shop in the Rue du Faubourg Saint Honoré. In the years that followed, Poiret altered the outline of women's clothing for good. First came his interpretation of the Empire line: long straight dresses falling from a high waist that emphasized the bust. Then there was the 'hobble' skirt, cut so straight and narrow that its wearer could take only tiny steps (somewhat undermining claims that his clothes 'liberated' women). Inspired by fantasies of the Orient and the exotic Ballets Russes, Poiret devised variants of the kimono and baggy harem pants. The latter caused a sensation because, in fashion as in relationships, women were not expected to wear the trousers. Poiret went on to blur the boundaries between art and fashion, recruiting painters such as Georges Lapape and Raoul Dufy to illustrate his catalogues, and decorating his store in a style that prefigured Art Deco.

Like Worth before him, Poiret had a practical yet sophisticated approach to promoting his products. In 1911 he became the first couturier to launch a branded perfume, which he called Rosine after his eldest daughter. Poiret picked out the fragrance and designed the bottle, the packaging and the advertising. That same year, he threw a lavish party called 'The Thousand and Second Night', a fancy-dress extravaganza to which guests came as Persian royalty or cohorts of Scheherazade. The designer himself sported a natty gold turban. The most fashionable names in Europe were there, along with selected members of the press.

Poiret opened branded boutiques in major French cities and organized travelling fashion shows. He designed dresses for the actress Sarah Bernhardt, his very own celebrity muse. Later, when he refused to sell any more dresses to a certain member of the Rothschild family – who had apparently dared to mutter a criticism at one of his shows – he made sure the decision was widely broadcast.

Not all of his marketing efforts were entirely self-serving, however. In that golden year of 1911, he opened an atelier in which Parisian girls 'from modest backgrounds' were trained to produce fabrics, rugs, lampshades and other accessories for the home. These were sold in a boutique and several department stores under the Poiret sub-brand 'Martine', this time named after his youngest daughter.

But despite his talent, his marketing prowess and his influence, Poiret could not halt the onward march of fashion. His star was already descending after the First World War, and by the 1920s he was locked in bitter rivalry with the woman who was to become the fashion icon of the era, Gabrielle 'Coco' Chanel. According to Guillaume Erner in the book *Victimes de la Mode?* (2004), Poiret referred to Coco as 'the inventor of misery'. Bumping into Chanel in her black ensemble one evening, Poiret exclaimed, 'You must be in mourning! But for whom?' Chanel is reputed to have replied, 'For you, my dear.'

Poiret wasn't quite ready to slip away. In 1925, during the Art Deco Exposition, he hired three vast Seine barges. The first he turned into a restaurant, the second a hairdressing salon, and the third a boutique selling his perfumes, accessories and furnishings. It was to be his last extravagance. In the words of Erner, 'While the barges stayed afloat, the business sank.'

Chanel, Dior and beyond

Gabrielle Chanel considered that Poiret's dresses were costumes rather than clothes, and a growing number of women seemed to agree with her. 'Eccentricity was dying: I hoped, by the way, that I helped to kill it,' she said, as quoted in the book *L'Allure de Chanel* by Paul Morand (1996). Rubbing salt into the wound, she added that it was easy to attract attention dressed as Scheherazade, but a little black dress showed more class. 'Extravagance kills personality,' she pronounced.

Whatever the truth of these claims, there is no arguing with the fact that Chanel took fashion into the 20th century. But the move had actually been precipitated by social change. During the First World War, women worked in factories and fields and grew accustomed to the simplicity of uniforms. When it was all over, they were underfed but hardy, and unwilling to slip back into the traditional housewife/goddess role. (Many of them had, in any case, lost husbands and fiancés.) This was also the era of the automobile, which led to a more practical approach: short hair, skirts above the knee and tweed car coats. Women became less overtly feminine. Chanel and others – notably Jean Patou – adopted and embellished the androgynous style.

With her quotable wit and her talent for mixing with the right crowd, Coco fits right in to our alternative history of fashion – one that emphasizes the power of marketing. We certainly shouldn't forget her perfume, simply named No.5 because it was the fifth in a series of samples she had to choose from. It was notable for being the first unabashedly synthetic scent, which contributed to its image of modernity.

While Chanel was busy twisting the fashion writers around her little finger, other designers were demonstrating that they also knew a promotional trick or two. Although her brand did not prove as resistant as that of Chanel (and, let's face it, few did), Elsa Schiaparelli was a formidable pre-war competitor. Salvador Dali collaborated on her dress designs – notably providing a cheeky lobster print – and the curvaceous bottle containing her perfume, Shocking, was supposed to have been modelled on the bust of the actress Mae West. Unfortunately, such publicity coups could not sustain her business through the dark years of the 1940s.

War, of course, changed everything again. Although a number of fashion houses sprang up in occupied Paris, Jacques Fath and Nina Ricci among them, the focus shifted to the United States. Until that time, fashionable American women bought expensive gowns that had been imported from Paris, or had more affordable copies run up closer to home. Even before the war, manufacturers on Seventh Avenue in New York had begun experimenting with synthetic fabrics, faster production techniques and light, interchangeable garments. This development accelerated in the 1940s, and New York became the birthplace of ready-to-wear. By the time peace broke out, the hegemony of Paris as the world's fashion capital was being challenged. Wartime innovations had shown that 'chic' need not mean personal dressmakers or 'haute couture'. For the first time, fashion was no longer the preserve of the wealthy elite.

Not that Paris had relinquished its importance. The 1950s saw the rise of Christian Dior, a man whose fervour for promotion outstripped even that of his predecessors. As well as being a visionary designer, the inventor of 'The New Look' was a moneymaking machine. He launched his first perfume in 1947 and a ready-to-wear store in New York in 1948. By the end of the decade, he had licensed his brand to a range of ties and stockings. He opened branches all over the world, from London to Havana. By the time he died prematurely, in 1957, he was employing over a thousand people – a situation previously unheard of for a couturier. More than anybody before him, Dior realized that luxury could be repackaged as a mass product. Not only that, he considered it the key to the survival and profitability of a brand. As quoted by Erner, he once commented, 'You know fashion: one day success, the next the descent into hell,' adding, 'I know lots of recipes, and one day ... they might come in useful. Dior ham? Dior roast beef? Who knows?' Perhaps it's no surprise that, today, the Dior brand is owned by the LVMH (Louis-Vuitton Moët Hennessy) empire – the ultimate expression of luxury as big business.

Beyond Dior, the dictatorship of the brand took hold. Even in the 1960s, when fashion was democratized and everyone claimed the right to be stylish, the marketers had the upper hand. When asked who invented the mini-skirt, herself or the French designer André Courrèges, Mary Quant replied generously, 'Neither – it was invented by the street.' Nevertheless, Quant was one of several designers who translated Sixties youth culture into profit, with considerable success.

Another such designer, on an entirely different scale, was Pierre Cardin, a man for whom extending the brand was little short of a crusade. A protégé of Christian Dior, naturally, Cardin noted very early on the decline of haute couture and acknowledged the potential of ready-to-wear (prêt-à-porter). He opened one store called Eve and another named Adam. He demanded, and got, a corner of the Parisian department store Printemps reserved exclusively for his brand. A darling of the media, he followed Dior's example by licensing his increasingly marketable identity, and today more than 800 different products around the world bear his name. In her (1999) book *The End of Fashion*, Teri Agins comments, 'There was always a manufacturer somewhere who was ready to slap "Pierre Cardin" on hair dryers, alarm clocks, bidets, and frying pans. "My name is more important than myself," Cardin once said.' Agins goes on to quote Henri Berghauer, who helped to manage Cardin's empire in the 1950s: 'Pierre realized early that he wanted to be more of a label than a designer. He wanted to be Renault.'

Although this strategy generated a vast personal fortune, it also undermined the sense of exclusivity that is the core value of any luxury brand. The Cardin label has languished in the purgatory of the un-hip since the 1990s, and is only now seeing the first glimmer of a resurgence. The future of the brand could depend on whether the designer, aged 82 at the time of writing, decides to sell his business – although buyers have apparently balked at the asking price. 'One billion euros, minimum,' he told a newspaper reporter in 2011. 'I work on the principle that, when I died, the business will be sold.

So it might as well be me who does it.' In the same piece, he estimates that he now has 700 licences in 100 countries ('Pierre Cardin: My name is worth a million', *La Provence*, 19 May 2011).

It's impossible to talk about the fashion brands of the 1960s – or indeed the 1970s – without mentioning Yves Saint Laurent. Initially the successor to Dior, Saint Laurent quickly broke away to follow his own path, and it soon transpired that he was able to have his cake and eat it too. He was hailed as a genius of haute couture by the runway-watchers, while at the same time luring shoppers to his 'luxury prêt-à-porter' store, Saint Laurent Rive Gauche, in Paris's Saint Germain district. YSL was keen on licensing, too, but, along with his business partner, Pierre Bergé, he kept a closer eye on quality control than Cardin had done. His biggest hit was a perfume, Opium, which launched in 1978 and remains popular today.

Throughout the 1970s the democratization of fashion continued apace. Art schools pumped out rebellious young designers, rock fell in love with avant-garde clothing, the fashion press exploded and the first generation of 'stylists' – those benign dictators of dress – told consumers what to wear and how to wear it.

In France, the *ancien régime* of haute couture experienced a paroxysm of self-doubt, as prêt-à-porter took the high ground and street-wear usurped aristocratic glamour. The French also faced a new challenge from across the Alps, where the Italian textile and leather merchants began developing their own brands. As early as 1965, the Italian leather goods and fur business Fendi was working with a talented young designer called Karl Lagerfeld, who helped to turn the small company into a ravishing brand. And Fendi was not the only Italian player; among the many others were Armani, Gucci, Cerruti, Krizia and Missoni, to name but a few. The London of the 1970s boasted plenty of fresh ideas, associated with names such as Ossie Clark, Anthony Price, Zandra Rhodes and the short-lived concept store Biba, but the real powerhouses of the future were being created in Milan. Until a French tycoon called Bernard Arnault began laying the foundations for LVMH in the 1980s, the Milanese seemed to have the monopoly on luxury as a business. They were traders at heart, and they knew how to marry art with commerce in a way that many French labels hadn't quite grasped.

The death of fashion

When did fashion stop being fashionable? To paraphrase Hemingway, it happened slowly, and then very quickly. Probably the rot set in around the mid- to late 1980s, provoked by a boom-to-bust economy and the emergence of AIDS as a powerful metaphor for the delayed hangover that followed the 1970s. The effect of the disease was terrifyingly real as it tore through the creative economy, robbing it of some of its brightest emerging stars.

Not that this grim decade was entirely devoid of hope. By now the most interesting thing on the catwalk was definitely in prêt-à-porter, with extraordinary creations from Jean-Paul Gaultier, Thierry Mugler and Kenzo. Elsewhere, Karl Lagerfeld was busy revitalizing Chanel – where he was appointed in 1983 – and Christian Lacroix was showing flamboyant dresses inspired by his passion for opera, folklore and the history of costume. This was, after all, the time of the New Romantic. The period also saw the emergence of the Japanese designers, notably Yohji Yamamoto and Rei Kawakubo (of Comme des Garçons), whose ethereal black numbers combined minimalist rigour with futuristic interpretations of traditional garb. More costume than dress, they served as inspiration for the monochrome severity that characterized the tail-end of the 1980s.

More than anything, though, this was the era of the yuppie, the young upwardly mobile professional, whose clothing signified success. 'Power dressing' became a buzz phrase. Giorgio Armani's unstructured but easily identifiable suits were worn as a badge of success. In the UK, while providing flashy City boys with eccentrically reworked interpretations of the tailored suit – his trademark 'classics with a twist' – Paul Smith also discovered the Filofax, a leather-bound 'personal organizer' manufactured by a tiny East End company. By popularizing this combination of address book and diary, which implied that its user had people to see and places to go, Smith handed the yuppies their ultimate accessory.

Meanwhile, on the other side of the Atlantic, Ralph Lauren had been steadily building one of the ultimate fashion brands. His rag-trade-to-riches story has been told many times before, but it's worth briefly repeating here.

Born Ralph Lifshitz in 1939, the United States' most upwardly mobile designer was the son of Russian Jewish immigrants from the Bronx. His father was a house painter, who changed the family name to Lauren when young Ralph was still at school. Ralph was brought up on the Hollywood movies of the 40s and 50s, mentally filing away images of Cary Grant and Fred Astaire so that he could recreate their style. He got his start in the fashion business selling suits at Brooks Brothers, and later became a wholesaler of ties and gloves in New York's garment district. Soon he began designing his own ties, choosing the name 'Polo' for its aristocratic associations. The stylish neckwear proved a big hit at Bloomingdale's, and by 1970 Ralph had taken over a corner of the Manhattan department store with an entire range of upmarket apparel.

According to Teri Agins, 'Lauren will go down in fashion history for introducing the concept of "lifestyle merchandizing" in department stores ... Lauren designed [his] outpost to feel like a gentlemen's club, with mahogany panelling and brass fixtures.' She goes on to say that Lauren's stores 'stirred all kinds of longings in people, the dream that the upwardly mobile shared for prestige, wealth and exotic adventure'. But Ralph Lauren is important for another reason. European luxury brands frequently dwell on their 'heritage' for marketing purposes, using a tradition of craftsmanship as a way of seducing consumers and justifying elevated prices (think of Hermès, Louis Vuitton, Dunhill and Asprey). Almost subconsciously, Lauren realized that, in the United States, history was irrelevant. This was the land of Hollywood, of fantasy for sale.

Lauren created a world of aristocratic good taste, but it was pure invention. In the end, his success rested on the quality of his clothes and his knack for branding. Lauren's shops were film sets, and his advertising campaigns – shot by Bruce Weber – were stills from movies that had never been made. It's no surprise to learn that Lauren designed the costumes for the film *The Great Gatsby*. In many ways, Lauren *was* Jay Gatsby – the man who created himself.

Ralph Lauren was the perfect brand for the 1980s, when fashion became less important than 'lifestyle'. In fact, with the rise of the supermodel, the media seemed more interested in how the models lived than in the clothes they wore.

Fashion clutched its chest and keeled over some time in the 1990s. In *The End of Fashion*, Teri Agins suggests that women lost interest in fashion because they were more concerned about their careers: '[They] began to behave more like men in adopting their own uniform: skirts and blazers and pantsuits that gave them an authoritative, polished, power look.'

In addition, the Paris catwalks had lost their relevance in the face of MTV culture and street-wear. Levi's, Nike and Gap seemed a lot more connected to quotidian reality than some ethereal vision on a runway. Tracksuit-wearing rappers and the chino-clad super-nerds of the dotcom boom were the new icons; 'casual Friday' elided into the rest of the week. Stores selling comfortable but unchallenging garments, mostly run up on the cheap in Asia, made dressing down not only affordable, but acceptable. The elitist stance once taken by fashion brands began to look stuffy and – horror of horrors – old-fashioned. Clothing became a commodity, spare and functional. Even supermodels began to look less 'super'. Kate Moss, in her first incarnation as a grungy teenager, had nothing of the femme fatale about her. Calvin Klein built a phenomenally successful brand around posters featuring Moss and other androgynous youths sporting baggy jeans and nothing else; it was the 'simple chic' ethic taken to the nth degree.

Finally, many fashion houses were acquired by or grew into vast corporations, selling clothing, accessories, make-up and furniture. As Teri Agins explains, 'Such fashion houses just also happen to be publicly traded companies, which must maintain steady, predictable growth for their shareholders ... Fashion... requires a certain degree of risk-taking and creativity that is impossible to explain to Wall Street.' Further, she observes that the utilitarian blandness of 90s clothing made marketing more important than ever. Branding played a critical role 'in an era when... just about every store in the mall [was] peddling the same styles of clothes'.

Today, while branding remains as crucial as ever, its raison d'être has changed. Nine years on from the publication of Agins' book, fashion has – inevitably – transformed itself again. Style has come out of the closet.

The rebirth of fashion

The glamour factory had been plotting its resurgence all along, humming away in the background throughout the late 1990s, while industry observers fretted about the rising tide of 'smart casual'. The next wave of upmarket fashion brands would come from Milan and from Paris; clearly, reports of the death of the French capital had been greatly exaggerated.

There is one name you can't escape when you attempt to write a history of fashion branding: Tom Ford. As Carine Roitfeld, then editor of French *Vogue* and a one-time collaborator of the American designer, said, 'In the history of fashion, there's definitely a pre-Tom Ford and a post-Tom Ford period. He was one of the first contemporary designers who really understood the power of marketing. He was not a snob about his work – he wanted to sell.'

The story of Gucci resembles an opera, replete with glamour, envy and murder. More on that later, but for now it's enough to say that Ford realized (like all the smartest designers, from Worth to Lauren) that the key to a successful fashion label lay not just in the garments, but in the 'universe' surrounding them. Or, as Roitfeld put it, 'He created a dream world.'

It was fine that in winter 1995 Ford showed a collection of sexy, sophisticated clothes that attracted the attention of Madonna and Gwyneth Paltrow. Even better that he reintroduced the bamboo-handled bags that had been the making of Gucci back in the 1950s. But he also redesigned every aspect of the brand, from print advertisements to stores, ensuring that everything gelled to create an 'ideal' of what the Gucci name meant. According to Guillaume Erner, 'The Texan turned the style of the brand upside down: previously everything that bore the Gucci name had been brown, soft, and rounded. With him, it became black, hard, and square.'

So what did the Gucci name mean, exactly? It meant sex. Ford brought lust back into fashion with a series of overtly erotic ads that were quickly tagged 'porno chic'. A famously over-the-top example showed a crouching man gazing at the Gucci logo shaved into a woman's pubic hair – beautifully photographed, of course. While outwardly deploring the trend, the mainstream media had great fun with fashion's filthy new image. Sex, as everyone knows, always sells, and many consumers wanted in. Even those who could only afford to buy their jeans from Gap found some extra cash for a Gucci belt. As Roitfeld observes, '[Ford] created clothes people wanted to wear, and then he explained to them that if they couldn't afford the dress, they could at least buy the sunglasses.'

Ford was not the only one giving the rarefied world of fashion a much-needed kick up the rear. At the same time, Miuccia Prada – with the aid of her husband and business partner Patrizio Bertelli – was blowing the dust off the old family luggage firm in Milan. Prada, too, understood that the brand message had to be carried right through from advertising to clothing to store. Taking the opposite stance to Gucci's sex-drenched imagery, Miuccia positioned her brand as creative, sensitive and politically engaged. New York intellectuals and London businesswomen loved it. The Prada bag replaced the Filofax as the status symbol of choice, and the shoes and clothing quickly followed.

But what was happening in Paris? By the end of the 1990s the city was a shadow of its former self, its image as the world's fashion capital eroded by the slow decline of haute couture and the rapid ascent of Milan, not to mention the dominance of US pop culture and the influence of American designers. As unlikely as it may seem, the resurrection of Paris as the world's most glamorous city can be credited to one ascetic, understated businessman.

Bernard Arnault was already on the rise in 1984, when he acquired Christian Dior. Two decades later, he is president of both Dior and LVMH, with a glittering portfolio of brands that includes Céline, Kenzo, Thomas

Pink, Givenchy, Loewe, Fendi, Pucci, Marc Jacobs and Donna Karan – not to mention Louis Vuitton itself. And although the two men have radically different personalities, Arnault's tactics are not dissimilar to those of Tom Ford.

'I met Bernard Arnault in 1985, and he was already nurturing the idea of a luxury brand that would be at the same time relatively accessible,' recalls the fashion marketing consultant Jean-Jacques Picart, who is also Arnault's personal communications adviser. 'Dior now has hundreds of boutiques around the world, so it can't be described as a luxury brand in the classic sense of the term, which implies exclusive. [Arnault's] stroke of genius was to bring marketing techniques to a world that had previously claimed to have no use for them.'

As far as Dior was concerned, Arnault's most inspired move was the appointment of a charismatic designer named John Galliano. (Legend has it that Arnault made his choice by arranging a meeting of the world's top fashion journalists, and asking them who they thought was the world's most creative designer.) Galliano didn't arrive at Dior directly: he was first appointed at Givenchy, following the reluctant retirement of the illustrious Hubert de Givenchy. But it seemed as though he was being groomed for Dior all along: when the Italian designer Gianfranco Ferré left the fashion house, Galliano was brought in to replace him. Rebellious Londoner Alexander McQueen then slid into the hot seat at Givenchy, further illustrating Arnault's penchant for shaking up the conservative world of French high fashion, and reaping plenty of media exposure in the process. Arnault would repeat the trick by bringing in hip New York designer Marc Jacobs to revamp Louis Vuitton.

In the opinion of Jean-Jacques Picart, 'One of the things that can enable a fashion brand to stand out is transgression. At the end of the 1990s, when fashion leaned towards the minimalist, John exploded on to the scene with a personal vision inspired by history and costume. It was baroque, excessive, warm, rich, flamboyant, brimming over with decadence and sex. It was also completely at odds with the existing image of Dior. It had the effect of a firework display.'

Gucci, Prada and Dior's formula of young, inventive clothes and afford-able accessories, plus aggressive marketing, seemed to reanimate the public's inner fashion victim. Ford and Galliano were personally photogenic and exciting – as entertaining in their own way as rock stars. Fortuitously, their makeover of previously moribund brands coincided with the media's increasing obsession with the cult of celebrity and the rise of magazines like

Heat and *OK!* When the paparazzi captured Victoria Beckham or Jennifer Lopez swathed in designer brands, millions of young women wanted to imitate them.

Of course, as we've already pointed out, few ordinary folk could afford a Prada suit or a Dior dress. Even if they could stretch to a handbag or a pair of sunglasses, where did they get the clothes to match? Enter Zara, H&M and Topshop – high-street brands employing talented young designers who produced fun, fresh creations that wouldn't look out of place on the Paris runways, and were sometimes directly inspired by them. (See Chapter 3: When haute couture meets high street.) By the end of the millennium, fashion was glamorous again.

Surviving the crash

As dream merchants, fashion brands are curiously resilient. In September 2001, a minor war had been preoccupying industry-watchers for several months. The conflict ranged Bernard Arnault against another French businessman, François Pinault, owner of the retail and mail-order conglomerate Pinault-Printemps-Redoute (PPR). The disputed territory was Gucci.

Arnault had been stealthily buying shares in Gucci with the intention of taking over the company. By 1999 his stake had reached 34 per cent. But neither Tom Ford nor Gucci CEO Domenico De Sole liked the idea of being swallowed up by LVMH, where they suspected they would lose control of the brand. Their white knight arrived in the form of François Pinault, who snapped up 40 per cent of Gucci's shares. He also acquired beauty and cosmetics company Sanofi, which owned Yves Saint Laurent. In a couple of swift moves, Pinault had created Gucci Group, a potential rival to LVMH.

The flurry of acquisitions that followed on both sides looked like a duel between billionaires – Monopoly played for real. As LVMH continued its rapid expansion, the Gucci Group took possession of Boucheron, Bottega Veneta and Balenciaga, and signed partnership deals with Alexander McQueen (who left LVMH's Givenchy amid considerable tongue-wagging) and Stella McCartney. Meanwhile, the bitter dispute over who had the right to take control of Gucci was tied up in court in the Netherlands, where Gucci's shares were listed.

Finally, in the economic dip provoked by the dotcom crash – and almost as if he sensed that he needed to conserve his resources for the difficult period ahead – Arnault gave up the fight. On 10 September 2001, he sold his

Gucci shares, allowing his arch-rival François Pinault to take full ownership of the company. The *guerre du luxe*, as the French press had termed the conflict, was over.

We all know what happened the next day. In New York, the fashion carnival was in town for the spring–summer collections. The huge marquees that would be the setting for many of the shows had been erected in Bryant Park, practically within view of the Twin Towers. The industry was therefore witness to the horror that was to cause its latest nervous breakdown.

It seems almost churlish to try to place an event as tragic and far-reaching as 11 September 2001 within the context of fashion. But the interesting fact is that, after a dramatic slump, the industry emerged from the disaster in rather better shape than anyone had a right to expect.

On 19 December 2001, an article in *The Independent* reported, 'Profits fall by half at Gucci and Italian fashion giant predicts no upturn until late 2002.' Fast-forward to 16 October 2003, and a headline in *The Guardian*: 'Fashion back in fashion as Gucci sales surge.' Later (23 January 2004), again in *The Independent*: 'LVMH's luxury defies the downturn.' In *Time* magazine's autumn 2004 Style and Design supplement, an article headlined 'Luxury Fever' commented, 'Despite rising interest rates, staggering energy prices... and the general state of unrest in the world, conspicuous consumption is back.'

Four years later the tables were turning again, as the world plunged back into recession. By then, however, luxury houses like LVMH and PPR were the guardians of a wide range of products across many different markets. As consumers in the West began to tighten their wallets, high-end fashion brands were able to focus their marketing firepower on the emerging markets of Asia, particularly China. As other sectors faltered, the luxury industry registered reassuring growth. Back home, Paris saw the emergence of mid-market fashion brands that had filled the gap by borrowing from the vocabulary of luxury while offering marginally more accessible prices: the likes of Sandro, Maje, Zadig & Voltaire and The Kooples.

Right now, confidence is returning. We need to take a break from fashion occasionally, but sooner or later we come back for more. And if they've been smart enough, our favourite brands are waiting for us.

Fashioning an identity

02

In a lot of ways, branding is simply telling a story.

Exploring the fashion world occasionally feels like gate-crashing an exclusive club. At least, that's the sensation I experience as I climb a spiral staircase in a building near Place Vendôme – the grand Parisian square that is home to the Ritz. César Ritz opened his celebrated hotel on 1 June 1898, and its rich patrons attracted the attentions of Cartier, Boucheron, Van Cleef & Arpels, and the other jewellery and luxury goods boutiques that crowd the square.

This particular building is the headquarters of a publishing firm, but its location is entirely appropriate. Over the past 10 years, Assouline has published a series of glossy books, each minutely dissecting the history of a legendary designer label. With offices in Paris, London and New York, it has become a luxury brand in its own right. I reckon that here, at least, I should get my first insight into what makes a fashion icon.

As so often on these occasions, the claustrophobic staircase and labyrinthine corridors of the old building lead to a large office, with a bright picture window overlooking the potted trees and shrubs in the courtyard. Martine Assouline, an elegant French woman, sits me down at a glossy slab-like table and considers her response to my question.

'We live in an era where the brand has an exaggerated importance,' she tells me. 'Designers like Tom Ford, John Galliano and Marc Jacobs injected new life into fashion. They fused it with the music and film industries in a manner that seemed very new, very attractive. This was not always the case – in the era of the supermodel, nobody really cared about brands. Naomi Campbell and Claudia Schiffer were the brands; the clothes were immaterial. But fashion has come down to earth – it appears more accessible, more affordable, even when this is not the case. People identify with Prada, Dior and Louis Vuitton in a way that they never did before.'

But do these brands have anything in common? What's the uniting factor that has enabled them to succeed and survive?

'It's a heritage that makes customers daydream, and the strength to live up to it. The question of succession is important: Chanel was lucky to have appointed Karl Lagerfeld, just as Dior was resuscitated by the arrival of Galliano. The wrong designer can wreck a brand. It is also vital to achieve the correct balance between marketing and creativity. I don't think it is fair to say that fashion is based entirely on marketing. You can do as much marketing as you like, but if the final product does not deliver, the brand loses its power. Pierre Cardin made millions licensing his name, but the products were not always of an acceptable quality. And so...'. She shrugs.

A few days later, in the rather different setting of a shabby-chic café called Chez Prune near the Canal Saint Martin, I'm sipping coffee with a trend-tracker called Genevieve Flaven, co-founder of Style-Vision, a company that specializes in monitoring and predicting consumer behaviour (see Chapter 6: Anatomy of a trend). Like Martine Assouline, Flaven believes that few consumers are convinced by marketing alone.

'Every consumer can now decrypt advertising messages, so traditional marketing has become less and less significant. Consumers want to know what's behind the brand – what it can give back to them. Sometimes it's just a question of value: the best quality for the price. When people buy a very high-priced garment, they want to see the patience and the craftsmanship that has gone into it. They are paying to possess a beautiful object. And sometimes, when it's a famous brand, they are paying to be part of the story.'

Flaven explains that iconic brands create – and occasionally rewrite – their own narratives. 'It resembles a novel that you, the consumer, can enter. Chanel is a good example. First, through her talent and the power of her personality, Coco created her own myth. And now the legend of Coco is inexhaustible. It's the thread that pulls us into the Chanel universe. Every time Chanel launches a new product, it emphasizes a link with Coco, urging us to own a little piece of the legend. When the jewellery range was launched [in 1993] we were told it was in the spirit of Coco – but in fact she disliked jewellery. In a lot of ways, branding is simply telling a story.'

Few people can create a myth from scratch, which is why many fashion entrepreneurs have chosen to buy in to existing stories. (See Chapter 14: Retro brands retooled.) Take Lambretta, for instance. Like the Italian scooters themselves, the name has plenty of retro buzz: Mods and Rockers battling on Brighton beach, natty suits, sharp haircuts and Cool Britannia all rolled into one youth-friendly package. The scooter launched by Ferdinando

Innocenti in Lambrete, Milan in 1947 had long been out of production by the time a UK licensing company acquired the name. In 1997, Lambretta re-launched as a British menswear label with a flagship store in London's Carnaby Street – Swinging Sixties Central. Playing on Lambretta's connection with British Mod culture, the store contained a scooter, a Union Jack-patterned sofa and a range of sleek but street-smart clothing. The clothes, the store design and the advertising skilfully edited the Lambretta story, downplaying the brand's Italian heritage and favouring its role in British popular culture.

Controlling the plot

But if consumers are invited to play a part in the story of a brand, what happens when they subvert it? Throughout the history of fashion, consumers have had an irritating habit of sweeping aside carefully constructed marketing strategies and bending brands to their own will. It is doubtful, for example, that Dr Martens encouraged the skinhead movement to adopt its shiny black boots. To its credit, however, the brand does not try to bury the association. Its website has its own explanation: according to its narrative, the original skinhead was a 'multicultural, politically broad-minded and fashion-conscious individual' with a liking for 'reggae, soul and ska'. It was only later that the look was 'hijacked by right-wing racists'.

Burberry faced a similar problem in the United Kingdom. Some time ago, it joined the pantheon of brands adopted by label-conscious but not particularly upmarket British youth, notably soccer fans. As a direct corollary, and most damagingly of all, Burberry – and particularly its iconic check pattern – became associated with 'chavs'. The etymology of the term 'chav' is unclear – theories range from the Romany word for 'child' to the straightforward acronym of 'Council Housed and Violent' – but it was widely adopted by the British media to describe a certain type of downmarket consumer. And the chav's signature accessory was a baseball cap in Burberry check. The plaid fabric became so closely associated with hooliganism that some pubs and clubs instructed door staff to refuse entry to young people wearing it.

The 'chav' association clearly went against the grain of Burberry's status as a luxury brand. And yet Burberry has emerged relatively unscathed. For a start, 'chavs' are a purely British tribe, and the UK market accounts for only a fraction of the brand's sales. In Europe and Asia Burberry has successfully maintained its official positioning as English, quirky and fashionable – a 'classic with a twist', *à la* Paul Smith. It has also toned down the trademark plaid.

Burberry's non-executive director, Philip Bowman (the chief executive of Allied Domecq), skilfully handled the potentially difficult issue by at first laughing it off – brandishing a copy of a book about chav culture during a press conference – and then suggesting that most of the Burberry items worn by the clan were fakes. In short, Burberry trod a delicate line between non-chalant acceptance and ingenuous denial of the phenomenon. In any case, the chavs did little to undermine the company's performance.

Lacoste faced the same challenge in its native France, where the prestigious sportswear with the crocodile logo was adopted as a uniform by tough teenagers from the *banlieues*, or suburbs.

In 1925 tennis ace René Lacoste was standing in front of a shop window in Boston with Pierre Guillou, captain of the French tennis team, shortly before a vital qualifying match for the Davis Cup. 'If I win,' Lacoste said, indicating a crocodile-skin suitcase, 'you can buy me one of those.' He lost the match, but an American journalist who had heard about the bet reported that 'the young Lacoste [did not win] his crocodile-skin suitcase, but he fought like a real crocodile'. From then on, Lacoste wore a crocodile embroidered on the breast pocket of his shirts. And when he launched a range of sportswear in 1930, it naturally bore the crocodile logo.

With its emphasis on quality and its roots in the exclusive domain of tennis, Lacoste had all the ingredients it needed to seduce upmarket consumers – and it did so, for decades. But when French hip-hop fans began casting around for a home-grown version of the sports brands worn by their US counterparts, they naturally turned to Lacoste. The logo implied performance, taste and money to burn. Plus, what could be more rebellious than that snappy little croc?

At first, Lacoste observed this turn of events with grave concern, fearing that it would lose its traditional older, wealthier French client base. Soon, though, it recognized an opportunity – one that, after a false start, it utilized with considerable subtlety. While a blatant attempt to target these new consumers might have succeeded in distancing both loyal customers and suburban kids – whose very fascination for the brand lay in the fact that they had 'hijacked' it – Lacoste adopted an oblique approach. It used the trend as a springboard to rejuvenate the brand. It hired a new designer, Christophe Lemaire (formerly of Thierry Mugler and Christian Lacroix), who introduced a range of 'elegantly functional' clothing: 'Though Lemaire was not allowed to touch the polo shirt – the company still regards it as a perfect classic – he used it as a reference point for his collection of sharp pullovers, hip track jackets, soft pants and sexy pleated skirts.' ('Courtoisie on the court', *Newsweek*, 27 May 2002.) Lacoste showed on the catwalks in New York and Paris, and opened smartly minimalist concept stores in France, the United States, Germany and Japan. Cult film director Wong Kar Wai was brought in to direct a globally-screened commercial in the languorous style of his movie *In the Mood for Love*, raising the brand's profile among culturally savvy consumers while simultaneously catering to the important Asian market. Even the crocodile logo was given a subtle retouching by the design agency Seenk, becoming simpler and more streamlined.

Bernard Lacoste, company chairman and the founder's oldest son, refers to the strategy as 'evolution rather than revolution'. The brand regained control of its identity, while giving a '*merci*' nod to the influential group that had helped perk up its flagging relevance.

The Italian connection

The connection between Dr Martens, Burberry, Lacoste and Dior is that they have a lengthy heritage to rely on. They may choose to highlight or mask different aspects of their past depending on prevailing trends, but the elements are readily available – a pick-and-mix bag of anecdotes and attributes. But what if you're starting from zero, without access to a resonant name, a dusty archive or a famous designer? How do you give your brand a compelling story?

There are two instructive – and very different – examples from Italy. The first is Tod's, the footwear and accessories brand. There is no Signor Tod, and there never has been. When company chairman Diego Della Valle created the brand in 1979, he invented the name JP Tod's to give his ultra-comfortable loafers an air of Anglo-Saxon classicism. But his real stroke of genius was an advertising campaign featuring black and white photographs of Cary Grant, Jackie and John F Kennedy, Audrey Hepburn and David Niven, with a single Tod's loafer superimposed at the bottom of the image. Della Valle was not claiming that these people had actually worn his shoes – let's be clear – he was simply linking the brand with a certain insouciant style. Add a high price point to underscore a suggestion of luxury, and the legend falls smoothly into place.

The second example is perhaps even more impressive. It concerns a young man from rural Italy who ran up a pair of jeans on his mother's sewing machine, and went on to build a global brand.

On the day I went to meet that young man, we were barrelling down the *autostrada* in a functional four-by-four, when my driver pointed out a gleaming flame-red car. 'Look at that – a Ferrari,' he said. 'Now that's what I call a car. *Che bella*!' He looked on with envy as the Ferrari roared to a pinpoint in the distance.

Diesel founder Renzo Rosso wouldn't be quite so impressed. He's more of a Harley Davidson, rock and roll sort of guy. He likes things beaten-up, frayed and oil-stained, preferably mixed in with a bit of retro kitsch. The Diesel universe frequently resembles a 1950s sci-fi movie, sometimes the attic of a junk shop, occasionally an 'Easy Rider' psychedelic road trip, and very often a blend of all three. Mostly, it looks like the contents of Rosso's own head.

'I bought a sports car once, when I was younger,' confesses Rosso later, over lunch in the small town of Molvena, where Diesel is based. 'It was a Dodge Viper. I drove it maybe twice. The second time I was sitting at the traffic lights and I became aware of the fact that everyone was looking at me. I didn't like that feeling. I sold the car not long after that.'

Rosso has come a long way from his parents' farm – but, in a sense, he is still in the same place. Diesel's surprisingly small light industrial unit is tucked within the folds of the hilly Bassano del Grappa region in northern Italy, not far from where he grew up. He remains close to his native soil, with the major difference that he now has his own farm, as well as a vineyard producing the red wine that we are currently sipping.

'I have some luxuries,' he says, 'a beautiful home; but I'm still the same person. Basically, I'm a meddler. When I was a kid, I used to take my moped apart and put it back together again, to see if I could get it to go faster. I've always been like that. I look at things and try to work out how they could be better, more fun, more amusing. I'm allergic to the ordinary.'

Rosso ran up his first pair of jeans at the age of 15, on his mother's Singer sewing machine, because he couldn't afford a pair of the flares that were fashionable at the time. 'A couple of my friends liked them, and asked me to make some for them too. Every night I sat at home stitching jeans for my friends. But it was okay, because I charged them 3,400 lire – about two euros. I said to myself, "You know; there might be a future in this business."'

This insight led him to the local technical college in Padua, where he studied textiles and manufacturing. Afterwards, he got a job as a production manager at a company called Moltex, which made trousers for various Italian labels. The enterprise was run by Adriano Goldschmied, who became

Rosso's mentor. Rosso is quick to acknowledge, 'He taught me how to survive in the fashion industry.'

A couple of years later, in 1978, Rosso approached Goldschmied with the idea of starting his own jeans label. 'So we went into business together, producing jeans for ourselves instead of other people.' It was Goldschmied who came up with the brand name Diesel. 'We wanted something that didn't sound Italian; that had an international feel. Did you know the word is pronounced the same all over the world?'

The business developed slowly. By his own admission, Rosso was young, inexperienced, and unwilling to risk the future of the joint-owned enterprise by trying some of the wilder ideas that lurked in the back of his mind. Then, in 1985, he bought Goldschmied's half of Diesel: 'That was when I started producing things that were a little more personal, a little more crazy. Everything I did was inspired by vintage. Now everyone uses that word, "vintage", but we were the first to do that. When I began producing stone-washed jeans and jeans with holes in them, retailers would send them back, saying the quality was not good enough. I was obliged to travel – to New York, to Stockholm, to Los Angeles – to explain the concept. It's hard to imagine today, but 25 years ago department stores weren't stocking a great deal of casual-wear, particularly in the States. It was rows and rows of suits. Imagine trying to convince them to stock jeans that already looked old.'

In addition, Rosso had set his prices high. 'Because of the production process that had gone into ageing the jeans, I was selling them for 80 or 90 dollars, when the average at the time was about 50 dollars. I remember going into a vintage store called Antique Boutique in New York, which I thought our jeans suited very well. The guy said no, but I told him, "Don't say no! I believe in this thing! Give me one metre of space, and if you don't sell them all, I'll buy the rest back."'

Needless to say, he didn't end up empty-handed. 'The reason this company has succeeded is because we're always trying to be different. We stand out from the crowd. For instance, in 1995 we started doing accessories. We produced a really strange pair of sunglasses [the cult 'Sister Yes' model] when there was absolutely no innovation in that market. Then we turned to wrist-watches, and gave them the Diesel treatment too. We've changed many aspects of fashion, although few people would give us credit for it.'

It's impossible to talk about Diesel's idiosyncratic style without turning to Wilbert Das, the brand's creative director and head of design. The Dutchman joined the firm in 1988, straight out of art school, having hassled Rosso for a job. 'I'd seen his clothes in small boutiques in Holland, and I could tell right away that what he was doing fit in with my ideas. Everyone had big catwalk dreams, but I wanted to design clothes that I would see on the streets. That's where the really innovative stuff in fashion was happening – and it still is.'

Das joined the company as assistant designer on the men's line, gradually working his way up the ranks to the top slot. These days he's as essential to the Diesel image as Rosso himself, enjoying an almost symbiotic relationship with the founder of the brand. So how does he define the Diesel identity?

'We've always been fascinated by things that are kitsch, colourful, decorative. Sometimes we refer to it as "retro-futuristic", but that doesn't quite capture it. We like to clash styles, piling references on top of one another. We go out of our way to challenge definitions of good taste. We're not interested in fashion – we prefer to create things that are entirely our own. Diesel is anti-fashion fashion.'

Rather than attending catwalk shows, disembowelling glossy magazines or hooking themselves up to the internet, Diesel's designers travel to urban hotspots around the world. They return with posters, postcards, CDs, club flyers – and, of course, second-hand clothes. Diesel's design studios are cluttered with racks of unlikely vintage items in lurid colours, migraine-inducing patterns and crackly fabrics; all of which might resurface in a mutated form as part of a Diesel collection.

'We have a lot of freedom because we design our clothes on an item-by-item basis, rather than by co-ordinated "looks". We've always considered our consumers to be intelligent, not brand junkies who go to a single store for an entire outfit. We expect them to mix us with other brands, with vintage clothes, with anything they like. These are people who expect a lot of choice. For that same reason, we offer them a huge range of jeans: something like 45 styles and 67 different washes in each collection. Multiply that by lengths and waist sizes and you can see that it gets quite insane.'

Insanity, or at least eccentricity, doesn't seem to be a disadvantage at Diesel. The company traffics in irony, a rare commodity in the fashion world. This is evident in its widely acclaimed advertising, which has played a crucial role in establishing the brand's notoriety. Although Diesel employs an advertising agency, which is unusual for a fashion brand (see Chapter 7: The image-makers), Das oversees the creation of all marketing materials: 'This is vital, because we look upon communications as one of our products. The same standards that we apply to our clothes, we apply to our external communications.'

Diesel's decision to embark on an international advertising campaign in 1991 was a turning point in its history. Its first agency was a small Stockholm-based outfit called Paradiset. The relationship lasted until 2001, by which time Paradiset had racked up shelf-loads of advertising-industry awards and Diesel had exploded into a global brand.

'Our distributor in Sweden recommended the agency to us. It was tiny, maybe four or five people,' Das recalls. 'As soon as we met them, we loved what they were doing. In our sector there are not many people who are brave enough to try different things. And in the advertising industry as well, people are not very courageous. But Paradiset really had balls.'

Paradiset came up with the slogan 'Diesel: For Successful Living', which referred to the improbable advertising promises of the past, while utilizing the company's trademark irony. Print ads resembled the centrefolds of ancient porn magazines, Bollywood movie posters, army recruitment campaigns, ads for superannuated domestic appliances – anything but fashion spreads, in fact.

Renzo Rosso says, 'Once again, we broke through by doing something completely different. If you think back to 1991, fashion advertising was all black and white: Donna Karan, Calvin Klein... Tasteful, beautifully shot, black and white. And then we came out with these ads that were colourful, brash and surreal – it's not surprising people noticed us.'

The company has switched advertising agencies a few times since then, but the strategy remains the same. Diesel's ads delight in causing offence, combining the garish and the beautiful, the twisted and the sublime. One ad, showing an improbably leggy model perched on a giant cigarette, was emblazoned with the words 'How to smoke 145 a day'. But the skull at the foot of the image indicated that this was an off-the-wall anti-smoking message. Rosso has often used Diesel's advertising to make acerbic observations about Western society. A poster showing a pistol-toting male model, a comment on gun culture in the United States, caused uproar in that country. A later campaign portrayed consumers as ageless, wrinkle-free drones. The images were accompanied by instructions offering the keys to eternal life. More recently, pictures of youngsters engaged in daring, foolish or reckless pursuits – leaning out of two speeding cars to kiss; diving into a post box – accompanied by the exhortation 'Be Stupid'. In Diesel world, 'stupidity' equated spontaneity and transgression; an appealing idea for the young (or young-minded) consumers targeted by the campaign.

Whether Diesel's advertising carries a genuine message, or whether it is merely designed to provoke, entertain and draw attention to the brand, it has certainly been effective. Diesel began as a small Italian jeans maker with 18 staff and a clutch of sewing machines. Now it is present in more than 80 countries, with more than 5,000 points of sale and 400 branded stores. It also embraces Diesel Kid and the high-end Diesel Black Gold. Through the Italian manufacturing company Staff International, which it acquired in 2000, it obtained licensing agreements to make clothes for designer brands Vivienne Westwood, DSquared and Martin Margiela. Later, under the holding company Only The Brave, Rosso acquired controlling stakes in Maison Martin Margiela and Viktor & Rolf. It even owns a hotel, the Pelican in Miami's South Beach, which, with its Art Deco façade and eyeball-frazzling interior, perfectly captures the Diesel vibe. In fact, when studied carefully, all these elements remain true to the brand's skewed, avant-garde outlook.

The rise of Diesel proves that building a fashion brand is as much about communication as it is about clothes. It's about creating a playground, a diverting fiction. Renzo Rosso is often quoted as saying, 'Diesel is not my company, it's my life.' But his real genius has been to sell the world the product of his imagination.

When haute couture meets high street

03

It's not enough to be fashionable – one wishes to appear intelligent as well.

In the end, the *New York Daily News* summed it up best of all. 'Fashion king Karl Lagerfeld is a mega-hit for the masses from Manhattan to Milan,' the newspaper gulped, the day after the pillage (13 November 2004). 'Throngs of style-seekers stormed H&M stores around the world to scoop up the first moderately priced collection from the world-famous Chanel designer. By the end of the day, the Karl Lagerfeld for H&M line had sold out at the chain's seven Manhattan stores and across the Atlantic in cities from London to Milan, Munich to Stockholm.'

It was the same story in Paris, where Lagerfeld lives and works. The great man may have even cast a bemused eye upon proceedings from the shadows as shoppers ransacked a store in Les Halles. The Scandinavian brand has since tried to repeat this coup – with, it seems, ever-diminishing returns. Designers who have followed in Lagerfeld's footsteps include Stella McCartney, Viktor & Rolf and Roberto Cavalli. By now, though, consumers have grown blasé about the idea. When it was announced, the launch of Lagerfeld's 'capsule' collection for H&M was the consummation of a long-time hot and heavy flirtation between haute couture and high street; the two disparate worlds had been moving inexorably towards each other for some time.

Strategic alliances

There may have been a time when fashion was constructed like a pyramid, with haute couture at the apex, designer ready-to-wear just below, challenger brands in the middle, and a big slab of mass retail at the base. This is no longer the case today – if, indeed, it was ever that simple. Hovering around the structure are street-wear, sportswear and semi-couture, among others. Consumers, too, rather than being content to stay in their allotted sectors, scurry promiscuously from one to the other, picking up a Louis Vuitton bag here and slinging it over a Zara jacket there; wearing a Topshop T-shirt and Gap jeans under a coat from Chanel.

'It's not enough to look fashionable – one wishes to appear intelligent as well,' remarks fashion guru Jean-Jacques Picart. 'There are two different shifts happening at once. First of all, Chanel, Dior, Gucci and the others will continue to develop luxury as a business. At the same time we are seeing a complementary reaction, which is that a consumer may accept paying for the latest Dior bag, very trendy, that she's seen in all the magazines and advertisements; but she'll see no shame in going to Zara and buying a T-shirt for 10 euros, because it's pretty and it's a fair quality for the price. Then she may go to another store, a bit more expensive but not as well known, perhaps run by a young designer, where she'll buy a skirt. And these items, when brought together, reassure her and send a message to others that she's an intelligent consumer, not dazzled by marketing, in charge of her own image.'

In other words, the era of slavish brand worship is over. Just as everyone today is to some extent a marketing expert, we are also our own stylists. The designer Alber Elbaz, of Lanvin, commented, 'We've reached a turning point. Nobody wears logos any more. People aren't hesitating to mix Lanvin with Topshop. Everything is becoming more democratic.' ('Mr Nice Guy', *Numéro*, August 2004.)

The thinking behind the partnership between Lagerfeld and H&M was simple: if the mass market was attracted to the rejuvenated luxury sector, even to the extent of saving up for the occasional pricey item, and if upmarket customers were getting their kicks from unearthing fashionable fripperies at inexpensive stores, then why not formalize the relationship? Luxury brands could show they knew how to talk street, the chain stores would benefit from the glitter, and there would be lots of free publicity for everyone.

The trend can be compared to a parallel evolution among sportswear brands. Rappers have long enjoyed mixing solitaires and sneakers, and multi-brand lifestyle stores such as the pioneering Colette in Paris have been selling sports shoes alongside designer dresses for years. So it's not surprising that names previously associated with the rarefied world of the catwalk have started hooking up with sportswear brands.

Perhaps the most successful of these chimeras is Adidas by Stella McCartney. The partnership was originally announced in September 2004 and now covers women's athletic apparel across the sporting spectrum, from running to swimming. The success of the line was crowned with a commission to design the British team's apparel for the 2012 Olympics. But although the clothing undoubtedly performs to a high level in the sports arena, it fulfils a valuable marketing function in fashion land. Neda Talebian Funk put it best of all in a piece for *Huffington Post:* 'Fitness is the new fashion... Remember working out in baggy shorts and big T-shirts? Not anymore. Flattering, formfitting and highly technical sportswear is being worn not only to the gym, but to lunch, on weekends and even in the office.' ('Fitness – the new "it" bag', Huffingtonpost.com, 5 April 2012.)

As fashion is overwhelmingly concerned with body image, it was inevitable that sport and luxury would join forces. Funk cites Technogym founder Nerio Alessandri: 'Fashion is looking good outside; wellness is feeling good inside. It's the new frontier of luxury.' But the venture works well for Adidas too. It adds a sheen to the brand's image, pushing it further from the locker room and closer to the loft conversion.

Chic battles cheap

Upmarket brands may have begun stalking mass consumers, but the trend labelled 'massluxe' (or 'masstige', take your pick) is more about chain stores smartening up. Gap, for instance, recruited the likes of Roland Mouret and shoe designer Pierre Hardy to try and inject some pizzazz into its outmoded image after a long period of declining interest from consumers. In a variation on the theme, cut-price UK brand New Look launched a range by witty British designer Giles Deacon, who once worked at Gucci under Tom Ford.

Several elements combined to drive this evolution. The post-9/11 economic fall-out forced luxury shoppers to tighten their belts, while casting around for a viable alternative that would fool as many observers as possible. High-street shoppers, having spent years soaking up articles about Lagerfeld, Jacobs, Prada and the rest of the fashion firmament, became design-savvy and demanding. And the retailers wanted to distance themselves from the flood of bargain-basement supermarket labels that was lapping at their heels – a tendency that has been accelerated by the end of textile-trade restrictions at the beginning of 2005.

The emergence of supermarket brands and 'value-led' fashion is worth a brief detour. The reference in the sector is Wal-Mart, the world's biggest store group. When Wal-Mart acquired ASDA in 1999, the British supermarket chain was already famous for its cut-price clothing brand George, created by Next founder George Davies in 1990. Although the store didn't offer a dramatic retail environment or imaginative marketing, it sold jeans for £4 – along with other cheap and cheerful garments that, while not exactly fashion-forward, were perfectly wearable. ASDA began crowing that George now sold more clothes than British favourite Marks & Spencer.

ASDA is not alone in this growing niche. Away from the supermarkets, 'value' outlets such as Matalan, TK Maxx and Primark are nibbling away at the mid-market retailers. One of the first into the sector, Matalan has been selling discounted high-street brands for 20 years. Customers must become 'members' of the organization before they can shop at its 170 or so outlets across the UK. With a loyal customer base thus assured, Matalan saves money by locating its stores out of town, buying clothing in bulk, and selling it in no-nonsense environments.

But Matalan faces major competition in the form of TK Maxx, which stocks genuine designer brands at rock-bottom prices. It's part of the US group TJX, which was founded in 1976 and now bills itself as the world's largest 'off-price' retailer. The magazine *Management Today* explained its approach as follows: 'Like others in the sector, [TK Maxx] keeps costs low with little in the way of merchandizing or advertising, although, as its fame has spread among the more well-heeled shopper in recent years, it has started advertising in magazines such as *Heat* and the *Sunday Times Style* supplement.' ('The low-cost retail revolution', March 2005.)

Marks & Spencer, which prided itself for years on the fact that it had never had to advertise to attract customers, appeared to be locked in a protracted and painful decline until it rejuvenated itself with a celebrity-driven ad campaign featuring swinging 60s icon Twiggy and a handful of younger models. The understatedly chic ads hit exactly the right note for the brand's conservative consumers, who wanted to play it straight but not dowdy. Seven years later, the Twiggy effect had proved so beneficial that the model launched her own line of branded clothing for M&S. The collection appeared to be the fashion equivalent of a family movie: 'Working closely with the M&S team, Twiggy tried to ensure the designs catered to everyone...

from 18 to 80.' ('Twiggy unveils debut collection for M&S', *Daily Mail*, 10 April 2012.)

'Masstige' has become the not-so-secret weapon of mid-to-downmarket brands. A whole range of previously uninspired retailers – Oasis, Target in the United States (fashionistas have taken to giving it an ironic French inflection, as in 'Tar-jay') – have ramped up their creativity with the aid of young designers.

Topshop is way ahead of the game, in the United Kingdom, at least. Even before H&M and Zara came along, its flagship store on London's Oxford Circus was the haunt of beady-eyed stylists and model agency scouts; which led to winking 'you didn't hear it from us' references in the glossies. And although its design has been a cut above the rest for some time, Topshop now has a massluxe range, positioned at a slightly higher price point as a signal to the discerning.

However, when writing about the democratization of fashion, there's no escaping the dynamic trio of high-street style.

Stockholm Syndrome

'What is it with you Swedes?' I ask Jörgen Andersson, the marketing director of H&M. 'First Ikea democratized interior design; now you're doing the same thing with fashion. Are you lot on a mission, or something?'

Andersson – who is, as you might expect, tall, good-looking and fair-haired – smiles at the thought. 'It's part of our heritage. We've been brought up with a Social Democrat government. Since we were young we've always been taught that everyone should have an equal choice. It's not just a business idea, it's a political one. Ikea was born out of the theory that you don't have to be rich to appreciate good design. We have the same standpoint on fashion. You can dress from head to toe in Gucci if you like – that proves you're rich, but it doesn't prove you have taste. It's more imaginative to wear your Gucci with some H&M. That's why *Vogue* readers are among our most loyal clients.'

H&M's base at Regeringsgaten 48, Stockholm, is certainly democratic in appearance. Located in the commercial centre of the city, just up the road from an enormous H&M flagship store, it is blocky and practical. The lifts, to be quite honest, could do with a bit of a makeover. Annacarin Björne, the company's press officer, tells me that this no-frills look is quite deliberate: 'We pride ourselves in being cost-conscious, so we can pass those savings on to our customers. We don't see the point of flashy offices.'

Company founder Erling Persson opened his first store in Västerås, a small town one hour south of Stockholm, in 1947. Persson had been inspired by a trip to the United States, where he had marvelled at a new kind of ready-to-wear boutique offering fashionable garments at affordable prices. He called his concept simply 'Hennes', or 'hers'. In the early 1960s the chain expanded into Norway and Denmark, and in 1968 it acquired the Stockholm store Mauritz Widforss, which specialized in hunting apparel and equipment. Crucially, the fusion allowed the newly created Hennes & Mauritz to add a masculine dimension to its collection. The first UK store opened in 1976.

In 1982, when Erling Persson's son Stefan took over as chief executive (he is currently chairman), the company entered a period of international expansion that continues to this day. At the time of my visit, H&M had just added Canada and Slovenia to the map, with Hungary and Ireland due to follow at any moment. The brand has been present in the United States since 2000. In total, it has more than 1,300 stores in 24 countries. It has an annual turnover of more than 68 billion SEK (US$ 10 billion).

H&M says that it owes its success to three factors: inventive design, the best quality at the best price, and efficient logistics. The team of 100 designers is based in Stockholm – and Björne stresses that, contrary to popular belief, they do not copy styles that have already appeared on the runways of Paris and Milan. 'They travel all the time and pick up any number of influences, from street trends, exhibitions, movies, magazines and trade fairs. We're a bit tired of being accused of copying famous designers. If we did that, we'd be up to our neck in court cases – and that's money we'd rather save.'

The company's basic products have long lead times – from six to eight months – but it aims to have high-fashion items in stores two to three weeks after the pattern has left the designer's PC screen. The company's 21 production offices (10 each in Europe and Asia, another in Africa), with a total of more than 700 employees, are responsible for liaising with around 750 factories. About 60 per cent of these are in Asia, the rest in Europe. H&M does not own any factories, but it has a lengthy code of conduct that all its suppliers must sign, as well as a team of quality controllers who can swoop in unannounced to ensure the rules are being followed.

According to Jörgen Andersson, 'Over the past 10 years, [H&M has] become preoccupied with the question of quality. We expect our suppliers to provide products of the highest possible standard at a very fair price, because that's our promise to the consumer.'

In terms of logistics, no fewer than 3,200 people are devoted to the task. The completed garments pass through a transit warehouse in Hamburg before being dispatched to distribution centres in individual markets. Only transport is contracted out; otherwise, H&M controls every step of the process, acting as importer, wholesaler and retailer. Computerized stock management ensures that new items arrive in stores every day.

This logistics approach is at variance with Zara's centralized distribution model, and there are other points of difference between the Swedish giant and its Spanish rival. One of them is marketing strategy. Unlike Zara, H&M has never shied away from advertising. Its simple but effective posters – showing models in casual poses against plain white backgrounds – have become a familiar part of the urban landscape. And, until recently, its Christmas lingerie campaign, featuring provocative shots of the hottest models, was a festive tradition attracting frank stares of appreciation, mutters of disapproval and free media coverage in equal measure. (A 1993 series of posters featuring the voluptuous Anna Nicole Smith in retro pin-up mode – right in the middle of the skinny-girl 'heroin chic' period – is regarded as a landmark in the brand's development.)

But all that has changed. In accordance with the new era of 'mass-clusivity', H&M is going upmarket. Jörgen Andersson says, 'What we have done very well throughout the 50 years of our existence is to keep our focus on the customer. We have a lean organization and a constant eye on the market so, as soon as tastes change, we change with them. We don't dictate style. Our style is whatever our customers demand.'

What the customers want now, according to Andersson, is glamour: 'Fashion always mirrors society. Many people today can afford a lifestyle that was previously only available to the rich. With low-cost airlines, they can travel to places their parents only dreamed about. You want to be famous? What's fame, today? You only have to go on a reality TV show to become famous. Celebrity seems just around the corner, so why not live it out while you're waiting?'

Enter Karl Lagerfeld. A decade ago it would have been hard to imagine H&M's young customers evincing much interest in either Chanel or its courtly, white-haired designer. The launch of Lagerfeld's collection for H&M was promoted worldwide with giant posters and a two-minute TV commercial, all of which replaced the traditional Christmas lingerie campaign. Andersson says, 'We had been running the underwear campaign for 10 or 12 years, and we felt that it had lost its relevance. We said to ourselves, "Hold on, we're supposed to be a contemporary company, a fashion company, we need to do something different." The underwear posters were very much focused on "this year's most famous model". But consumers don't care about that any more. They have become interested in design. They want to know what the new collection looks like.'

H&M linked up with Lagerfeld through the Paris-based freelance art director Donald Schneider. Andersson recalls, 'Donald created our new customer magazine and worked with us on our advertising. Through his work for *Vogue* he got to know Karl, and we had a conversation about whether Karl might be interested in doing something with us. A short time later, Donald called to say that Karl would like to meet us. So we flew to Paris and after sitting and chatting for a while, Karl said, "Let's do it – when can we get started?"'

Andersson says Lagerfeld was attracted to the 'youthful and creative' elements of the H&M brand. Lagerfeld himself confirmed as much in a flurry of interviews. He told French news magazine *L'Express*, 'One day I was in the elevator at Chanel with one of the girls who worked there. She looked very pretty in her tweed coat, and I complimented her on it. She told me, "It comes from H&M – I don't have the money to buy one here!" Obviously, I hadn't seen the buttons or the lining up close, but it had a lot of style; modern and well-cut.' ('Karl Lagerfeld, couturier chez H&M', 20 September 2004.)

In the same article, Lagerfeld mentions that when H&M sent him a suit for publicity photographs, 'I didn't have to make a single alteration.' He adds, 'Naturally, the fabric and the finish make a difference, but it's honest work – certainly more so than the second lines of some designers, [which are] criminal in their condescension and dullness.'

It doesn't take a marketing genius to grasp the value of quotes like that to H&M. Partnerships with leading designers have now become an important component of the retailer's strategy. Not with Lagerfeld, though, who complained to German magazine *Stern* shortly after the line's launch that not enough of the clothes had been made available, adding for good measure the suggestion that H&M's larger sizes did not flatter his designs. The statement did no harm to either party: the Karl Lagerfeld for H&M line remained a rare one-off, collectable for ever more, and Lagerfeld retained his dignity; H&M was the overall winner, in terms of publicity and prestige.

But Andersson observes that a shift in perception is not enough – the upward sweep must be visible at every intersection with the customer. 'As well as the qualitative aspects of the garments and the production process, we have been working very much with the appearance of stores. We've begun to radically rebuild and redecorate. We know that our customers love to shop – they consider it entertainment. And if the store is the main contact with the customers, we have to enhance that experience.' (See Chapter 5: The store is the star.)

Aware that its slick new image could create a distancing effect, H&M is building closer links with consumers in other ways. It has tentatively launched a web-based loyalty scheme, available in Sweden and Denmark at the time of writing. Those who sign up receive the H&M magazine – a cross between a catalogue and a traditional glossy – as well as e-mail bulletins, special offers and discounts.

In Andersson's view, 'If there's a group of loyal consumers who love H&M, we should foster that relationship. Mass communication is not always the answer – it's more efficient to address those who are the most receptive to the message.' Above all, Andersson believes it is crucially important to keep sight of the brand's core values, which he lists as 'fashionable, exciting and accessible'.

'Traditionally, fashion has been aloof and superior. You look at the advertising; it takes itself very seriously. H&M is not like that at all. I want people to come to the store because they're going out that night and they need a new top. And they don't hesitate – they buy something for 10 euros, because, let's face it, why not? For that price, you can give it to the Salvation Army the next day if you want. It hardly costs more than a couple of glasses of wine.'

Viva Zara

The reception at Inditex is very big and very white. It is, in fact, a glistening expanse of white tiles, with a horseshoe-shaped reception desk way over there in the distance. The walls are pale too, and entirely picture-free. I'm later told that this minimalism is for the benefit of employees: we're in Galicia, in grey and rainy northern Spain, and these spacious, pristine, light-deluged surroundings keep staff cheerful and motivated during the winter months.

Less than an hour ago, a taxi picked me up outside my hotel in La Coruña, the faintly raffish port that is the nearest large town. It feels a long way from cosmopolitan Barcelona or frenetic Madrid. This is the kind of place where fishing boats pull into the harbour every morning; where lunch is a slice of tortilla and a beer; where couples promenade in the square at dusk, surrounded by kids kicking footballs and observed by creased oldsters nursing coffees. The shopping district is a grid of well-preserved streets dotted with affordable boutiques, many of which belong to Inditex. One of them, in Calle Juan Flórez, is the first-ever Zara store.

It was in a shop window in La Coruña, so the story goes, that Zara founder Amancio Ortega and his fiancée saw a beautiful silk negligée with a barely believable price tag. Ortega, then working at a local shirt-maker, ran up a variation on the high-priced number. His fiancée loved it, and Señor Ortega started his own business producing glamorous but affordable nightwear. He later moved into general fashion, with the affirmed aim of bringing catwalk style to the street. He opened the first branch of Zara in 1975. Originally the store was to be called Zorba, after the character played by Ortega's favourite actor, Anthony Quinn, in the film *Zorba the Greek*. He couldn't obtain permission to use the name, so he played with the letters until he arrived at Zara, which sounded feminine and exotic. (The name should be pronounced the Spanish way: 'Thara'.)

The chain grew steadily throughout the 1980s but did not open its first store outside Spain until 1989, when it hopped across the border to Oporto, Portugal. Paris followed, then New York. The store didn't reach London until 1998, by which time the fashion pack had carried news of the brand back from shopping excursions to Barcelona. On opening day, the place was mobbed. In May 2001, the brand launched on the Madrid Stock Exchange – and Amancio Ortega's billionaire status was assured.

Today, the Inditex group embraces Zara – which provides 70 per cent of its income – and a clutch of other brands: Bershka (young mainstream fashion); Pull and Bear (urban street-wear and accessories); Oysho (lingerie); Massimo Dutti (classic fashion); Kiddy's Class (children's clothing); and Stradivarius (fashion and accessories). Zara Home, which aimed to do for interiors what Zara had done for fashion, launched in 2003 as a separate chain.

The secret to Zara's appeal is that, although shopping there is cheap, it doesn't *feel* cheap. The stores are large, swish and centrally located. The clothes are given room to breathe and usually – unless it's a Saturday afternoon during the sales – so are the customers. And then there are the clothes themselves. Zara is renowned for whisking budget interpretations of catwalk styles into its stores with breath-taking speed. A designer dress photographed on a model during fashion week won't arrive in department stores for months – but something very like it can be spotted hanging in Zara in a couple of weeks. This infuriates the designers, but delights customers who can't stretch to the originals – or no longer see the point of trying.

'I am sorry, but I don't think it will be possible for you to interview any employees,' apologizes Carmen, the press officer who will be my guide at Inditex, after greeting me in the blinding-white reception area. This is not entirely surprising, as the company is famously enigmatic. Before its stock-exchange flotation, few journalists had set foot in the Inditex headquarters. Even today, Señor Ortega never, ever gives interviews. (I glimpse him during my tour, though: a sturdy, tough-looking figure with the sleeves of his white shirt rolled up, as hands-on as he has always been, even though he is one of the richest men in the world. Later, I spot him again – this time in the staff canteen.)

The company prides itself on having spent hardly a penny on conventional advertising throughout its history. No posters, no print and certainly no TV. Carmen tells me, 'The reason for not spending money on publicity is that it doesn't bring any added value to our customers. We would rather concentrate on our offering in terms of design, prices, rapid turn-around of stock and the store experience. That's why we have stores in the smartest locations and devote a lot of attention to façades, interiors and window displays. Our stores are our way of communicating.'

Everything about Zara is streamlined for efficiency. The building I'm standing in is the hub of the brand, and there are very few stages between here and the customer. Design, purchasing, pattern-making, samples and visual merchandizing are all handled in-house. More than 50 per cent of the clothes, particularly high-fashion items, are made in Zara's own factories in Spain, most of them close to its headquarters. An enormous 480,000-square-metre logistics centre is capable of handling 60,000 garments an hour, whizzing orders twice a week from the green suburbs of La Coruña to stores all over the world.

'Each order contains our latest items as well as those requested by the store managers,' Carmen explains. 'The store managers are a vital part of our strategy. They monitor the tastes and demands of their customers, and tailor stock accordingly. That's why different Zara stores in different cities – or even two stores in the same city – rarely stock exactly the same products. The clothes reflect the profile of the customers.'

Zara's product managers keep in touch with stores, seeking feedback from customers and monitoring the popularity or otherwise of items. Tills are computer-linked with headquarters, providing a constant stream of sales data: 'We know within a day or so whether or not a product is successful.'

The tour takes me through each element of the production process. In the design area, I comment on the pile of fashion magazines next to a designer's computer terminal. Carmen says, 'We don't invent trends, we follow them. Styles, colours, fabrics – we don't guess any of these things. We are a business catering to a demand, and we've never made any secret of that. But we need to know what the trends are, so we follow them through magazines, fashion shows, movies and city streets. We use trend-trackers and forecasting companies. We keep our eyes open.'

Zara has been accused of flagrant piracy, which it denies. And there's perhaps a certain amount of snobbery in the implication that a company from an obscure corner of northern Spain has no right to ape catwalk styles. In fact, the region has a strong fashion tradition, and is home to leading Spanish designers such as Adolfo Dominguez, Roberto Verino and Purificacion Garcia. It is true to say, however, that Zara specializes in 'fast fashion', cranking out some 11,000 different models a year.

As I continue my tour, we come across a visual merchandizing specialist laying garments flat on the floor, then standing to see how the colours look together. When she's happy with the arrangement, she transfers the clothes to shelves that mimic those in the stores. ('That's another reason for the white floors,' remarks Carmen.) Nothing about the stores is left to chance. Passing through a doorway, we emerge into a ghostly street of 'pilot stores', where window and interior displays are mocked up before being transmitted to branches around the world. Although it is June, the windows are dressed for winter. (I make a mental note to snap up a dandyish black corduroy jacket.) The posters inside the stores – the closest Zara ever gets to advertising – are the responsibility of the corporate image department.

Breaking for lunch in the Inditex canteen, I can't help remarking on the college refectory atmosphere. In fact, with its modernity, bustle and hordes of scrubbed, trendy young people, the entire building resembles a college campus. Carmen tells me that the average age there is 26. There are romances, relationships, even marriages. Apparently, Señor Ortega approves: 'He likes the idea of a family atmosphere. He tries to make working conditions pleasant because he wants to attract talented people, and to keep them here. After all, it's not an obvious place to live and work, compared to Barcelona or Madrid.'

We hop into a car to tour the peripheral buildings that make up the Inditex estate. Our next stop is a factory floor, where four cutting tables can cut as many as 8,000 garments a day. The highlight, though, is inevitably the logistics centre, whose immense size defies description. It works rather like a mail-sorting office, except that the envelopes and parcels are boxes or hanging plastic sheaths of garments. Each of the system's 1,200 slots corresponds to an individual store somewhere on the map. 'Everything is computerized, and there are very few errors,' says Carmen.

After what seems like half a lifetime of writing about advertising, I'm slightly numbed by Amancio Ortega's achievement: a global fashion brand with barely a photographed pout in sight. But it's not entirely accurate to say that Zara's stores are its only form of communication. There are also those dark blue paper carrier bags, dangling smartly from wrists on buses and trains and in the street, in every city, everywhere.

A unique brand from Japan

While the French had been flirting with Uniqlo for a while, they embarked on a full-blown love affair with the Japanese brand in October 2009. That's when it opened its first store in the city centre – just behind the Opéra Garnier, to be exact – after testing the concept in the outlying district of La Défense.

The result was an inversion of a familiar Paris spectacle. Strollers had grown used to seeing Japanese tourists queuing up outside the Louis Vuitton flagship in the Champs Elysées. But now, Parisian shoppers stood in line outside Uniqlo. And they did so right in the middle of a recession.

Coincidentally, a couple of months earlier, I'd been in Cannes for the advertising industry's annual jamboree, the Cannes Lions. And there was Uniqlo, sponsoring the festival's official T-shirt and winning awards for its quirky online advertising, including a downloadable screen saver that told you the time while cute girls danced in the brand's streamlined clothing (the Uniqlock). Innovative, quirky and innocently sexy, it seemed very Japanese – and it told you a lot about the brand.

The roots of Uniqlo stretch back to 1949, when a menswear store called Ogori Shoji was founded in Yamaguchi Prefecture. This morphed into Ogori Shoji Co in 1963, which in the globalized way of things later changed its name to Fast Retail, Uniqlo's parent company. In 1985 it opened its first unisex store, The Unique Clothing Warehouse, in Hiroshima. Less than 10 years later there were 100 Uniqlo outlets across Japan. The company moved into a higher gear in 1997, when it placed design, merchandizing and production under one roof and began 'buying high-quality materials at low cost through direct negotiations with, and bulk purchases from, material manufacturers globally' (**www.fastretailing.com**).

It shrugged off the idea that Japanese consumers would not buy items sourced in China – and in fact they loved the store's well-designed, good value basics. International expansion began with the UK in 2001 and has accelerated since, although at the time of writing only 10 per cent of the company's sales come from overseas. Uniqlo wants to fix this; overseas sales should surpass domestic revenue before the end of the decade ('Uniquely positioned', *The Economist*, 24 June 2010).

Uniqlo's strategy is different to those of Zara and H&M. It offers a comparatively short range – about 1,000 pieces – and steers clear of cutting-edge fashion so it can stock items for longer. Having said that, it sells the same models in many alluring colours: shoppers entering the French flagship that first week fell drooling over a rainbow array of cashmere v-neck sweaters. Shrewdly, the brand distracts from the rather mundane aspect of its designs by injecting Manga-style quirkiness into its stores and internet presence. In Paris, it's hard not to trip as you read the LED messages that flicker across the stairway. The brand has added a thin layer of fashion funkiness – like the red stripe in toothpaste – through partnerships with Jil Sander and Lady Gaga designer Nicola Formichetti. It has also done well with its HeatTech range of T-shirts and undergarments, which are made of rayon and milk protein. They work by using your 'body moisture' (read: sweat) to generate heat. With technology a key value of brand Japan, they lock into the retailer's image.

No HeatTech is required on the Côte d'Azur, however. Clad in my standard Cannes Lions Uniqlo T-shirt, I settle down at the festival's headquarters to talk to the brand's chief operating officer, Naoki Otoma (who is wearing a black polo and khakis). The first thing I do, of course, is ask him about the clockwork girls I downloaded from the website. It's clear that Uniqlo has decided to take an unconventional approach to advertising.

'We find that conventional advertising does not deliver the return on investment we require,' he replies. 'By communicating in an innovative way, we encourage people to talk about us. In that way, the customer comes to us and is fully engaged with the experience when they arrive at the site. It's the opposite of TV where you're trying to make yourself heard among many other brands. In fact we prefer not to think of what we do as advertising, but as communication with our customers. That's why it often has an interactive element.'

Talking to the customer is a pillar of Uniqlo's strategy: it says its Customer Centre receives around 70,000 comments a year and these are often fed back to the design team. The HeatTech range, for example, has been tweaked over the years to satisfy a desire for softer fabric, more colours and so on.

I note aloud that the humour of Uniqlo's advertising is in direct contrast to the understatement of its designs. Is that because it has its eye on a fairly young target group? Mr Otoma responds: 'The humour is a way of standing out in a world where people are bombarded with information. Nobody will pay attention to your communications unless it is attractive and entertaining. But to answer your question, we don't believe in market segmentation. Our clothes are for everybody, every day. For the same reason, you'll never find a logo on our clothes. We don't see ourselves as a fashion brand. People can adapt our clothes to suit their daily lives and their own unique personalities.'

The brand does have a distinct image, though. Even though it has gone global, it makes no attempt to disguise its provenance. 'We're proud to be seen as "born in Japan", because it implies quality, refinement and attention to detail. Our goal is to provide well-designed casual basics of the best quality at the most affordable prices. The retail space is important, too: it should be spacious, accessible and fun. We want customers to have a good time at our stores, so they look forward to coming back.'

Your clothes aren't made in Japan, though? 'About 90 per cent are made in China, although the materials are often sourced from elsewhere, such as denim from Japan, for example. As you can imagine, quality control is a hugely important issue for us. We have 300 Uniqlo employees in China supervising 70 manufacturers. We also have 30 experienced employees called *takumi*, or "masters", who are responsible for overall quality control and who oversee two or three sites each. It's also important to point out that we are not a "fast fashion" brand, so we don't need to put pressure on sites to churn out the latest trends.'

He adds that the recession had a positive impact on the company, as consumers turned their back on frivolity and became more exacting about quality and value for money. I mention the forthcoming store in Paris and ask him if overseas stores have a different format to those in Japan.

'We have different strategies for Europe and Asia. In Europe and the US, where our name is less familiar and there is less affinity with Japanese culture, we're opening large flagship stores to give us plenty of visibility. Competition is tough, so we're relying on the stores to express our image and demonstrate our offering. In Asia, where many customers already know us as a leading clothing brand, we've adopted a domination strategy: opening many stores in lots of different formats in order to combat the likes of Zara and H&M.'

Talking of those high street giants, isn't there a danger that Uniqlo's basics could be perceived as dull compared to their more fashion-forward designs? Can Uniqlo sell the same black polos and v-neck cashmere sweaters forever? Mr Otoma smiles in a 'you don't really get it, do you?' kind of way. He says, 'Basic items don't remain stable – they evolve. Silhouettes change, fabrics become more sophisticated, colours become more or less popular. By changing with our customers, we will continue to meet their demands and their expectations.'

The fact remains that H&M and Zara are still far bigger than Uniqlo when it comes to overseas sales. But they are undoubtedly looking over their shoulders.

The designer as brand

04

I don't follow trends. It's my job to create trends.

Snapshot number one:

Galignani, a cavernous bookstore on rue de Rivoli, Paris. Even on a Saturday afternoon, it is the kind of place where the only sounds are the turning of glossy pages and the pleasant creaking of varnished floorboards. Fiction is available here, but customers really come for hefty coffee table tomes about art, interior design and – yes – fashion.

I am looking through a book about 1950s furniture when I hear a familiar voice behind me. The language is French, but there is a metallic hint of something else: not English, but European. It has a vaguely aristocratic air about it; a Baron from the pages of Proust. I turn around and there he is: Karl Lagerfeld.

He's surrounded by an entourage of black-clad young men – and very quickly, by a team of enterprising booksellers – but he is quite unmistakable. The slender frame tightly bound in black jeans and a black jacket; the white shirt with its high Edwardian collar, cinched by a ribbon of black tie. The long pale face, impassive behind dark glasses. The white hair, tied in a pony-tail, which may well be powdered like that of an 18th century dandy.

Lagerfeld is the perfect incarnation of what most people think of as a 'fashion designer'. He is the head designer of a legendary brand, Chanel, while collaborating with Fendi and running his own brand. Nearing 80 years old, he has a relentless energy and, as those who have seen him on French television can attest, a fully functioning sense of humour.

He is also perfectly aware of his own image. In recent years, with his permission, his unmistakeable silhouette has appeared on a Coca-Cola bottle and been transformed into a rag doll – no facial expression required, just a black suit, dark glasses and that pony tail.

In short, Karl Lagerfeld is a logo.

Snapshot number two:

An exhibition about the history of Louis Vuitton – in particular, the work of its womenswear designer Marc Jacobs – at the Musée des Arts Décoratifs, right next door to the Louvre. The lower floor of the show is devoted to the heritage of the Vuitton brand: luxurious steamer trunks. But upstairs is a Marc Jacobs wonderland.

'I love those boots – the white ones,' says one young tourist, gazing at a selection of footwear displayed on kicking clockwork legs, like the disembodied limbs of cabaret dancers. Suddenly you have the impression that the show is a huge shop window (the boots are from spring–summer 2002). It's certainly an efficient exercise in public relations.

One of the highlights of this section is 'Marc's World', a video wall displaying a collage of films and stills, from the kitsch to the sublime. Tucked away among the images is a rather disturbing series of clips: all of Jacobs' appearances at the end of his runway shows for Vuitton. It's customary for designers to take a bow at the end of their shows, but one rarely sees a decade or so of curtain calls tagged end to end, like this.

I'm shocked by Marc's metamorphosis. He starts out as a diffident, bespectacled young man; faintly preppy, like a character from a Wes Anderson movie. As time rolls on, his clothing becomes more flamboyant. His hair lengthens and is then sheared into a Caesar cut. His body is reined in, moulded, pumped up by the gym. His tattoos flourish. He gains jewellery and a tan. By the end of the series, he has become an action figure. I mean that quite literally: the Marc Jacobs action figure is on display at the end of the show. A few inches of tan plastic in a little skirt.

In his own way, Jacobs too is the official face of the fashion designer.

Snapshot number three:

Rush hour on the metro. As you hurry through the labyrinth towards your platform, your eyes skim across the advertising posters. You spot one for the Galéries Lafayette department store. A familiar figure leaps out at you: cropped hair, a beaming smile, sailor stripes across his chest.

Jean-Paul Gaultier. A fashion icon, as familiar to most French citizens as a TV presenter. He was, perhaps, one of the earliest examples of a designer who crossed over into the realm of the pop star: indeed, back in 1989, he actually made a record – 'How To Do That' ('Ow To Do Zat'). His boundless energy and inventiveness have always appealed to the media and the public alike.

Designers are useful figures because they incarnate their brands; like strokes of shorthand, they embody the complex messages and values the brand is asking the public to buy in to. But these are dangerous times to be a designer. Alexander McQueen committed suicide. John Galliano, the flamboyant genius who embodied Dior, left under a cloud, embroiled in a scandal that began with a sordid argument in a bar. Other major figures have been linked with burnouts and drug abuse.

Because designers are more than just figureheads. While they are obviously supported by hardworking teams, they're asked to conceive an increasingly large number of collections: not just spring–summer and fall–winter (sometimes for both men and women), but also pre-collections, cruise collections, trunk shows and partnerships with chain stores. They are under pressure to be creative, but commercial; to represent mystique, but to keep their heads.

Tom Ford – another perfect example of the designer as brand – found it so exhausting that he left womenswear after his wildly successful stint at Gucci to concentrate on something less stressful: like making an Oscar-nominated movie. He has since moved back into the fashion spotlight, but with the distance and wisdom of a battle-scarred veteran.

Galliano and Ford are perfect examples of designers whose personal image helped to transform brands. A dead or dormant brand, whose founder has passed on or ceased to be involved, often needs an identifiable figurehead to make it relevant to consumers and the media. The designs must be compelling, of course, but that's only part of the job. Just as Ford became linked with Gucci, Galliano breathed new excitement into Dior when he was installed as its womenswear designer in 1996. Over a decade earlier, Lagerfeld had achieved much the same transformation at Chanel. Until certain chain stores began adopting the same strategy, a glamorous star designer – parachuted in for a huge fee, like a successful soccer player – was the main factor that separated a luxury brand from a high-street one.

These days, the process has become so familiar that it is beginning to sound formulaic. With each new appointment, we read that the incoming designer has foraged in the archives of the brand, uncovering a system of codes and values that they can use to inform their own vision. In this way they don't reproduce the original designs, but reinterpret and remix them to arrive at something entirely new – while at the same time giving a respectful nod to the owner of the name they are about to inherit.

British designer Ozwald Boateng arrived in Paris to design Givenchy's menswear collections in 2003: 'I looked in the archives. I took inspiration from the elegance of Hubert de Givenchy... That's how I discovered the emblem of the tulip, a flower that could often be seen in a vase on his desk. The polka dots that you can see in the linings of suits and hats or on pocket handkerchiefs recall the motif of his favourite ties.' ('Ozwald Boateng: Paris–Londres', *Le Monde*, 8 October 2004.)

When Nicolas Ghesquière became head designer at Balenciaga in 1997, he was forbidden access to the archives by their imposing-sounding guardian, Madame Jouve. As he recounts, 'They must have thought I'd make poor use of them. I discovered [Cristobal Balenciaga's collections] by another means, in the museums of the United States and in Irving Penn's images, which at the same time meant that I was not overloaded with references, didn't end up making reproductions.' ('Nicolas Ghesquière sort de l'ombre', *Le Figaro*, 28 September 2004.)

Ghesquière has since become one of the most fêted designers in Paris, praised for having turned Balenciaga back into a mega-brand by combining his own 1980s influences – the high-tech experimentation of Issey Miyake, the glamour of Versace, the daring of Gaultier – with the Spanish designer's architectural sensibilities. It doesn't hurt, either, that Ghesquière's clothes have been enthusiastically adopted by French actress and fashion icon Charlotte Gainsbourg.

At the time of writing, a new round of musical chairs has seen Hedi Slimane settling into the hot seat at Yves Saint Laurent, while the cool Belgian Raf Simons has taken over at Dior. Two of the most admired names in fashion, facing off. Exciting for us, daunting for them.

Once, designers seemed all-powerful. But now we know where the power lies: with corporate bosses and shareholders. Today, designers know that are replaceable, even those who've founded their own brands. How do they feel about that? What will happen to Paul Smith, the brand, when Paul Smith, the designer, decides to retire? Mulling over the question, Smith said, 'I always have a hard time thinking of myself as a brand, even though I occasionally talk about this entity called "Paul Smith", as if it's not my own name. I got into this business because I loved it, then woke up one day and realized

I was locked into this system of marketing. I suppose we'll just have to wait and see. The business is structured so that everything is taken care of, except my own personality.'

Fashion designer may seem a desirable profession – almost a dream job, like actor or sports hero. But the showmanship of a Jacobs and the fluid *bons mots* of a Lagerfeld put a smooth façade on an abrasive industry. As a choice of career, fashion designer makes even freelance journalist seem a responsible and financially secure way of earning a living. Despite John Galliano's acclaimed degree collection at Central Saint Martin's College of Art, he struggled to obtain financial backing in London. When he first arrived in Paris, he was forced to sleep on friends' floors while he created his next collection. It was only when Anna Wintour, the editor of US *Vogue*, helped him to secure backing that his career began to take off. Ford, meanwhile, worked as an assistant to two designers in New York before moving to Gucci in 1990 – where his clothes were barely noticed until a breakthrough collection in 1995.

Every year, at fashion school degree shows, awards ceremonies and competitions, one or two names are proposed as the future of fashion. A very few make it. Stephanie Finnian, owner of the careers advice service The Fashion Careers Clinic, states clearly that 'talent is not enough'. She says, 'It's often the better designers who are missing out on jobs, simply because they've been told how amazing they are by tutors and parents... While there's clearly nothing wrong with praise for a graduate, it's dangerous if the said graduate then thinks a job will fall at their feet. I've seen many graduates who have had lots of press after their university show and been featured in news articles and photo shoots yet haven't secured a job in the six months to a year after graduation. Graduates should be aware that they need to be proactive and persistent.' ('Becoming a fashion designer', *Guardian Careers*, 5 April 2011.)

Some have a brief burst of glory before dissolving into the design teams of the established brands. Many are never heard of again.

How to be a designer brand

I am hurrying down a street in the centre of an unexpectedly hot London, perspiring heavily and late for an exclusive interview with one of the city's favourite designers. Matthew Williamson and his business partner Joseph Velosa have agreed to put some time aside for me and my book.

Williamson burst on to the scene, as they say, during London Fashion Week in 1997. His debut collection was modelled by, among others, Kate Moss, Helena Christensen and Jade Jagger. Not bad for a start, and the press couldn't fail to notice. The show made front pages in the UK and Williamson was soon being fêted not only by the UK edition of *Vogue* – which had known about him for some time, as we'll see later – but by glossies all over the world.

These days, his clothes are stocked in more than 170 stores worldwide, and he has standalone boutiques in London, New York, Dubai and Qatar. A celebrity magnet, his designs have been worn by Madonna, Sarah Jessica Parker, Gwyneth Paltrow, Kirsten Dunst and Nicole Kidman. And to top it all, at the end of 2007 the Design Museum in London staged a special exhibition celebrating his 20th year in fashion.

At the time of our meeting, Williamson's business is located in a beautiful townhouse in a street off Tottenham Court Road. It is colourful and cluttered and very neo-Bloomsbury; and the first thing I do on entering is almost trip over a small dog. 'You've met Coco, then?' says the receptionist, when the shiny-eyed spaniel follows me into her office. A few moments later, I climb the stairs to what seems like the top of the house, getting glimpses of people working in warren-like spaces; a PC here, a pile of drawings there. The walls are painted in warm, rich shades that recall Morocco or India – locations that have inspired Williamson's designs. Joseph Velosa – a dark-haired young man with a calm, measured voice – shows me into a bright and spacious office. My eye is drawn to the colourful illustrations tacked to the far wall – Williamson's next collection, which he'll be showing in New York in September. This would have started life as a 'mood board': colourful pages torn from books and magazines, images and objects, scraps of fabric … a magpie collection that defines the tone and feel of the resulting show.

Velosa and Williamson met when the designer was still at Saint Martin's. At the time Velosa was doing a philosophy degree – something that sits oddly with his obvious talent for marketing. Mutual attraction evolved naturally into a partnership, with Velosa taking care of the strategic side while Williamson concentrated on designing and giving the brand a public face. But the delineation between the two is much less strict than it appears, as Williamson is quick to point out. 'It's always presented as though [Joseph] is poring over bank statements while I'm mincing around with a pencil,' jokes the designer, whose faint Manchester accent gives him a sardonic, self-deprecating air. 'In fact I love the business side – and Joseph is very creative.'

The arrangement is not without precedents. Perhaps the most obvious comparison is the partnership between Pierre Bergé and Yves Saint Laurent. Partners in life as well as in business, they founded their company in 1961, with Bergé as managing director – the same position occupied by Velosa. The museum in Paris devoted to Saint Laurent's work is called the Fondation Pierre Bergé/Yves Saint Laurent.

Williamson is slight and energetic, and the rakish beard he has adopted can't conceal a certain boyish quality. This should not be confused with lack of seriousness or ambition, however. He is one of those rare people with a vocation: 'I always knew what I wanted to do. Even at the age of 11 or 12 I knew that I wanted to be involved in art or design, and shortly after that I realized it was fashion I was really interested in. It was instinctive, somehow. I'd been good at art all the way through school, and I was interested in clothes. I was always sketching. By the time I applied for a foundation course at Manchester Polytechnic, the woman there took one look at my portfolio and told me it would be a waste of time: I should apply directly to Central Saint Martin's.'

He did so – and was accepted after his first interview. 'I didn't think I had the slightest chance of getting in, so I must have come over as rather blasé,' he recalls, smiling. 'They misconstrued what was actually nervousness as coolness and confidence.'

He studied fashion design for four years, specializing in textiles and print. But life at the famous college – whose alumni include John Galliano, Alexander McQueen and Stella McCartney – was not to Williamson's liking. In fact, he's one of the few designers to have spoken out against the school: 'It has a phenomenal reputation, but I didn't really fit in there. They're not interested in the business side of fashion. I had the feeling you were left to sink or swim. And either you flourish and become fabulous, or you don't. I was a bit of a black sheep because I was the antithesis of what they try to promote. They're interested in fashion as art. So while I was trying to design clothes that somebody might actually want to wear, my fellow students were doing things like going to mental institutions to seek inspiration. It wasn't the greatest period of my life.'

During his third year at the school, in 1993, Williamson got a placement working for the legendary British designer Zandra Rhodes. 'I loved working in her design studio and watching the pattern cutters bring her designs to life,' he recounts, in one of the notes accompanying the Design Museum exhibition. At the end of the day he would sweep up the unused scraps of material, which he assiduously set aside for himself. A patchwork fabric made from these scraps eventually became a shift dress that appeared in his triumphant graduate collection.

After leaving Saint Martin's, Williamson went to work at Monsoon, the ethnically inspired chain store. He was there for two years as a freelance designer, dealing largely with the accessories division. 'After Saint Martin's it was an incredible release. I was doing my own thing, I was gaining experience... Part of my job was to go to India at least twice a year, but usually three or four times. I learnt a lot through, firstly, working for a massive company – because even though it's high street, the same principles apply – and, secondly, the travelling. The trips to India were inspirational, but they also provided the first sign of a resource. Before that, I had no idea how to go about sourcing fabric.'

After two years at Monsoon, Williamson associated with two suppliers in India and started his own label. 'At first I just made scarves, because I was still too scared to make clothes. I wanted to get some publicity, so I opened a copy of British *Vogue* and scanned the editorial page. I thought going straight for the editor might be a bit over-ambitious, so I chose a writer called Plum Sykes, because I liked her name.' He laughs at the naivety, which, at the beginning of his career, turned out to be his greatest asset. 'I sent her a letter with a scarf. She was impressed by that and invited me in to the *Vogue* offices. So I took a box full of scarves and swatches and a few trinkets, and suddenly I had about 20 women around me, all *screaming*, telling me that they loved this stuff and that I had to make dresses for them all. That was my first order. I went home to Joseph in a state of shock – and told him I'd have to make some clothes. Joseph became involved organically from that moment on.'

Velosa recalls, 'He came home saying something like "I've got what I wanted – now what do I do?" So we sat down and worked out how much it was going to cost to produce the garments, what the mark-up needed to be in order to make it worth our while... and before we knew it we'd created this cottage industry.'

On *Vogue*'s advice, the pair trotted along to a Knightsbridge store called A La Mode. Although at that point Williamson had made only two dresses, the buyer immediately placed an order for several dozen pieces. Williamson says, 'I was overwhelmed, but Joseph reckoned that if we could get into A La Mode, we could get into [the temple to style on London's South Molton Street] Brown's. So we went around the corner to Brown's and got another order for 50 to 100 pieces. By then we were getting very excited with ourselves, so we started thinking about Barney's in New York and Colette in Paris.'

Fired up with enthusiasm, they got on a plane to India and started the production process. Velosa says the anecdote is illustrative of fashion's insatiable hunger for novelty: 'It shows you how little you really need to do in order to impregnate the market. As it's based on change, fashion is inevitably attracted to anything new. Clearly, Plum [Sykes] saw something in Matthew's work that appealed to her, but I don't think there is any other industry that is so accepting of this kind of approach. As you go on, of course, you realize that, while there's a certain amount of tolerance for new talent, it's actually quite a conservative industry, with almost scientifically defined parameters.'

In this respect, Williamson's overnight success has a perfectly logical explanation. Velosa elucidates: 'It's known as "confetti buying" or "confetti press". Whether you are a buyer at Barney's or the editor of a fashion magazine, it's the same principle. You have to dedicate 80 per cent of your floor space to your mega-brands, or 80 per cent of your editorial to your biggest advertisers. So you're left with 20 per cent of what's called "confetti" – the fun, new and innovative stuff that you sprinkle around to make your store or your magazine look fresh and interesting.'

The problems start when you want to hang around for a while. Velosa says that the British fashion scene, in particular, is extremely fickle; the latest big thing can turn into yesterday's news in the blink of an eye. 'Sooner or later you realize that, like any other industry, fashion is controlled by money. If you have money, you have advertising muscle, so you can control your editorial presence, which then affects how the customer perceives you, which in turn maintains the buyers' interest in your label.'

For the same reason, the label no longer shows during London Fashion Week. Velosa explains that New York was chosen because the Paris and Milan collections are dominated 'by huge advertising brands and heritage brands'. 'With the heavyweights controlling everything, it's almost impossible to get a good slot in the schedule – and if you don't, you're immediately regarded as B-list. New York is less crowded, so you can get a decent slot, yet everyone goes there. London Fashion Week is known as exciting and innovative, but it's also seen as a distraction. Because young designers receive little support in the UK beyond an initial burst of enthusiasm, few of them make it to an international level. So London has come to be seen as interesting, but not serious.'

Matthew Williamson has survived by adopting smart marketing tactics that have not, by and large, required a great deal of outlay. Most importantly, he has used his natural charm and his ability to attract supporters, mainly in the shape of beautiful young women. The first in a long line was Jade Jagger, whose papa is a Rolling Stone but who, as a jewellery designer, is these days better known for gemstones. After modelling a neon-pink Matthew Williamson dress for society mag *Tatler*, she contacted him to find out where she could get her hands on another one. Velosa, who answered the phone, told her very innocently how much it would cost her. He recalls his partner's reaction: 'When I told Matthew, he said, "Are you crazy? She needs to be wearing it! And we should give her some others too." So he arranged to see her and they had what I can only describe as a meeting of minds.'

Williamson admits that he saw the potential of the relationship – but he stresses that all his celebrity links are driven by genuine admiration. 'I am inspired by people who have a certain sense of style and way of life. So I've built this little... collective, if you like. But it's always a creative relationship. When I met Jade there was a spark creatively – we loved each other's work and we were drawn to the same things.' By the time Helena Christensen, who had seen the same dress in *Tatler*, called up, Velosa had got wise to the strategy: 'I asked her whether, in exchange for a few free frocks, she'd agree to model them for us.'

Another key member of the coterie is Bay Garnett, who styles Williamson's shows. Actress Sienna Miller is also a fan. Williamson adds, 'Socializing with these girls and delving into what they're thinking has been crucial, because obviously as a guy doing womenswear you need to get some insight and feedback. But it doesn't have to be famous women – it can just as easily be my mum or my sister.'

Away from his limelight-grabbing celebrity links, Williamson has embarked on a number of business collaborations designed to raise sponsorship cash and generate PR coverage. These have included a limited-edition bottle design for Coca-Cola, a range of rugs for The Rug Company and exclusive stationery for Smythson of Bond Street, as well as a line of Williamson-designed clothes for department store Debenhams. Williamson and Velosa maintain strict control of the brand's image, and have no desire to go on a Cardin-style licensing spree – but, at the same time, they clearly envisage a future filled with Matthew Williamson sunglasses, shoes, bags and other accessories.

Years after that initial meeting at *Vogue*, Williamson still regularly meets up with Plum Sykes, and he works with the same factories in India. But these days his clothes are sold all over the world. 'On the surface it's still about me, but increasingly I'm a cog in the wheel,' he says, almost apologetically. 'Joseph always says the things we produce are at their best and most pure when they come directly from me, so I realize that I have to remain heavily involved in the design process. But as the business grows, my job becomes more fractured and I have to deal with a number of other things. It's overly romantic to think that I sit around designing 24/7. And I'm not sure I'd want to, because developing the business is important to me. I'm a businessman.'

He's certainly down to earth (although he claims to have a more exaggerated 'fashion' persona that he can wheel out when required). Williamson says he's not an intellectual designer 'intent on changing the way we dress'. He designs for women who want to look sexy and of the moment – and that's it. 'I don't think fashion is theatre, so my clothes aren't costume or avant-garde. A critic might say that they don't have any content other than being whimsical, feminine and decorative. But I don't have an issue with that. I think you have to find out what you're good at and then do it to the best of your ability.' Nor does he pay much attention to the vagaries of fashion. Like most designers at his level, Williamson is intent on creating his own style: 'I don't follow trends. If anything, I think it's my job to create trends.'

So how big could the Matthew Williamson brand be? Does he want to be a Gucci, or a Prada? He shakes his head. 'I think we're niche. But you can be niche and global at the same time. I'm particularly thinking of Missoni, Chloé, Pucci and Marni. Those four labels are international fashion brands, but they're not necessarily household names. And that's where I think our future lies, when I'm at my most optimistic.'

The store in Bruton Street is a strutting peacock of an establishment, embracing all the elements of the Williamson brand: colour, glamour, ethnicity, and even an unexpected Arts and Crafts sensibility. Needless to say, it sent interiors magazines into ecstasies of delight. 'Matthew Williamson's Mayfair jungle,' blazed the cover of *World of Interiors* in July 2004.

According to Velosa, 'The store is the cornerstone of why we're here today – how we can even discuss the future. We weren't an advertising brand; we were a small British designer brand struggling to break through to an international market. We thought about ways that we could stand out, and we realized we had to compete with the likes of Stella McCartney and Alexander McQueen. Even though their stores were backed by the Gucci organization, we knew we had to come in at the same level, at least in terms of perception. It was no good fading into the background with a little boutique in Notting Hill. So we raised the money through the Debenhams venture and by re-mortgaging our own properties.'

It was a risky venture that appears to have paid off – at the time of our interview, Velosa says takings are six times higher than predicted. 'It's unprecedented in that we've been able to open a retail operation without the backing of a major conglomerate. It also provides a fantastic expression of the brand and an invaluable contact with consumers.'

He points out that the fragrance works on a similar, but micro, level. 'You literally have to condense everything you stand for into a box. I think you've got a very successful brand if you can do that.' Williamson describes creating his fragrance as 'one of the most satisfying projects I've ever worked on'. 'The man who was responsible for the bottle design was a very chic, elegant character from Paris. He sat opposite me and said almost nothing as I struggled to explain my point of view and where I was coming from. I'd cobbled together a few... odds and ends, for want of a better expression: a tea-cup; a Venetian mirror; various objects that had inspired me over the years. And he nodded and went away, and I said to Joseph, "That was probably the worst meeting of my life."'

Three months later, the bottle designer reappeared. This time he donned white gloves and placed eight black velvet pouches on the table. 'I opened the first one, and it was, "Oh my God!" The next one was the same. In the end, I loved all of them. The guy had not only listened to every word I'd said, but he'd perfectly interpreted my ideas.'

The fragrance launch was supported by the brand's first print advertising campaign, created by the agency M&C Saatchi. But Williamson is keen to emphasize that his approach has not changed. As he underlines, 'I've overseen every detail, from start to finish. I wouldn't do it otherwise. After all, with each product area you go into, you're still trying to express your personal vision. However big your company ultimately becomes, it's vital you keep control over that.'

The store is the star

05

Customers today expect shopping to be a brand experience.

In London's New Bond Street, on a chilly November afternoon, the Asprey store is dressed for Christmas. Thousands of fairy-lights twinkle enticingly around its windows, and in the central atrium a splendid Christmas tree (could it actually be in British Racing Green?) soars almost to the ceiling. But there is nothing tacky about the festive décor because, along with the aromas of pine and scented candles, Asprey exudes class.

'Good afternoon sir, can I help you?' enquires a smartly suited doorman, seconds after I've stepped into the fragrant trap. I reply that I am just browsing, thank you, and he discreetly retires with a faint sketch of a bow, as if he is my brand-new butler.

Asprey has been selling luxury goods and jewellery from these premises since 1847, but in past decades it is unlikely that anybody with an eye for fashion would have paid it a visit. All that changed in May 2004, when Asprey's new owners, investors Laurence Stroll and Silas Chou, re-opened the store after a two-year, £50 million refit. The pair had acquired Asprey & Garrard from Brunei royalty in 2000. Asprey was known for selling prestigious but hardly pulse-quickening items such as silver and leather goods, watches, porcelain, crystal, rare books and gems. But Stroll and Chou promised to turn it into 'the ultimate British luxury lifestyle house' – Louis Vuitton with an English accent. When the refurbished Asprey threw open its doors, it was backed by an advertising campaign featuring the British actress Keira Knightley and styled by New York-based art director Fabien Baron. On display in the store, alongside an extravagant array of baubles and accessories, there was a line of ready-to-wear designed by Hussein Chalayan.

Once Asprey had had a chance to settle in to its spiffy new image, it became clear that the space itself was the star of the show. Before the revamp, the store was a stuffy warren formed by five 18th-century townhouses clustered around a concealed courtyard. Architect Norman Foster – whose previous, rather larger, refurbishment projects include the Reichstag and the British Museum – uncovered the courtyard, sheltered it with glass, and added a grand sweeping staircase reminiscent of a luxury liner. Interior designer David Mlinaric – who refurbished Spencer House, the former home of Diana, Princess of Wales, in 1990 – retained and recovered historic elements such as decorative pillars and an 18th-century fireplace, without undermining Foster's modernity.

The 6,000-square-metre retail space feels even bigger, thanks to a mirrored wall alongside the staircase. There is an air of understated elegance that invites shoppers to linger, to wallow in the luxury. The carpets are plush underfoot; cream leather sofas beckon here and there. Various touches indicate that this is a branding concept as well as a retail one: the subtle references to the 1920s, the last period when Asprey was remotely fashionable; and, more obviously, the use of a signature hue. This colour, a purple so deep that it is almost aubergine, is seen on the banner outside the store, in the suits sported by Asprey's doormen, and in a branded fragrance called Purple Water.

'The store is absolutely the key to the brand,' said Gianluca Brozzetti, then CEO of Asprey & Garrard Group, shortly after the re-opening. 'Customers today expect shopping to be a brand experience. As they move from store to store, they move from atmosphere to atmosphere. And Asprey has an atmosphere that is absolutely unique.'

Surveyed from the staircase, the store has a nostalgic, other-worldly atmosphere. Perhaps, long ago, all department stores were like this.

Retail cathedrals

Buying clothes has never been a simple pleasure. In recent times we've grown familiar with the concept of the 'brand experience' – but more than a century ago retailers understood that they had to make shopping an adventure. In his book *Au Bonheur des Dames (The Ladies' Paradise)* Emile Zola presents a lightly fictionalized version of the Bon Marché department store in Paris, which he describes as 'devoted to consumerism'. The store's roguish manager, Octave Mouret, unhesitatingly equates shopping with lust. The sight of women scrabbling to get a look at the latest silks leaves him breathless: '[They] paled with desire and leaned over as if to see themselves, secretly fearing they would be captivated by such overwhelming luxury and unable to resist the urge to throw themselves in.' In another scene, he catches one of his salesmen laying out swatches of silk in harmonious gradations of colour, blue next to grey. Mouret pounces on the man, exhorting him to 'blind them!' with red, green and yellow. Zola portrays his hero as the best *étalagiste* – display artist – in the whole of Paris. The year is 1888.

Many of the earliest department stores are still open for business today. The Bon Marché, which opened in 1853, is generally accepted to have been the first. Its owner, Aristide Boucicaut – the model for Zola's central character – was a retail pioneer and marketing visionary. At the beginning of the 19th century French shopkeepers were still mired in a positively medieval system. Historically, access to trades and professions had been regulated by a system of unions. Traders were required to specialize in a single product or service and could not, legally, branch out into other markets. Firms were passed from father to son, and business was done with regular customers on a one-to-one basis, often by appointment. Clients rarely ventured beyond their local vendors. Prices were not displayed, and bargaining was expected. This meant there was little need for advertising, window displays, or any other form of visual merchandizing.

The system was scrapped in 1790, but for more than 30 years traders stuck tenaciously to the traditional structure. It was only in the 1820s that a new type of boutique, called a *magasin des nouveautés*, began to appear. Grouping textiles, parasols and other items under one roof, these small shops developed revolutionary techniques like tempting window displays, clearly marked prices and the division of merchandise into aisles. It was in one of these stores that Aristide Boucicaut started his career in 1830. Some 20 years later he formed a partnership with one Paul Videau to run a more prestigious concern. Located at the corner of Rue de Sèvres and Rue du Bac, it was called Le Bon Marché, or 'The Good Deal'. Thanks to Boucicaut's innovations, notably discounting and the rapid rotation of stock, in a few years its profits rose from 450,000 French francs to more than 7 million. At that point, Boucicaut bought out his partner and embarked on an ambition expansion plan.

Boucicaut's idea was to create not merely a 'shop of novelties', but a shopping emporium. He brought in none other than Gustave Eiffel to help him build his dream. Eiffel was an expert in manipulating iron and glass, which meant he could construct the huge display windows and open shopping spaces that Boucicaut had in mind. The new, improved Bon Marché store opened in 1870. It was a veritable cathedral of commerce, with light pouring through lofty skylights and departments accessed by swirling stair-cases. The structure covered 52,800 square metres and eventually employed 3,000 people. The techniques that Boucicaut used to ensnare customers were astonishing in their modernity: home delivery, reimbursement, sea-sonal sales, illustrated catalogues and commission for sales staff were just some of the advances he brought to the retail business.

Of course, Le Bon Marché was not alone. In the cities of Europe and the United States, economic growth driven by industrialization was creating an eager market of consumers, and giant stores were springing up to serve them. In 1862, A T Stewart opened New York's first department store, strad-dling an entire city block at Ninth Street and Broadway. Macy's – originally a smallish haberdashery – expanded in the 1900s to become the world's largest department store. In 1851 William Whiteley opened a small shop in the unfashionable Bayswater quarter of London. As his business grew, he acquired the shops around it, becoming one of the city's most successful entrepreneurs. Whiteley was murdered in 1907 by a man who claimed to be his illegitimate son. The department store that bore his name – today a shop-ping mall – opened in 1912. Six years earlier, an American entrepreneur called Harry Gordon Selfridge had opened his eponymous store in London. Just around the corner, in Regent Street, Liberty was closer in ambience and clientele to today's Asprey; opened by Arthur Lasenby Liberty in 1875, it catered to a craze for fabric and *objets d'art* from the Orient. Like Whiteley, Liberty gradually acquired neighbouring properties, and his emporium soon became London's most fashionable shopping venue.

For decades, the department store remained an appealing 'destination', reflecting Gordon Selfridge's foresighted philosophy that shopping should be a form of entertainment. Unfortunately, though, the stream of innova-tions that had originally lured customers into the stores began to dry up, and eventually trickled into nothingness. A century after their creation, the giants began to seem more like dinosaurs. Certainly they would have looked familiar to Boucicaut and Selfridge. While bright, spirited chain stores such as Topshop began taking cues from high fashion, department stores were bogged down with dull own-brands and risk-averse buying.

Selfridges was one of the first to break out of the time bubble. It com-menced a five-year overhaul in 1994, pulling in a host of cutting-edge brands and refiguring the store to target young, upmarket shoppers. These days it's the unassailable home of fashion on Oxford Street. On the other side of the Channel, in 2009 the venerable Printemps department store completed a €280 million refurbishment that included, among other things, recruiting a team of artisans to restore its 19th-century façade and hiring interior architects Yubu Pushelberg to rip out three floors and replace them with a spectacular atrium. Entering the luxury accessory department on the ground floor, visitors now find their gaze drawn upwards, almost impelled to step on the escalator that rises through the 15-metre space.

One UK name that has been linked with fashion since the 1990s is Harvey Nichols, which as well as its Knightsbridge flagship has stores in Birmingham, Leeds, Manchester and Edinburgh. Affectionately known as 'Harvey Nicks', it was championed by the shopping- and Champagne-addicted Edwina and Patsy in the cult sitcom *Absolutely Fabulous*.

Benjamin Harvey opened his linen shop in a terraced house on the corner of London's Knightsbridge and Sloane Street in 1813. In 1820 the business passed into the hands of his daughter, who went into partnership with a certain Colonel Nichols to sell oriental carpets, silks and luxury goods. The existing Knightsbridge store was opened in the 1880s. With its award-winning window displays and tempting array of designer brands, Harvey Nichols is an ideal place to examine the interplay between a department store and its customers.

Creativity drives consumption

April Glassborow, senior buyer for international designer collections at Harvey Nichols, drifted into her career by accident. 'I'd left university having done a French degree and took a temporary job at Liberty, working in the jewellery department,' she recalls. 'At one point the buyer fell ill, so I took over her job for a while. Later, when she moved departments, I took over full-time. Subsequently I bought accessories; then I moved to Harvey Nichols to buy jewellery and womenswear.'

Glassborow says buying for Harvey Nichols involves something of a balancing act: 'We're expected to be a step ahead, so we are constantly look-ing for new labels. We take risks with young designers who may not sell a great deal for three or four seasons, until a buzz generates around them. But at the same time, we want to reflect the demands of our customers, so we stock the more commercial designers too. In general, though, I don't think our type of customer is content to blindly follow the herd.'

As well as monitoring all the usual sources – magazines, the web, mutter-ings on the fashion grapevine – Glassborow receives intelligence from the store's representatives around the world, who are often its first point of contact with young designers, forwarding photographs and background information. Crucially, she decides where each brand will be located in the store. 'The amount of space you are going to give to each designer clearly dictates the buying, so it's impossible to separate the two. Once again, you have to evaluate the "hot" aspect of a designer compared with the commercial reality: just how well is this label going to sell? And then, of course, the decisions you make about placing the clothes affect sales. You are aware that a certain type of customer goes for a certain type of designer, so the idea is to keep them flowing from one boutique to another, almost unconsciously, because they keep seeing things that catch their eye. I can't tell you how I do that – it becomes instinctive.'

Instinct also drives the work of Janet Wardley, the store's visual merchandizing controller, who handles window displays as well as interior mannequins and display points. 'I'm lucky because, at Harvey Nichols, the display function is separated from the marketing department, which is not the case in many places. It means there is no pressure on me to favour certain brands, or to give the entire window display over to one brand because a deal has been struck. We ensure that the Harvey Nichols brand comes out on top. That situation gives me a lot of freedom.'

She endeavours to evoke an atmosphere that enhances the clothes, rather than being led by them. At the time I interview her, she's just created a dark, autumnal theme with Halloween overtones, featuring giant metal insects. 'For spring I'm picking up on blue, which is going to be big next season. You have to be on-trend, not just in terms of fashion magazines and runway shows – which of course I study – but also in terms of the general feel of the times. You're reading newspapers and listening to the radio, soaking up influences. One of the interesting things about Harvey Nichols is that it is considered a trendsetter, so we can't really get it "wrong", so to speak.'

Interestingly, Wardley never receives official feedback about whether her displays have driven sales inside the store. 'It's considered one of the last artistic professions, so to be monitored in that way would take away our freedom and the ability to take risks. It's precisely because we don't have to answer to commercial concerns that we can do something entirely different. After all, we're supposed to be the leaders in our field.'

Wardley heads a team of 10, including five prop builders and two graphic designers (who take care of signage). Harvey Nichols has its own workshop and, on the rare occasions it sources materials from outside the company, it tends to use the same trusted suppliers. Mannequins get to travel, as they are rotated around the group's stores. Occasionally they are renovated.

Wardley – who rarely looks at the windows of rival stores in case she is 'inspired by someone else without realizing it' – has none the less noticed the return of the mannequin, the humble shop-window dummy, as a display device. 'There was a time when all the chain stores were using posters and bust forms in their windows. I imagine it was because they'd spent so much money on their advertising that they wanted to squeeze maximum value out of it, so they put the posters in the window, too. It was a classic case of what happens when the marketing department drives the display side. Now it seems to be swinging back the other way – you're seeing mannequins again and more creative displays.'

Of all the marketing tricks in the retail book, window displays are the oldest and, still, the most alluring. Every year in the run-up to Christmas, crowds jostle in front of breath-fogged windows in Regent Street, Boulevard Haussmann and Fifth Avenue. Historically, French fashion houses were judged by the sophistication of their window displays. In Paris, the house of Hermès on the Rue du Faubourg Saint Honoré has long been famed for its enchanting fairy-tale displays created by Leïla Menchari – who has been with Hermès since 1977 – which combine silk and leather goods with jewellery, flowers, sculptures, and even leaves and seashells. And all this from a company that claims with a straight face that it does not do 'marketing'.

In a world where luxury is big business, even the most exclusive brands rely on marketing – and their stores are the most spectacular manifestations of their ambition.

Luxury theme parks and urban bazaars

'Maison Hermès understands that the shop window is more than a platform for showcasing the latest bag or belt. 'The window... communicates what the brand represents,' wrote Kanae Hasagawa in the interior design magazine *Frame* (May/June 2004). 'At the big Maison Hermès outlet in Ginza, Tokyo, the retailer has worked with no fewer than ten international artists and designers on a series of rotating displays since the store opened in 2001. Designed by Renzo Piano, Maison Hermès is a serene ten-storey edifice wrapped almost entirely in blank façades of glass block.'

As Hasagawa suggests, the communications potential of a store goes way deeper than the window. Architecture is an element of brand communication: the choice of location, the façade, the height of the ceiling, the size of the changing rooms, the attitude of the sales staff, the colours and the name of the architect all express the values of the brand you've come to explore. They are, in effect, expensive packaging.

Luxury brands are in competition to see which of them can open the most immense, sense-scrambling spaces. In 2005, to mark its 150th anniversary, Louis Vuitton took the wraps off its biggest store so far: more than 1,500 square metres on Paris's Champs-Elysées, previously hidden behind a colossal monogrammed suitcase while the work was being completed. More recently, in Rome, Vuitton opened a flagship in what was once Etoile, the city's first cinema. It included a library and a screening room. As well as allowing it to 'support the Italian film industry', it also enables Vuitton to screen the elongated advertising spots that it regularly debuts online. There could hardly be a clearer indication that stores have become entertainment complexes as well as showcases for product.

In Milan, visitors to the Espace Armani in Via Manzoni can stroll through the entire price range, from suits to jeans, while pausing at a café, a bookshop, an exhibition space or a branch of hip Japanese restaurant Nobu.

Some of the most powerful expressions of architecture-as-branding come from Prada, whose stores perfectly express its intellectual image. The locations are designed by the hippest architects: Herzog & de Meuron (best known in the UK for the Tate Modern art gallery) in Tokyo; Rem Koolhaas in New York and Los Angeles. Exteriors provide no trace of the Prada name – smart Prada consumers, undoubtedly up to their ears in newspapers and architecture magazines, are expected to know where they are headed. This concept is taken to the ultimate degree in Los Angeles, where the entire front of the store is open to Rodeo Drive, taking advantage of the clement weather and tempting passers-by to drop in. A subtle wall of air keeps breezes and raindrops at bay when needs be – and at night an aluminium screen rises from the ground to seal off the space. Shop 'windows' are giant reinforced portholes set into the floor, so customers trot over the mannequins. The interior is pure science fiction. Plasma screens blink fragmentary images and clips of the day's news, and glass changing rooms turn opaque at the touch of a floor-switch. Lighting controls enable customers to see their desired garment at various times of the day. Elsewhere, laminated screens change in tone and hue depending on how many bodies are present. At the press launch, Koolhaas told journalists, 'We give people the freedom not to shop … by devising alternative sources of interest.' ('Down with shopping', *The Guardian*, 20 July 2004.)

There are suggestions, however, that many consumers are veering away from one-brand shopping destinations. If clothing is an expression of identity, then shoppers require a range of brands to choose from, mixing and sampling like DJs until they've transformed their selection into something entirely personal. Such consumers wish to peruse items of the highest quality, however, so a vast department store will not do. Instead, they turn to pre-edited collections of brands, chosen for them by one-off stores such as Colette in Paris and 10 Corso Como in Milan. These destinations typically also contain gadgets, furniture, CDs, books and art – the keys to a fashionable lifestyle. 'Such stores are not created, they are curated,' says Genevieve Flaven of trend-tracking agency Style-Vision.

Carla Sozzani, the founder in 1991 of Milan's 10 Corso Como, prefers to think of her operation as a contemporary European take on an oriental bazaar. Sozzani's 4,000-square-metre space fringes a shaded courtyard restaurant and incorporates a photographic and design gallery, a bookshop, a music outlet and boutiques selling clothing and accessories.

The ancient concept of the bazaar, or quite simply the market, has also been re-appropriated by fashion retailers. 'I have always loved the energy and anarchy of good markets,' Rei Kawakubo, the designer behind Comme des Garçons, told the *International Herald Tribune* ('Kawakubo's commune: a retail rebellion', 7 September 2004). Kawakubo was speaking at the opening of The Dover Street Market, her eclectic retail concept housed in a six-storey Georgian building in London. Along with clothing created by Kawakubo and fellow designer Junya Watanabe, there were contributions from various 'guests': furniture designed by Hedi Slimane; a white collection from Lanvin's Alber Elbaz; jewellery by Judy Blame; unique pieces from Azzedine Alaïa; the labels Boudicca and Anne Valery Hash; an outpost of cult Los Angeles vintage store Decades.

The design of the store resembles a stage set, with boutiques housed in battered wooden huts, screened by silk curtains or standing before theatrical backdrops. There is art inspired by Picasso, and even a recreation of a French bakery. 'Shops are clothes just put in a gorgeous box. But for me, the box itself is as important as the clothes,' Kawakubo has pointed out.

It has to be said that she is more innovative than most when it comes to creating retail experiences. Running in tandem with the Dover Street venture, she also introduced the concept of Guerrilla Stores. These hit-and-run outlets open for only a few months at a time, taking over empty spaces in the edgiest districts of cities. After all, if fashion is ephemeral, why shouldn't stores be equally transient? The stores are designed to be discovered by word-of-mouth, as their target market chatters about them in clubs and on the web. The strategy acknowledges that, being naturally suspicious of anything 'corporate', the new generation of consumers prefers to mine its information from underground seams. The stores flatter consumers who take pride in discovering and inventing trends. Fatigued by the infinite buying opportunities around them, they look for the eccentric and the rare.

Whether fashion retail spaces resemble markets, art galleries or palaces, they are being forced to work harder to engage the attention of consumers. This is an era of mix and match, of experiment and personalization, not to mention web shopping. Today's shoppers don't like to stay in a box for long, no matter how gorgeous it is.

Anatomy of a trend

06

Trends have expanded beyond fashion.
What colour is your mobile phone this season?

When a fashion-conscious friend of mine saw a poster of Uma Thurman decked out in a bright yellow motorcycle jacket and matching trousers for the movie *Kill Bill*, she turned to me and hissed, 'Shit – that means we're going to look like bananas all summer.' Actually, Uma's violent yellow outfit never quite caught on – although her sneakers, made by the Japanese brand Asics, did. Movies, particularly when they become popular culture phenomena, clearly have an impact on fashion trends, along with the music industry (see Chapter 10: Celebrity sells).

Apart from these obvious sources, though, where do trends come from? Why are the stores full of pink one season, green the next, blue the season after that? Why does cowgirl follow flapper; 1940s take the place of 1970s? Is it some kind of conspiracy? Do the fashion companies get together in a top secret location every autumn and decide what they're going to foist on us the following year? Not quite – but almost.

'I'm not always entirely sure where trends come from,' admits April Glassborow, senior buyer for international designer collections at Harvey Nichols. 'But I tend to think they're started by the fabric mills.' Fabric suppliers are indeed among the first links in the fashion chain. One of the most influential events of the year is Première Vision, the fabric trade show held in Paris at the end of September. As many as 800 fabric manufacturers from all over the world – Italy, France, Japan, Portugal, Switzerland and the UK are some of the most influential markets – display their wares to design teams and buyers. It's one of the few trade shows where you can spot designers stalking the aisles.

The fabric merchants are armed with formidable marketing skills. They have regular clients, and new wefts and weaves to sell to them. Occasionally they'll be asked to come up with a specialized fabric for a designer, but they may let slip details of the product to a rival. Similarly, if an influential designer has picked up on a certain fabric, clients who arrive at the stand later may be tactfully encouraged to follow suit. Technology naturally affects trends, too: the resurgence of tweed was provoked by manufacturing developments that made the fabric lighter, more supple and easier to manipulate. Every year there's a new way of treating denim, to give jeans a look that is subtly different from the year before.

At the other end of the chain, if retailers tacitly agree to support certain colour or fabric trends, it means heightened customer demand, guaranteed sales, and less remaindered stock – which they might have been saddled with if they'd veered off-message. Hence, fuchsia one summer, lavender the next; this season linen and denim, next season velvet and corduroy.

But if the secret meeting suggested above does not actually take place, how do they know to stock similar stuff at exactly the same time?

The style bureau

Sitting in front of me is a man in a sky-blue v-neck sweater. He is casually yet stylishly dressed. And he runs one of a handful of companies that, ultimately, have a significant impact on what we wear.

Pierre-François Le Louët is chief executive officer of Nelly Rodi, a 'style bureau' (**www.nellyrodi.fr**). Based in Paris, the company has offices in Italy and Japan and a network of affiliates worldwide. Its clients come from the fields of fashion, textiles, beauty, retail and interiors. They include, in one category or another, L'Oréal, LVMH, Mango, H&M, Liz Claiborne, Agnès B, Givenchy, and a clutch of brands across Asia. There are other, similar agencies, including Promostyl, Peclers and Carlin International, but Nelly Rodi (Le Louët's mother) was one of the pioneers of trend counselling in Europe. She remains chairman of the company, while he handles the day-to-day running of the business. In the early 1970s she looked after communications for the designer Courrèges, before being appointed in 1973 as manager of an organization called the International Fashion Committee, which had been created by the French government two decades earlier.

Nelly Rodi's son takes up the story: 'In the 1950s, ready-to-wear was an American phenomenon, and it was felt that the French offering was disorganized and behind the times. Following a trade mission to the United States to see how the industry was structured over there, the French government created the committee, which was essentially a state trend coordination agency financed by the textiles industry. Why coordinate trends? Simply, to reduce incertitude: if you give the same intelligence to those who sell the clothes, those who design them, those who buy the fabrics and those who supply them, there are enormous economic advantages for the fabric manufacturers, because they know what material will be in demand and where to concentrate their efforts. Similarly, if the retailers are all stocking violet that year, it inevitably creates a demand for violet, so they sell out their stock. The idea was to reduce the margin for error in the extremely risky field of fashion.'

This was the organization Nelly Rodi joined in 1973, and where she learnt many of her skills before quitting to form her own agency in 1985. In 1991 she purchased the newly privatized International Fashion Committee, ensuring beyond a doubt that she would become the trend counsellor of choice. Today, inevitably, the company has a team of trend-trackers who jet around the world monitoring social phenomena, observing the emergence of youth tribes and taking note of obscure trends, which they might pluck from the streets of Rio or Tokyo to turn into global fashions. As well as supplying such information to its clients, the agency can advise on brand strategies, produce marketing materials, organize events, provide stylists, and even design entire collections (its 30-odd staff come from both design and marketing backgrounds). 'We are the mercenaries of fashion,' Le Louët smiles.

But Nelly Rodi's most celebrated products are its 'trend books'. These hefty tomes, filled with photographs, illustrations and fabric swatches, as well as explanatory texts, resemble luxurious scrapbooks. They round up the agency's predictions of forthcoming trends and act as inspirational tools – or, more accurately, as prompts – for designers looking for the next big idea. Every season, the agency produces a dozen separate trend books covering categories such as ready-to-wear, knitwear, lingerie, colours, prints, fabrics, lifestyle and beauty. It even provides a 'perfume trend box set' containing little bottles of notes, blends and scents. Each book costs around €1,400 and only about 200 are printed in each category. Retailers and the beauty industry are the biggest buyers. Le Louët says, 'The luxury brands don't often buy them, because they see themselves as trendsetters. Nevertheless, I know that photocopies can be found in many designers' studios.'

To illustrate his point, he opens a trend book at a page detailing a 'heritage' theme. It features an atmospheric photograph of a handsome tan

Chesterfield sofa on a carpet with a muted paisley pattern. Then he leafs through a recent copy of *Vogue*, and shows me an ad for a well-known Italian designer label. There is the moody photography, the carpet and the Chesterfield sofa – only this time with a lithe model reclining on it. The resemblance is striking. Le Louët grins. 'And, as I say, they are not one of our clients.'

A team of independent experts helps to create the trend books. Each October, the agency rounds up 18 personalities from the fields of fashion, design, sociology and the arts for a brainstorming session. Smaller meetings, aimed at strengthening the resulting theories and synthesizing them into text, last a month and a half. As Le Louët explains, 'There is a regular core of contributors, and an outer circle that changes from year to year. We are careful to choose people who can look beyond the media of today and give us an original perspective on the future, without relying too much on their personal opinions.'

The theory is that these people are constantly creating and absorbing fashion shows, art events, exhibitions, literature and social phenomena, and can divine which of these will have an impact on consumers' appearance and lifestyles in the near future. It's like watching stones being thrown into a pond and analysing how far the ripples will spread. As a fictitious example, let's say we know that a major exhibition about Art Nouveau will be staged at the Metropolitan Museum of Art in New York next summer. In all probability, as designers often attend such shows, we will see fashions inspired by the style of the early 1900s emerging on the catwalk a season or so later. Visualizations of the resulting fabrics and designs will appear in the trend book. Another trend could just as easily be sparked by street kids in Mexico City personalizing their T-shirts by hacking complex patterns into them.

Once all these theories and insights have been gathered, a team of photographers and illustrators brings them to life. The resulting books, as plundered by Nelly Rodi's clients, have an impact that may trickle down to consumers a year and a half later. Chain stores such as Zara and H&M, with their quick turnaround, can act on the prompts much earlier than designer brands, which is why their clothes are 'trendier' than those of their more expensive counterparts.

'I'm not saying we're indispensable – some brands are perfectly capable of anticipating or creating trends by themselves,' stresses Le Louët. 'But we're one of the many ingredients that have an impact. It's also important to note that trends, particularly colours, have expanded beyond fashion to take in beauty products, interiors, and even electronics – what colour is your mobile phone this season?'

The new oracles

With fashion in constant flux, there is a strong argument for producing a trend book that can be updated not every season, but every day. An online service called the Worth Global Style Network (**www.wgsn.com**) has dramatically changed the way trends are monitored.

Created in 1998 by the brothers Julian and Marc Worth and later acquired by publisher Emap, WGSN is the Bloomberg of the fashion industry. Based in London, it has more than 150 staff, and outposts in New York, Paris, Hong Kong, Tokyo, Los Angeles, Milan, Barcelona and half a dozen other cities. As well as daily fashion business news, it delivers interviews, analyses, surveys, city reports, coverage of trade shows, and thousands of photographs of stores, runway shows and street life from around the globe. With a click of the mouse, its subscribers can see what fabrics were on show at Première Vision the previous morning, or what teenagers on the streets of Shanghai are wearing today. Not surprisingly, its extensive client list covers everybody who is anybody in fashion and retail, from Abercrombie & Fitch to Zara.

The WGSN headquarters in London resembles the bustling editorial floor of a major newspaper, with dozens of journalists tapping away at keyboards. And I'm assured that there are many others, out snapping the latest trends with digital cameras. WGSN does not so much predict trends as provide vital intelligence for a multi-billion-pound industry. But of course, part of its job is to monitor cutting-edge trends, and to explain how those might be interpreted for the mass market.

Other trend-trackers act not so much as consultants to the fashion industry but as observers of cultural shifts that may have an impact on product development. One such agency is Style-Vision, founded in 2001 (**www.style-vision.com**). Alongside its bi-monthly 'mega-trends' reports, it produces surveys of individual industries (not just fashion, but also food, personal care and technology, among others) and regularly holds roundtable conferences on evolving consumer trends. Usually staged at exclusive hotels or villas in the south of France, these events attract leading marketing directors, advertising creatives, designers, architects, branding experts and journalists.

Style-Vision's business development director, Genevieve Flaven, says, 'Our goal is to provide a rational analysis of societal changes, as well as forecasting developments that may have an impact on design. We're also interested in mixing consumer insights and expertise from different industries. We're very practical – there's no crystal ball, and we're not gurus. The main thing we strive to avoid is treating consumers as if they're malleable and somewhat naïve. We realize that we're all consumers – intelligent human beings with highly complex responses to the world around us.'

In fact, says Flaven, the agency is less concerned with predicting trends than in getting inside consumers' heads. 'We're interested in individuals in the context of society. Through our research among consumers and opinion-formers, we imagine future scenarios, how consumers will react to them, and what kind of products and services they might require within those scenarios.'

Ironically, though, the only people really in touch with the latest trends are those who create them – on the streets. Consumers themselves, particularly young ones, are more iconoclastic, inquisitive and inventive than any designer armed with a WGSN password and a stack of trend reports. No sooner has a marketing executive told adolescents that this is the correct way to wear a pair of jeans, than they've torn off the waistband and started wearing them differently. The classic argument runs that, once a trend has crossed over into the mainstream, it is already out of date.

The fashion industry is the ultimate fashion victim.

The cool hunter

I find the prospect of meeting a cool hunter rather daunting. After all, as somebody who mixes with rappers, graffiti artists and Mexican gang members to get a line on youth trends for a music television channel, Claudine Ben-Zenou has got to be one of the coolest people on the planet. Accordingly, I fix our rendezvous at the trendiest bar I know, and go along dressed in ancient jeans and a black T-shirt advertising the 1984 Winter Olympics in Sarajevo, as purchased on a market stall there a few months earlier.

I needn't have worried: Ben-Zenou is not some thrusting style maven in shades, but a friendly, discreetly well-dressed woman in her mid-20s. However, for somebody so outwardly normal-looking, Claudine has some very specialized areas of interest that have made her invaluable to a wide range of brands. She recently quit a full-time post as MTV's official trend-tracker to set up her own agency, called Vandal, with a colleague.

'I've always been immersed in subcultures and youth trends,' she says, without pretentiousness. 'I've been involved in the hip-hop scene for more than 12 years – I was part of a hip-hop collective called Sin Cru when I lived in London. I was also into skateboarding from about the age of 14 and had a lot of friends involved in that culture. Later I got interested in the urban music scene and the rave scene. But, while I found all this fascinating, I didn't have a clue that I could put it to any practical use.'

She studied marketing and advertising, but at the age of 19, while still at university, she got a job at a small marketing agency in Hoxton. At the time, the area was beginning to emerge after years of neglect as one of London's most vibrant districts, a veritable Petri dish of trends. 'The agency specialized in underground and youth marketing, and as I got more involved I realized that I had inside knowledge and connections that could be very useful,' she recounts. 'We were working on [beer brand] Fosters Ice and doing lots of stuff with street art and graffiti. It really opened my eyes to the possibility of using subcultures for marketing. Collaborations between mainstream brands like Nike and Adidas and underground designers are very common today, but we were among the pioneers.'

Since that first job, Ben-Zenou has acted as a consultant for global brands such as Levi's, Casio G-Shock, Pepsi and even Disney, always providing them with the inside track on street culture. 'The way I position myself is that I'm equally at home in the boardroom and on the street. I'm the connection between the two. I can talk to kids on their own level without coming across as a suit. What they're doing is not some abstract concept to me – it's very real.'

She also describes herself as 'a huge geek', and she has forged many of her underground connections via internet chat-rooms. 'A lot of the people I got close to in the early days have since become quite famous in their fields. I'm able to pick up the phone and talk to a friend who's a graffiti artist or a hip-hop MC. And, as they're my mates, I'm not trying to interpret these quite complex scenes as an outsider. Youth brands that try to connect with these communities have a habit of getting things wrong and basically getting everyone's back up. I feel strongly about trying to avoid that.'

Brands who try to target niche opinion-formers without doing their homework often find themselves exposed to ridicule. 'You can miss a step very easily. The key is to work closely with influential people within the communities, and listen carefully to what they say. Graffiti is a good example. I hear all the time about brands that've plucked some random kid off the street. If you're using somebody who's not a respected artist, the result may not be obvious to you but it's extremely obvious to people within the scene, which undermines your credibility as a brand. It's very important to develop long-term relationships, rather than just latching on to a scene in the short term and sucking everything you can out of it in a parasitical way.'

I ask Ben-Zenou if she ever feels in danger of being regarded as a sort of double agent – a suit in hip-hop clothing. 'Most of the people I deal with know exactly what I do,' she replies. 'I've always tried to make a positive contribution, encouraging brands to create events that will bring money back into these scenes and elevate artists who might not have been able to make it in other circumstances.'

For a while, she acted as an agent for a group of graffiti artists and break-dancers, liaising with brands on their behalf. 'A common attitude among marketing executives was that they were just dealing with a bunch of kids doing graffiti, so they didn't need to pay them or even particularly acknowl-edge their contribution. But these people are extremely talented and often do a lot for brands, so I'm keen to get them the recognition they deserve.'

Later she worked for the MTV website, but talked the broadcaster into creating a new role after observing that 'although we were very good at mainstream research, we didn't seem to be monitoring trends'. (And yet the stars of MTV's music videos have always had an impact on trends – brands such as Tommy Hilfiger and Dolce & Gabbana swear by the access the channel provides to a young, logo-oriented public.) In addition to providing regular e-mail newsletters, she wrote a quarterly trend report called 'Switched On', which was sent to MTV's advertisers and their agencies, as well as acting as an internal primer for staff. 'It was a creative tool designed to inspire people and give them a snapshot of what's happening out there. I picked up on micro-trends rather than huge shifts in behaviour.' Following her own rule of working within cultures, she often asked hip-hop artists and DJs to write their own articles. 'I think it's important to get people to talk about their scenes in their own voices.'

The position was based in Chicago, where she is now installed at the helm of her own agency. 'I'm moving away from trend-spotting into more of a consultancy role. Lately it has become in vogue to say you're a trend-spotter. Trend-spotting has become a trend. What clients are asking us for now is not just information about emerging trends, but advice on how to use this knowledge.'

Although she's one of the global elite of cool hunters, Ben-Zenou doesn't feel part of any such group. 'I'm aware of people who do a similar job and I've met a few of them, but I always have the impression that I'm taking a somewhat different approach. They tend to come from a research background, while my training is in marketing. I suppose the main difference is that I'm not approaching it objectively – I'm deeply, passionately involved. I still go to hip-hop events, my boyfriend is from that community... What some people don't realize is that you can't just turn up one day and break into these scenes. I get a lot of respect because I've been involved for years. If I didn't do this for a living, I'd be doing it anyway – always reading magazines, going online, chatting to people at parties and trying to find out how they think.' Hence her recent brush with Mexican gang members. 'I met them at a party and got talking to them. It wasn't a work thing – I just found them interesting. I'm like a cross between a journalist and a sociologist.'

Perhaps because I'm a decade older than Ben-Zenou, it occurs to me to ask if there's an age limit for being a cool hunter. Isn't there a danger that, one day, she'll no longer be able to relate to icons of hip? She says, 'I've occasionally wondered about that myself, but I think attitudes to age are changing. I've got lots of friends who are older than me and who are still very much involved in the scene. There's a graffiti artist called Futura 2000 who's 50 years old and still considered an icon of cool. He's recently done some work with Nike. Then you've got someone like Vivienne Westwood, who's still very influential. As for me – let's face it, I've got 200 pairs of trainers. I can't see myself suddenly giving up everything I love and dressing in beige anoraks.'

The image-makers

07

> *There's inevitably something appealing about an imagined better world.*

The relationship between fashion brands and other product categories is rather like the one between celebrities and normal citizens: they are aware of one another's existence, they occasionally share the same space, but they rarely mingle. While other brands hire international advertising agencies such as J Walter Thompson, Saatchi & Saatchi or BBDO, fashion brands tend to work directly with a narrow pool of freelance talents.

According to art director Thomas Lenthal, who has worked for brands such as Dior and Yves Saint Laurent, 'In fashion, there are probably only about a dozen well-known art directors, great photographers, stylists, make-up people, and so on. You don't need an advertising agency: you just need an address book with a handful of names in it.'

Many upmarket fashion brands don't have a marketing department or even a person with 'marketing' in their job title. The designer – often known as an 'artistic director' – is responsible for advertising imagery too. For instance, while Louis Vuitton works with the advertising agency Ogilvy & Mather on several aspects of its communications, its fashion imagery is entirely under the control of the brand's designer, Marc Jacobs.

With this in mind, a few years ago Hervé Morel set up an organization in Paris and New York called ADM – Art Direction Management. Morel does not have an agency, but he is an agent, handling a group of art directors and other creatives that includes Thomas Lenthal, Donald Schneider (H&M, Van Cleef & Arpels, *Vogue Hommes International*), Mathieu Trautmann (Oscar de la Renta Perfumes, Issey Miyake Perfumes, *Jalouse* magazine), Steve Hiett (Kenzo Perfumes), and Laurent Fétis (Cacharel Perfumes, Bless), among others. According to Morel, it was ADM that introduced Donald

Schneider to H&M, which eventually led to the store's publicity-generating partnership with Karl Lagerfeld.

Morel says, 'Designer brands may employ an agency to buy their advertising space, but they don't work with agencies on the creative side. It's more cost-effective to work directly with an art director, who can then bring together the other elements – the photographer, the model and so forth. Agencies tend to put forward teams that include a copywriter. But international fashion brands, which use the same images worldwide and work purely with visual stimuli, don't need copywriters. Plus, art directors have usually gained experience on fashion magazines, so they are comfortable in that world.'

Lenthal echoes his views: 'The structure of an advertising agency makes it an unwieldy vehicle. The one thing an ad agency fears above all else is losing a client, and in order not to do that it ensures that the creative process is as risk-free as possible. There are a lot of meetings involving eight people sitting around a table with somebody making notes, so everything is agreed with back-up in writing. The agency has a huge team consisting of the creative director, the art director, the copywriter, the account director, the strategic planner... they try to mirror the structure of the large corporations they are working for. But a fashion house is a much smaller unit.'

The fashion community feels that traditional agencies don't have people who understand the nuances of a fashion brand. For their part, advertising agencies say that the cliquish fraternity fashion brands work with means that their ads are often indistinguishable. And indeed it's doubtful that many fashion images could pass the marketing test that involves taking a bunch of print ads, covering up their brand names, and seeing which of them has a recognizable visual identity. Advertising for designer brands – whether clothing or accessories – is frequently sensual and elegant, but it can also be clichéd, humourless and chokingly pretentious.

Meanwhile, advertising agencies have been behind highly successful campaigns for fashion brands. The UK-based agency Bartle Bogle Hegarty has created consistently award-winning campaigns for Levi's in a relationship that stretches back to the 1980s. Its ability to constantly refresh the brand in the mind of the fickle young consumer – and in a highly competitive market – is certainly admirable. Diesel is another company that has worked with a series of advertising agencies. However, the brand's founder, Renzo Rosso, has ultimate control over its advertising messages, and admits that he prefers to work with small, energetic agencies that he can mould in his image.

There is also a considerable gulf between a hip jeans brand and a global luxury giant such as Chanel or Yves Saint Laurent. Here, perhaps, a more elitist approach is required.

Portrait of an art director

Thomas Lenthal has been fascinated by fashion since the age of five, when he enjoyed cutting pictures out of glossy magazines. 'Fashion is all about idealizing, and there's inevitably something appealing about an imagined better world,' he points out. In his early 20s he worked as assistant at a French fashion magazine called *Femme* (it no longer exists) with famed Swiss art director Peter Knapp as his mentor. From there, Lenthal moved on to the French edition of *Glamour*, where he formed a creatively rewarding working relationship with the editor Babette Djian.

Lenthal recalls, 'We were doing something very different at the time. The French magazine market has improved immeasurably since the 1990s, but back then publishers were determined to deliver exactly what they thought the female population was expecting. We didn't want to produce a women's magazine, but a fashion magazine. We discovered that 30 per cent of our readership was male – not just gay, but straight too. They liked the girls we used, and there was solid arts and culture coverage.'

Djian and Lenthal went on to found *Numéro*, still one of the most highly regarded French fashion magazines. In the first year of the title's existence, Lenthal was contacted by Dior, which recruited him on a part-time basis to take care of advertising, as well as related communications such as window displays. During that period, Lenthal recommended the photographer Nick Knight, 'because I felt he would be the perfect person to work alongside [Dior designer] John Galliano'.

Lenthal says that establishing a relationship with all the parties involved in a brand campaign is one of the art director's greatest challenges: 'Usually you are working closely with a designer, so it's very important that there is an atmosphere of respect and trust between you. But very often you also find that you're the liaison between the designer and the management. You become a combination of diplomat and translator, because most of the time they speak quite different languages.'

The combination of Galliano, Lenthal and Knight resulted in one of the best-known examples of the style that became known as 'porno chic'. 'Guilty as charged,' says Lenthal. 'We did a controversial campaign featuring two gorgeous models [Gisele Bündchen and Rhea Durham] embracing each other and sweating. It was almost a new start for Dior, because it was bold, extreme and arrogant – everything a great fashion house should be, or at least needed to be at the time.'

Lenthal had already gained an insight into Galliano's style by looking at the designer's runway shows. 'I knew there was a certain stylish brashness and brutality about his designs. The campaign was overtly erotic, but it was also an exaggerated version of the interaction between French women, who are much more touchy-feely than the British, for instance. Nick's photography was sharp and luscious, which turned the image into something iconic. Dior was, after all, a fashion icon. There are clouds in the background – what you're looking at is Dior's version of heaven. Many of the elements made perfect sense.'

Lenthal's explanation brings to mind a theory I've heard often while investigating fashion marketing, which is that the brand references are extremely subtle. Although ads can look similar, codes saturate the image, and the target audience receives the message almost subliminally.

Dior's glam-trash new look was a hit. Lenthal says, 'To their credit, the management [LVMH] backed the idea wholeheartedly, even though it was outrageous, especially for Dior. Bernard Arnault was incredibly supportive. I think it was the first time John had really felt at home there. They were encouraging him to be himself, so this was his way of saying, "You want young? You want sexy? All right, I'll show you – because I guess you haven't been in a nightclub for a while."'

Later came the collection Galliano called 'Trailer Park Chic'. The related advertising imagery, says Lenthal, consisted essentially of 'tarts covered with grease on a scrap heap'. He cackles delightedly at the recollection: 'Once again, it wasn't exactly something you'd associate with a French fashion house. The consumers loved it.'

Perhaps inevitably, after leaving Dior Lenthal ended up working with the Gucci Group's star designer, Tom Ford, on Yves Saint Laurent beauty products. 'At first I wasn't sure I could work with Tom, because his aesthetics were so well defined that I didn't know if I would have any room to experiment. The good thing was that he was already in the mood to do something different; and particularly with Yves Saint Laurent he felt that he needed to differentiate it [from his work for Gucci]. This time we stuck quite closely to the roots of the brand, as envisaged by Yves Saint Laurent himself. The interesting thing about my job is that you are reinterpreting codes and values that may have been established many years ago. And you can either decide to push the imagery a long way from the core of the brand, or hover more closely around it. The important thing is to always be aware of the brand's origins.'

Tom Ford left Yves Saint Laurent – and the Gucci Group – in early 2004. In Lenthal's view, 'He did an extremely valuable job in that he put the brand back in the spotlight, when before there was a feeling that nothing had been going on there for a while.' Since then, Lenthal has been working with the label's new artistic director, the Italian Stefano Pilati, who is deeply respectful of the Saint Laurent heritage. Lenthal feels that the brand is 'particularly rich' – starting with the YSL logo, designed by the poster artist Cassandre in 1963, which remains unchanged. He says, 'With Saint Laurent you have so much to explore, particularly the way he makes colours clash instead of trying to get them to blend together. He is famous for his daring colour palette. He also designed for a certain type of woman, so when you're doing the casting you naturally look at the kind of models he used in the 1970s. For me, today, [the model] Karen Elson is the quintessential Saint Laurent girl, with her red hair and very pale skin.' Interestingly, the actress Catherine Deneuve, who has worn Saint Laurent in a number of films, has also expressed a particular view of the typical Saint Laurent woman; she once said that the designer created clothes for 'women who have double lives'.

Lenthal believes that the same team should create a fashion brand's communications in its entirety – for clothing, accessories and beyond – even though, with branded perfumes usually licensed to large beauty companies, this is not always the case (see Chapter 13: Accessorize all areas). At the time of our interview, Lenthal had just begun to work on the fashion element of YSL, as well as the beauty side, and said it is his intention to 'try and link the two': 'I like to think that once you understand a brand, you can imagine every element within its specific world, even down to the objects. Is there a particular Saint Laurent chair, telephone, or lamp? The answer is "yes".'

The alternative image-maker

One of the most talked-about companies in branding is not an advertising agency, a marketing consultancy, a public relations adviser, or an events organizer. It is all of these things – and none of them. With offices in London and Los Angeles, Exposure is based on the concepts of networking, leveraging influence channels and brand advocacy. It can handle everything from getting a fashion brand into a music video or on to the back of a celebrity, to linking seemingly unrelated brands for mutually attractive partnerships, and much more besides. It was Exposure that teamed Matthew Williamson with Coca-Cola for the series of limited-edition bottles mentioned in Chapter 4.

Raoul Shah founded Exposure in 1993. He had graduated in textiles management and did a short stint at Agnès B in Paris before joining Pepe Jeans back in the UK, where he became closely embroiled in the company's marketing strategy. He recalls, 'The brand was growing phenomenally at the time. Most of the marketing was done in-house, so I learnt how to do everything, from dressing windows to point of sale. It was an incredible experience; by the time I left, I knew how to market a brand in every conceivable way.'

Shah decided to use his knowledge to found his own business. His simple but effective concept was to build brands by introducing them to the right people. 'I realized that, thanks to my time at Pepe, I had this network of people that crossed fashion, music, film, clubs, the drinks industry... and I thought that by using my contacts and my friends, and by bringing brands together with them, I could create some extremely interesting marketing opportunities.'

Exposure's joint managing director, Tim Bourne, who came from a sales promotion background, brought an additional commercial element to the business. 'We created a dual pillar structure,' explains Shah, 'with fashion and lifestyle on the one hand, and FMCG [fast-moving consumer goods] – sales promotions, sponsorships and so forth – on the other. But the idea was that they should cross over. We saw even back then that many mainstream brands were beginning to take on the characteristics of fashion and lifestyle brands, in that they wanted to look for alternative ways of reaching an audience.'

Exposure has worked with a wide range of clients, not only in fashion (Burberry, Dr Martens, Converse, Dockers, Levi's, Nike, Quiksilver and Topshop, to name but a few), but also in beauty, retail, FMCG, catering, movies, automotive... you name it. It even manages the European media coverage of the hip-hop star Damon Dash. The organization is now divided into a number of interconnected divisions, including media relations and publicity, partnerships and product placement, sales promotion and events, design and production, consumer insights and brand consulting, and digital marketing. It also has its own gallery and showroom.

A handful of Exposure case studies would take up many thousands of words (take a look instead at **www.exposure.net**), but the key to its success, it appears, is to shake up brands in a way that creates a surprising, media-friendly cocktail. Hence Dr Martens boots customized by the likes of Vivienne Westwood and Jean-Paul Gaultier; or a serious museum exhibition about 'trainer culture' for sports-shoe retailer Foot Locker. Exposure asked lingerie brand Agent Provocateur to customize a Triumph motorcycle – the appropriately named Thruxton 900 was given a pink paint job featuring pin-ups in a state of *déshabillé*. Then it got the magazine *Tank* to design a coffee-table book for Oxo.

The beauty of Exposure's operation is that the elements that make up its network are constantly spinning off and reconnecting. The brands, creative talents and celebrities with which the agency has a relationship can be mixed and matched to suit the task in hand. None of this is rocket science – and other agencies have since copied the format – but Exposure seems to generate an inordinate amount of respect among the notoriously prickly fashion and celebrity community.

'The key to it all is that as a company we're very people-oriented,' explains Shah. 'We're honest about what we do, we don't over-promise, we're professional. People who work with us enjoy the experience, so they trust us the next time. We do very little of our own publicity – it's all by word-of-mouth.'

Shah seems vaguely surprised that there are still brands that haven't got the message. 'Fashion advertising is very formulaic, and sometimes I question the validity of that formula. When you consider that you can make the phone ring off the hook in a store just by placing one jacket on the right celebrity for the right party, traditional advertising is not tremendously cost-effective. The really exciting brands are the ones who take risks: I'm thinking here of Helmut Lang placing his ads in *National Geographic* magazine, or on the top of New York taxi cabs... We've reached a stage where consumers and the media are so saturated with demands on their time that brands have to work much harder to get noticed at all.'

They shoot dresses, don't they?

08

> *The photographer has an enormous influence on the branding process.*

I'm standing under the portico outside the Victoria & Albert Museum, sheltering from a summer storm that has raced in from nowhere to dash the streets with raindrops the size of boiled sweets. Beside me, tourists mutter exclamations and unfurl umbrellas, or haul vivid cagoules over their clothes. Frankly, I'm grateful for the enforced pause in the day, because it gives me time to think. I've just seen an exhibition of fashion photography so disturbing – so downright weird – that it has shaken up my idea of what the alluring métier of snapping models in dresses is all about.

A couple of days earlier, the photographer's name, Guy Bourdin, had been only vaguely familiar to me. But a friend recommended the show, and I'd found the promotional poster intriguing. It was at the same time compelling and repellent, showing a girl's long white legs splayed over a sofa as if she had collapsed face down. She wore scarlet high-heels. The sofa was orange, and so was the bottom of her very tight, very short dress, which along with the curve of her buttocks was all that remained visible before she was cut off by the frame. The image was strongly ambiguous: could this be a corpse; or was she in an alcohol-induced coma? It certainly didn't look like standard fashion photography.

The other pictures reinforced this idea. They were often erotic, frequently perverse and mostly eerie; reflections in TV screens in cheap hotel rooms; the suggestion of unseen figures lurking outside the frame; latent violence. Bourdin seemed to be equating fashion with lust, and imagining its potentially terrible consequences. Elsewhere there were hints of dark satire: a group of models striding past a shop window display looked barely more human than the mannequins trapped behind the glass. Each picture was lit with the icy clarity of a crime scene; an idea taken to its logical conclusion with a picture of a discarded pair of shoes next to the chalk outline of a dead body. Some of Bourdin's work resembled that of another ground-breaking fashion photographer, Helmut Newton; but to me the images had more in common with Hitchcock and Edward Hopper.

Bourdin worked for French *Vogue* and shot a series of advertisements for Charles Jourdan shoes – a project that allowed him to give full reign to his fetishist imagery. Despite the fact that most of the pictures in the exhibition dated from the 1970s, they had hardly aged. This was not surprising, because I discovered that, although Bourdin died in 1991, his influence continues to saturate fashion advertising today. Contemporary art directors such as Thomas Lenthal and photographers such as Nick Knight acknowledge a huge debt to Bourdin. He is generally regarded as the first fashion photographer to have shifted the focus away from the product and towards the imagery. Before Bourdin, fashion advertising used fairly conventional depictions of female sexuality to sell products. Bourdin subverted the form. Instead of entire bodies, he showed fragmentary images of limbs. Models and actresses were dismembered by his lens, or mutated by make-up into ashen-faced cartoons of femininity. His fashion spreads were narratives, resembling stills from surreal thrillers. Bourdin realized that fashion advertising was not just a picture of a dress or a pair of shoes; it was an imaginary universe. In doing so, he placed the photographer at the forefront of the process that transforms a garment or an accessory into an object of desire.

Brand translators

'Fashion photography is about translating a brand into a concept,' says Vincent Peters, the German-born, London-based photographer whose list of credits includes British, Italian and French *Vogue*, *Arena*, *Dazed and Confused* and *Numéro*, as well as ads for Dior, Bottega Veneta, Celine, Miu Miu and Yves Saint Laurent. 'Often, when a client comes to you, they have a product and a brand identity, but they aren't certain how to combine the two. Your job is to achieve that transition; to create the image that brings the brand to life. Sometimes the client has a reasonable idea of how you're going to do it – after all, that's why they've hired you – but in my experience they like to be surprised. This means that the photographer has an enormous influence on the branding process.'

Peters began taking pictures on a trip to Thailand in the 1980s, with the results being published in a travel magazine. In 1989 he moved to New York, where he got a job as an assistant photographer. Soon he branched out on his own, moving into fashion photography. After a while, though, he developed an ambition to become an artistic photographer, and relocated to Paris to pursue his goal. Although his work was exhibited throughout Europe and published in leading art photography magazines, he grew disenchanted with the scene and decided to refocus his efforts on fashion photography: 'I remember I had a season when it all suddenly began happening for me. I shot a campaign for Miu Miu, and that made a difference. Things evolved quite quickly after that.'

Fashion photographers have always combined commerce with art. The earliest practitioner with something of the star status accorded today's snappers was one Baron Adolphe de Meyer, nicknamed 'the Debussy of the camera'. (Although he was not from an aristocratic background, he married into nobility.) From 1913 to the early 1930s he brought an other-worldly lustre to his photographs of socialites, actresses and dancers, first for American *Vogue* and then for *Bazar* (which later evolved into *Harper's Bazaar*, picking up an extra 'a' along the way).

In 1923, de Meyer was replaced at *Vogue* by another pioneer, Edward Steichen, whose pictures already looked more crisp and modernist than the soft-focus confections favoured by his predecessor. Steichen may have taken the first colour fashion photograph, but he was far more interested in the art of photography than in fashion. In the early 1900s he'd been a friend of the sculptor Auguste Rodin, and he later co-founded, with Alfred Stieglitz, Photo-Secession, an organization whose sole aim was to elevate photography into an art form. Between 1947 and 1962 Steichen was director of photography at the Museum of Modern Art in New York.

Another founding father of fashion photography, whose background was almost as aristocratic as that of de Meyer, was George Hoyningen-Huene. Born in Russia, he had escaped the revolution with his family and pitched up in London before moving to Paris after the First World War. He started out as a backdrop designer for shoots before moving on to photography with the encouragement of French *Vogue*'s editor, Main Bocher. Hoyningen-Huene, too, was later lured away to *Harper's Bazaar*. His photographs of Josephine Baker, Joan Crawford and the model Lee Miller – eventually an influential photographer in her own right – have a frosty monochrome poetry about them.

In this respect, Hoyningen-Huene's work resembled that of his protégé, Horst P Horst, who was inspired by Greek statues and Renaissance art. Technology had not yet freed the camera from the studio, so their pictures inevitably look stiff and enclosed, and reliant on props and backdrops for atmosphere. Cecil Beaton, the final member of this precursory quartet, used props to sometimes surreal effect, deploying sculptures of papier-mâché and aluminium backdrops. Born in London in 1904, Beaton had been captivated as a child by postcards of glamorous society women; and this influence is still apparent in his costume designs and art direction for films such as 'My Fair Lady', for which he won an Academy Award in 1964.

By the Second World War, Leica was producing cameras with faster shutter speeds – an advance that urged fashion photography outdoors and encouraged breezy spontaneity. This ushered in the era of Irving Penn, Richard Avedon and Norman Parkinson. There is the gulf of a generation between Horst's stony goddesses and Avedon's early photos of models frolicking on a beach; or Parkinson's exotic, sun-drenched location shots.

Parkinson, known to one and all as 'Parks', formed a stylistic bridge between the pre-war practitioners and the emerging generation of the 1960s, who added sexual liberation to photography's physical freedom from restraint. Working for British *Vogue*, Parks brought an impish spirit to his pictures of strong, provocative women, which did not look at all out of place beside the images being turned out by the rebellious trio of David Bailey, Terence Donovan and Brian Duffy (see Chapter 9: This year's model). With their unambiguous, cool-yet-accessible aesthetic, these photographs look as innocent now as they must have seemed decadent at the time.

In the 1970s, a seismic shift caused tremors that are still being felt today. It was provoked by Bourdin and, of course, Helmut Newton. Vincent Peters cites Newton, who died in early 2004, as one of a handful of icons who sought to change fashion photography in particular, as opposed to photography in general: 'Guy Bourdin's world was not about fashion. What makes Helmut Newton so irreplaceable is that he really was about fashion photography – he was determined to push it as far as it could go, to make it sexy and dangerous rather than cold and bourgeois. He did for dresses what James Bond did for suits. In the 1970s there were no rules, no formulas, so if you had the talent you were free to experiment.'

In the 1980s, fashion photography benefited from an evolution within the fashion media itself. New magazines such as *Blitz*, *The Face* and *i-D* – the latter started by Terry Jones, a former art director at British *Vogue* – had an irreverent, slash-and-paste style that owed far more to punk than to catwalk shows. They proved fertile ground for photographers like Nick Knight, Corinne Day, Juergen Teller and Terry Richardson, whose pictures pushed clothes – and sometimes models themselves – further into the background, relegating them to mere ingredients in entertaining tapestries. Photography took on a hyper-real, snapshot air, with the merciless light of the flashgun illuminating seedy domestic scenes, drug-fuelled nightclubs, or parties that seemed to have dragged on far too long. These pictures were personal and observational, pulling the viewer into the world of the individual who had taken them.

Corinne Day became notorious for creating the so-called 'heroin chic' look, with a series of photographs featuring Kate Moss. The pictures, which appeared in the June 1993 issue of British *Vogue*, showed the model looking wan and undernourished, clad in vest and knickers and posing in a dingy flat. The shoot, which spawned hundreds of pale facsimiles, contributed to the 'grunge' fashion trend.

Richardson's lurid, funny, blatantly sexual pictures – famously shot on an old Instamatic – continue to provoke controversy today. In an interview with online fashion magazine *Hint*, he refers to his playfully erotic advertising work for the fashion brand Sisley. 'We tried to put a picture of a girl with pompoms over her tits on a poster in SoHo [New York]. They said no, because a little of her areola was showing... They said it was too sexy and it would be too close to a church and a school. It's all so silly and conservative.' Despite his involvement in fashion, the photographer's attitude to clothes has a timeless ring about it: 'To me, photographs are more about people than clothes. I'm not one of those photographers who says, "Ooh, that dress is just making me crazy".' (**www.hintmag.com/shootingstars/terryrichardson**)

Photographers can take comfort in the existence of magazines such as *Visionaire*, a format-shifting blend of fashion publication and portable art gallery in which clothes definitely take second place to ideas. It has occasionally provided a setting for the work of photography duo Inez Van Lamsweerde and Vinoodh Matadin, who utilize digital technology to produce the kind of images Bourdin might have come up with, had he used a computer. Disturbing and disorienting, the pictures are filled with digitally contorted limbs, manipulated expressions and artificial landscapes. All of these photographers have lent their talents to advertising, as well as contributing to fashion magazines. And with their peers they continue to blur the boundaries between art, fashion and marketing.

The limits of experimentation

Other, more pragmatic industries might have shied away from the idea of artistry to promote a product. In fashion, however, it has traditionally been seen as a brand value. But Vincent Peters fears that, in the advertising field, photographers now have fewer opportunities to take risks: 'The fashion business, like Hollywood, is increasingly controlled by people who don't come from the creative tradition. It's a stock-market product.' This, he believes, encourages blandness and fuels criticism that all fashion advertising looks alike. 'Nobody wants to throw money away, so of course they're going to look at what's worked before and go down a similar route. Fortunately, there are still enough clients left who want something challenging.'

In terms of trends, he believes that fashion photography has become less narrative and more conceptual: '[Advertising clients] are looking for the big idea. This is a huge challenge for the photographer, because sometimes you're called upon to invent a brand with a single image. At the same time, it's good for us, because it makes us indispensable to the process.'

Art director Thomas Lenthal would agree. During our conversation about his work for Yves Saint Laurent, he said, 'I've always advocated the fact that if you're working for a brand, you've got to build a visual alphabet for it. Within that framework you can tell a great many stories, but I think it makes sense to link them through that visual alphabet – and the easiest way of doing that is to use the same photographer.'

Having said that, a fashion photograph is a collaborative effort, requiring the participation of art directors, stylists, make-up artists and assistants, all bustling around the central figure of the model. As Vincent Peters confirms, 'It takes an incredible amount of time and finesse, almost like making a movie. A lot of money is being spent on this one key image, so you have to get it right. Is the sun shining, is the hair and make-up the way you want it? Every detail counts. When people outside fashion say that all the advertising looks the same, they aren't paying attention to the details. But at the luxury end of the market, where I tend to work, consumers notice details.'

He adds that the life of a fashion photographer is not always an easy one: 'Don't forget, we're all freelances, and in fashion your fortunes can change very quickly. There's always somebody standing behind you. To a certain extent, you're only as good as your last piece of work. It's a delicate balance, because you want to maintain a personal style, while striving to provide something different each time. If you do three shoots in the same way, people think you're getting lazy. So we're under a great deal of pressure.'

For a while, it looked as though photographers might be losing ground to fashion illustrators. Established artists such as François Berthoud, David Downton, Charles Anastase, Jordi Labanda and Yoko Ikeno became increasingly influential, both in publishing and advertising circles. In 2002, Stella McCartney engaged the artist David Remfry to create an advertising campaign, sparking numerous articles about the trend. One of them, in *The Observer*, opined that this approach was 'valued for being warmly personal' and went on to explain that 'the expressionist, abstract aesthetic of illustration is increasingly seen as a fresh, more subtle – and attention-grabbing – alternative to computer graphics and photography'. ('Sketch show', 29 June 2003.) In the same piece, Alice Rawsthorn, director of London's Design Museum, commented, 'It's part of the general trend towards a richer, more romantic aesthetic. We're yearning for the individuality of hand-drawing at a time when our lives are more automated.'

For now, though, the yearning seems to have passed. Although fashion illustration has rightfully regained the respect it had lost over the previous decades, it is unlikely to replace photography as the medium of choice for fashion branding.

Fashion photographers, in any case, often take their cues from artists. Although Vincent Peters' work is frequently artistic – his prize-winning 2002 ad for Dior's Poison scent, for instance, was a painstaking recreation of a 19th-century Gothic illustration – he sees no contradiction in using his skills for commercial purposes. 'Quite honestly, when I was involved in the art scene, I found it more superficial and pretentious [than fashion]. Again, I don't think people realize how much effort we put in to what we do. The people I work with have a real appreciation of beauty. It's something of a paradox. When you shoot a fashion picture, whether for an ad or a magazine, you're trying to create something beautiful. That depends, of course, on what your concept of beauty is, and we all have different sources we're feeding off. My own are quite classical, because my mother was an art teacher and I take a lot of inspiration from paintings.' He adds that, in any case, great art has often been commercial: 'Look at Renaissance painters, or look at Mozart: their best work was commissioned by wealthy patrons.'

This year's model

09

> *A fashion picture is never a picture of a dress –
> it's a picture of the woman who wears it.*

'I can be whatever you want me to be,' Gisele Bündchen told the US edition of *Esquire* magazine in October 2004. 'If you want me to be the sexy girl, I can do that. If you want me to be the weird girl, I can do that. And if you want me to be the classically beautiful girl, I can do that too.'

The word 'supermodel' sounds a bit tired these days, but it's difficult to find a more appropriate term for Gisele. Somewhere between goddess and pin-up, these women are prized by designers, brands and magazines as the perfect denizens of fashion's fantasy land. 'Almost every other model looks ugly when you stand her next to Gisele,' says the photographer Vincent Peters. 'Gisele is a star – she's an action movie. But sometimes, you want a relationship movie.'

Peters confirms that choosing a model is part of the branding process. 'Most models have a precise image that either works for the brand or it doesn't. Some of them are more couture, others are sexy... And it's important to get that right for the shoot. [Art director] Alexey Brodovitch said, "A fashion picture is never a picture of a dress – it's a picture of the woman who wears it." When you're doing a fashion shoot, you're creating characters.'

Models have existed for as long as there have been fashion brands. Worth used first his wife and then other women to model his designs; Poiret followed the pattern. In early editions of *Vogue*, dresses were worn by wealthy socialites – although they were gradually replaced by 'normal' girls. For many years, models were little more than clothes-horses, as their glacial expressions and disdainful poses suggested. Although some of them became famous within their profession, they were not 'stars' in the sense that many of them are today.

The London of the 1960s changed all that. Young photographers like Terence Donovan and David Bailey began to take pictures of girls in a manner that suggested there might be more interesting things going on when the shooting stopped – and there usually was. In Michael Gross's compelling (1995) book on the subject, *Model: The ugly business of beautiful women*, Donovan is quoted as saying that, until he and Bailey came along, 'in England all fashion photographers were gay'. Donovan says this was important because, as a straight bloke, he feared he didn't understand how clothes and jewellery worked together: 'And then suddenly you realized... all you had to do was take a strong picture of a girl.'

Bailey, meanwhile, shot stunning pictures of a girl he had fallen in love with – Jean Shrimpton, rechristened 'The Shrimp' by the tabloid press. 'She and Bailey became the archetypes of a new breed of photographers and fashion models,' writes Gross. 'By letting the heat of their sexual relationship into their pictures, by letting their models seem touchable... they transformed themselves into fashion's first real celebrities outside fashion.'

But Swinging London's most famous model stood at a distance from the frenzy going on around her. Lesley Hornby, a sweet girl from Neasden, was initially represented not by a modelling agency, but by her mentor and boyfriend Justin de Villeneuve. Her colt-like frame, all arms and legs, earned her the nickname 'Twig', which evolved into 'Twiggy'. When she let a hairdresser use her as a model for a new style – a short, elfin cut that emphasized her enormous blue eyes – her future was assured. She climbed quickly from the pages of the *Daily Express* to *Elle* and *Vogue*. Soon, clothing brands and car manufacturers were beating a path to her door with offers of sponsorship deals. Gross writes, 'She wasn't a model like any before her; she was a marketing miracle... the first model to achieve genuine international celebrity.'

But Twiggy earned only a fraction of the sums that were reaped by the stars who followed her. Kate Moss, discovered by the Storm agency in 1988 as a Croydon schoolgirl, is often compared to Twiggy. At the beginning of her career she was described as a 'waif'; and although she had been championed by iconic style magazine *The Face*, her rise to global fame was due to a landmark series of ads shot by Patrick Demarchelier for Calvin Klein's CK brand. It was the first time CK's young target consumers had seen a model with whom they could identify, somebody who – although pretty – might conceivably live around the corner.

Long after the waif era has faded into fashion's distant past, Moss has proved her adaptability. Her streetwise looks were instrumental in winning Burberry a new, young audience. The Moss style has proved as suited to the elegance of Chanel as it is to the accessible cosmetics brand Rimmel. A *W* magazine article about the Moss phenomenon suggests that her human imperfections – the scattering of freckles and ever-so-slightly crooked smile that offset her lofty cheekbones and pouting mouth – have enabled young women across the globe to identify with her. The photographer Inez Van Lamsweerde describes her as 'a generation's muse'; while the artist Alex Katz – who painted her portrait for a *W* cover – says, 'She's completely ordinary. That's what makes her so extraordinary.' In the same piece, Tom Sachs explains why he chose to photograph her in the setting of a fast-food restaurant: 'Of course her face is a brand – she's a commodity.' ('All about Kate', *W*, September 2003.)

Models grow used to regarding themselves as commodities, to expressing a set of values that can be utilized by marketers. At the beginning of Gross's book, Cindy Crawford tells him, 'I see myself as a president of a company that owns a product, Cindy Crawford, that everybody wants. So I'm not powerless because I own that product. When you start thinking that your agency owns it and you don't own it, you have a problem.'

Packaging beauty

It's not my intention here to explore the seamier side of the modelling business, which is thoroughly described in Gross's book. (Milan, particularly, is portrayed as a morass, in which playboys circle modelling agencies like sharks.) Perhaps the profession's darkest hour was the aftermath of investigative journalist Donal MacIntyre's BBC documentary about agencies in 1999. As part of the series 'MacIntyre Undercover', the reporter used an array of bugging devices to present an industry riddled with sexual predators and drug abuse. There were recriminations and legal action – but by then the programme had confirmed what many members of the public already suspected.

The subsequent poor image of modelling agencies upsets John Horner, managing director of UK agency Models 1. 'I deplore the way the industry is represented by the media,' he says. 'In the UK, we have one of the most professional businesses in the world. [Internationally] the industry is badly let down by a few grubby agencies that sully its reputation. Most of the UK agencies are managed by women, so they're not the ones doing the damage. And men in the business have a responsibility to behave professionally. You have to be protective – I mean, most of the time these are young, vulnerable kids. When we send them to shoots in Italy – which even within the business has a poor reputation – we make sure that they are professionally chaperoned. Often their parents go with them.'

Horner, particularly, understands the value of models to marketers – after all, he worked in advertising for more than 30 years. He started out in 1965, wrapping parcels stuffed with promotional products at an agency called Dorlands. Over the years he went on to work for some of the most famous agencies in the ad industry – including Leo Burnett and J Walter Thompson – start two businesses, sell both of them at a profit, and play a key role in high-profile mergers. In 1998 he began advising the two head bookers (modelling-speak for agents) at Models 1, Karen Diamond and Kathy Pryer, who had been offered a management buy-out by the agency's founders.

'Gradually they realized that they didn't have the necessary business skills; they weren't sure how to raise the money or write a business plan. But the future [of the agency] looked bright enough, so we did what is unfortunately called a BIMBO – a buy-in management buy-out – because I joined the team by buying into the business. And so, in January 1999, I became a model agent.'

Horner says that, as the managing director of the business, he works behind the scenes. 'On arrival, I did exactly what you'd expect a marketing guy to do, which was to re-establish the brand identity. Obviously we had a great brand name, because the agency had been going for 35 years. It also had a number of brand values, which I kept and strengthened. It's very important that we behave correctly as an agency – that's a key part of our positioning. We pay our models on time, there's no misbehaving or impropriety whatsoever. It's absolutely vital that we are second to none in that regard. It's an interesting challenge because you have to reassure the parents [of teenage models] while making the brand funky enough to appeal to youngsters too.'

Models 1 has an illustrious history. Founded in 1968, it has played an instrumental role in the careers of models such as Twiggy, Jerry Hall, Yasmin Le Bon and current favourite Karen Elson. Today it's the biggest model agency brand in the UK (in competition with Select) and has a database of 7,000 clients, some 2,000 of which are active. International clients count for 25 per cent of the business. The operation is divided into four divisions: women, men, new faces and classic. The 'classic' division handles personalities – notably Patsy Kensit and Faye Dunaway – and established or mature models. 'New faces' is obviously looking for beginners.

While he was working on the brand repositioning – a process that involved, among other things, interviewing key clients and every single member of staff – Horner discovered that the agency was known as 'reputable, but a bit dusty'. 'We had to make the place a little more dynamic. We wanted to become exciting enough so that youngsters would aspire to being part of Models 1. At the time, our new faces division was not doing as well as it should have been. It was one of the reasons we relocated from the wrong end of the King's Road to the heart of London [in offices near Covent Garden].'

Horner points out that, because the fashion industry thrives on novelty, attracting fresh faces is critical to the performance of a modelling agency. With this in mind, Models 1 ran a press relations campaign targeting the youth media, organizing a number of events that brought together journalists, photographers and representatives of the new faces division. The result is that now, when schoolgirls dream about becoming a top model, Models 1 is again among the agencies they consider approaching.

Modelling agencies are also famous for their 'scouts', the talent-spotters who cruise the gathering places of adolescents, as well as constantly keeping their eyes peeled for suitable candidates. Horner admits that this is by no means his field. 'I don't have an eye – but fortunately my job is to run the business rather than to find models. It's very instinctive: a scout "knows" when somebody has potential. We're not after a particular look – it's rare that we set out to find a redhead or a quirky look or whatever. We don't create trends. The photographers do that.'

Whether a walk-in or one of the scouts' finds, the potential model is invited to the agency, always with a parent or guardian. Polaroid photos are taken, after which the agency's experts debate the candidate's potential. If a genuine talent is thought to be present, test photography is done. On the basis of the results, a decision is made.

Models are not expected to contract to the agency for their entire working life, or even for a set period. They sign an agreement that they will not work with any rival UK outfits, but as their career develops they are free to fire their existing agency at any time. Horner says, 'If you think about it, we're taking on youngsters between 16 and 18, mothering them, looking after their careers, so the relationship between model and booker becomes very close. For them to change agencies is quite a wrench.'

In the earliest days of their new career, the young saplings are sent on 'go-sees' – they show their face at magazines and meet photographers with the hope of being hired for a shoot. For those who live outside London, the agency keeps a 'model flat', sleeping six at a time for two- or three-night periods. ('They always wreck the place,' jokes Horner. 'Don't forget – they're teenagers.') The newcomers stay in the new faces division for up to a year before moving on to what is called 'the main board'. There is also a separate 'image' division for what Horner calls 'high-profile, fast-track models' – the kind who end up in *Vogue*. But what outsiders don't realize is that they may be better off working for catalogues.

'A fast-track model can burn out quickly, sometimes inexplicably – she has such a strong image that she goes out of fashion. A bread-and-butter model working for catalogues and mainstream brands can have a solid career for years. And the simple fact is that *Vogue* only pays about £75 a day. Working for the fashion media in general, you'll only earn a maximum of £350 for a shoot. But the media know it's important for the model's career, because then she might get access to a big brand name.'

And that's when the bigger fees start – not only because the model is expected to commit to the brand for a long period of time, 'but also because she is contributing to that brand's essence'. Horner agrees that the right model can transform the fortunes of a brand. He cites the example of Christy Turlington, who became the face of the cosmetics brand Maybelline in the United States (a contract said to be worth £1.8 million a year).

A brand in its own right, Models 1 is among the best known in the fashion industry. 'In the client community, awareness is as high as it could be. But of course we keep in constant contact with our clients, by mail and telephone. My advertising background means I know roughly when clients are going to start thinking about their next campaigns. We make appointments to go and see them. Alternatively, they may ring us to say they are casting for a project, so we send them cards [photographs and statistics] either by mail or online. Each model also has a book of photographs that is constantly updated.'

The agency has about 2,000 models on its books, with a nucleus of 600 who get a steady turnover of work. The decision about which model to use can be made by various parties: the advertising agency, the art director, the photographer or the client, depending on the situation. Often, it's the photographer – and their choices can make or break careers.

Mathilde Plet, in charge of casting models at the French magazine *Numéro*, has cited celebrated photographer Steven Meisel as one of the greatest talent-spotters in the business. 'His mastery of fashion gives him an enormous influence with the agencies,' she said. (*Le Monde* magazine supplement, 20–21 June 2004.) Meisel played a key role in the 'supermodel' phenomenon, shooting Christy Turlington, Naomi Campbell and Linda Evangelista.

John Horner comments, 'Photography is a deceptive process. You can look at a girl and think "she's going to make it", but the photographs tell a different story: exaggerating a jaw, making a nose look too big. The camera is the ultimate judge.'

Perfection and imperfection

'We don't wake up for less than $10,000 a day,' Linda Evangelista famously told *Vogue* in 1991. The quote was the defining phrase of the supermodel era, when the clothes faded into the background and the women wearing them became stars. Things are different now. Fees have settled down – for most models they were never that high in the first place. Dawn Wolf, of the agency IMG/France, told *Le Monde*, 'I've never read an article about the price of models that was right.'

Linda Evangelista is now on the books of Models 1, although agency boss John Horner agrees that the supermodel craze has faded. 'Versace really put supermodels on the map. He decided he'd pay whatever it took to get the best models, which started the whole inflation process. Eventually, though, they became too expensive. It began to be debatable whether they added enough value to the brand in relation to the price the advertiser was paying.'

But Horner also hints that, in terms of sheer professionalism, those few supermodels might have been worth it. 'We did a campaign with Linda Evangelista for Wallis, and it was as much about us selling her to Wallis as it was about the brand wanting a model of that calibre. They did the shoot in America. Normally you do a test day, with a fitting and so forth. But in this case they just turned up with the clothes, and she's such an amazing model that the second they were on, they looked a million dollars. Erin O'Connor is another one: quite unusual-looking, very tall; but the second you put a garment on that girl, she's instantly into model mode.'

Cindy Crawford calls her model persona 'The Thing'. The writer Michael Gross describes the process as follows: 'She fluffs her hair and strikes a pose, and suddenly The Thing is in the room.' Crawford tells him, 'I'm becoming this other character, and all of a sudden – I don't know why – all of a sudden I'm brave, I'm telling jokes, I become much more theatrical... and then I wash it off.'

Perhaps it takes a bit of pantomime to create a fairy-tale. Horner dislikes the term 'clothes-horse', but admits that models play the role of a blank canvas. 'They are there to interpret and enhance a product. The more flexible their face or body, the more easily they can create a distinctive image for the client.'

How much digital trickery goes into moulding that image is open to debate. Horner says that the very best photographers disdain re-touching, as they can achieve the desired effect through lighting, make-up and their own skill. But he admits that cosmetics advertisers and fashion magazines remove blemishes with a few judicious clicks of the mouse.

One of the things a computer can't change is ethnicity. The pages of fashion magazines are far more cosmopolitan (no pun intended) than they used to be, but black models are still a comparative rarity. Veronica Webb, Grace Jones, Iman, Naomi Campbell, Waris Dirie and Alek Wek are memorable partly because they broke through the barrier. According to one fashion journalist, who wishes to remain anonymous, 'It's simple practicality. When you put a model on the cover of a magazine, you're promoting cosmetics as well as clothes. And if most of your readers are white, they want to identify with that image. The black community has its own fashion magazines.'

Colour is one thing – but how about shape? In the same way that fashion models are young for practical reasons (energy, clear eyes, smooth skin), they are also skinny. When designers create clothes for their collections, they make items in one size. Therefore, models also come in a standard size. And the received opinion is that a dress is flattered by a slender frame. But John Horner strongly refutes allegations that modelling provokes eating disorders. 'Anorexia begins before modelling. We have never had an anorexic model on our books, and if we believe somebody may be veering in that direction, we send them away to get help. If models are skinny, it's often because they're born that way. They eat perfectly healthy meals. We even considered putting paid to the myth by producing a book called *Model Food*, in which they'd list all their favourite recipes. Of course, if they get overweight, they don't work. But we certainly don't want them to be all skin and bone. Some photographers like fuller figures.'

Yet various groups, from the British Medical Association to the National Eating Disorders Association in the United States (whose public face is the former model Carré Otis), have expressed concern that fashion magazines promote unrealistic body shapes. It's a case of supply and demand. In the Western world, where a growing percentage of the population is officially obese, slenderness has become idealized.

Horner observes that an agency must have, within reason, models of all shapes, sizes and racial backgrounds on its books: 'And even ages. Some models have a short working life, often because they decide to pursue other careers or raise families. But Yasmin Le Bon has been working for 20-odd years. We also have a model called Daphne Selfe, who is in her 70s. [She featured in a Dolce & Gabbana campaign.] There is a market for different types of look.'

Lately, though, fashion brands have been favouring well-known faces over the blank canvas of models. Celebrities, while not always perfect, are undeniably powerful.

Celebrity sells

10

*When a celebrity wears something,
it has a direct impact on sales.*

In 1975, Giorgio Armani sold his Volkswagen. The money went into a pool of US$10,000 that Armani and his partner Sergio Galleoti had got together to open their Milanese fashion house. Having left medical school to enter the fashion business in 1957, Armani had worked as a buyer for the department store La Rinascente. But it was as a designer at Cerruti, which he joined in the early 1960s, that he learnt the techniques that were to make his career. The charismatic Nino Cerruti was a master of marketing: he once convinced Lancia to paint a fleet of cars in the same shade as his new range of suits, and then enlisted the curvaceous actress Anita Ekberg to break a bottle of champagne over one of them for the cameras. The effectiveness of such publicity coups was not lost on Armani, who would use relationships with celebrities as the cornerstone of his marketing strategy.

Armani's clothes alone were impressive enough – although the casual deconstructed look of his suits is familiar today, it was revolutionary at the time – but it took a movie star to transfer the designs from the fashion press to the public eye. The star was Richard Gere, and the vehicle was a film called *American Gigolo* (1980). Designers had been dressing stars for years – Hubert de Givenchy was famous for outfitting Audrey Hepburn – but this was arguably the first time a set of clothes had played such a prominent role in a film, almost becoming an extension of the main character. After Gere wore his suits on screen, Armani's sales soared. Since then, by nurturing a close working relationship with Hollywood, Armani has provided the wardrobe for more than 300 movies, always ensuring that his name appears in the credits. His marketing department has also seen to it that movie stars are regularly invited to his shows and outfitted in Armani for high-profile events – especially the Oscars. For a long stretch of the 1990s, Oscar night was Armani night.

Armani can be considered as having pioneered the link between fashion and Hollywood. His dressing of *American Gigolo* was a milestone that led to an enduring relationship. It's part of the brand value – its customers appreciate its association with stardom.

Armani is not alone in developing such relationships. Designers such as Valentino and Versace have also displayed a knack for deploying star fire-power. At Louis Vuitton, the brand's artistic director, Marc Jacobs, has moved on from using supermodels to pop stars and actresses in its advertising. In the UK, as we've heard, Matthew Williamson makes no secret of the fact that dressing a string of well-known young women enhanced his profile. Male fashion is not immune either (see Chapter 15: Targeted male). During the run-up to Oscar night, designer brands begin a mating dance with stars and their publicists, often sending racks of free clothing in the hope that a garment will make it on to the red carpet.

The benefits are as blinding as a spotlight: stars give brands a well-defined personality for a minimum of effort, and bring with them a rich fantasy world to which consumers aspire. In addition, consumers have a 'history' with stars. Even though they've only seen them on the screen or in the pages of magazines, they form an attachment to celebrities, regarding them as friendly faces and reliable arbiters of taste. Models, with their distant gazes and alien bodies, can't compete.

April Glassborow, senior buyer for international designer collections at Harvey Nichols, recalls, 'When Victoria Beckham was photographed in a green satin Chloé dress by the *Sunday Times Style* section, it created a demand. It's not a theory. When a celebrity wears something, it has a direct impact on sales.'

By now there must be few readers of glossy magazines who still believe that, when an actress is photographed carrying the latest 'must-have' bag, she has actually paid for the item. Celebrities occasionally go shopping like everyone else, but generally they are bombarded with free gifts and offers of sponsorship deals. Designers will practically slit one another's throats to get a dress photographed on a star during Oscar night or at the Cannes Film Festival.

In terms of cost-effectiveness, a public appearance that might lead to a photo in a magazine is far more desirable than a multi-million-pound contract. Agencies such as Exposure in London (see Chapter 7: The image-makers) offer brands the possibility of rounding up stars for events, or placing clothes on influential figures, as part of their service. Such deals can work both ways, too: the actress Liz Hurley's career sky-rocketed after she wore 'that dress' – a daring low-cut Versace number held together by safety pins – to the premiere of the film *Four Weddings and a Funeral* (1994).

The relationship is a delicate one, however – for both parties. The designer's marketing adviser must ensure that the chosen celebrity flatters the brand. And the stars, aware that their every move will be made in the full glare of the media spotlight, must be absolutely sure that the garment flatters them. Just as many fashion brands hire agencies to develop relationships with celebrities, the stars themselves seek the counsel of professional stylists.

Andrea Lieberman has counted among her clients Jennifer Lopez, Gwen Stefani, Kate Hudson, Dido, Drew Barrymore and Janet Jackson. 'A star's image is today their major asset,' she told *Elle* magazine (Styliste de Stars, 6 September 2004). 'With the music industry in transition and piracy undermining their income, they've expanded into other fields like designing lines of clothing, launching their own perfumes, and tours. To be credible, they have to maintain a certain style. And they're under a lot of pressure: the slightest fashion faux pas and they're skewered by the media.'

At the beginning of her career, when she left Parsons School of Design in New York, Lieberman was forced to take a job as a waitress before finding a post with the designer Giorgio Sant'Angelo. Later, after being inspired by her travels in Africa, she opened a jewellery and ethnic accessories store called Culture & Reality. Soon she found herself styling upcoming New York rock bands, and was eventually introduced to the hip-hop performer Sean 'P Diddy' Combs. This led to a meeting with Jennifer Lopez. It was Lieberman who put Lopez into a much-photographed diaphanous green Versace dress, split to the navel, for the Grammy awards.

One stylist who has achieved star status is Patricia Field, who styled Sarah Jessica Parker for the fashion-fixated television series *Sex and the City*. Field is in fact a professional costume designer with several TV and film credits to her name. She opened her eponymous boutique in Greenwich Village in 1966 and started designing for television in 1980, creating the costumes for a series called *Crime Story*, about the Las Vegas Mafia. By putting 'SATC's' Carrie Bradshaw in a combination of designer labels and pretty thrift-store finds, Parker and Field created a bohemian mix-and-match look that resonated with consumers. How many pairs of Manolo Blahnik shoes were sold thanks to Carrie's love affair with the sleek sling-backs?

Having moved from the small to the big screen, *Sex and the City* is still a product placement magnet. But the TV show helped to convince image-makers that the buying public related more to the perceived 'realness' – however illusory – of actresses than to the unattainable beauty of models. Stars began to replace models on the cover of fashion magazines. Interviewed by *Time* magazine's *Style & Design* special edition (September 2003), Grace Coddington, the creative director of US *Vogue*, hinted that this might be a bone of contention: 'There are no models on covers any more. They're all actors because they're what sells. An actor often dictates what you're going to get. I find that annoying. And I'm incredibly shy, so they scare the pants off me. But I feel perfectly comfortable with the models. They're like my kids.'

Designers such as Matthew Williamson, Zac Posen and Marc Jacobs have been lucky enough to attract the attention and friendship of celebrities, who wear their clothes and attend their shows as a gesture of appreciation and support. Brands that don't have such an appeal merely dig into their wallets to ensure that the right people are seen in their front row. For upcoming and mid-range designers, however, celebrities aren't always an option.

There are signs, in any case, that the celebrity craze may be dying out. Upmarket brands, particularly, have started wondering when glitter becomes kitsch. In the view of Lanvin designer Alber Elbaz, 'The red carpet has gone from elitist to popular. Everyone has access to it, even if only on the internet or through magazines. Since fashion is an integral part of celebrities' lives, it's become a kind of permanent red carpet despite itself. But I don't think this phenomenon of identification is going to last much longer.'

When celebrities become designers

As fame fatigue sets in and consumers become increasingly sceptical about the relationships between brands and stars, it has become necessary to integrate celebrities more closely with the design process. Rather than being expected to buy an item of clothing merely because it is worn by a star, shoppers are now sold products that have – they are told – actually been created by their idol. To a certain extent, the trend grew naturally out of the stars' penchant for creating their own lines of clothing. Another celebrity seems to join the list every day: Jennifer Lopez launched a fashion brand back in 2001; Beyoncé and Gwen Stefani launched their lines in 2004; French fashion model Milla Jovovich teamed up with designer Carmen Hawk to launch Jovovich-Hawk in 2003 (the line ran out of steam in 2008). British pop singer Lily Allen entered the fray with Lily Loves. Sienna Miller and her sister created the line Twenty8Twelve. The Olsen twins have a whole clutch of lines: an upmarket, adult brand called The Row, as well as a vintage-inspired range called Elizabeth and James and collaborations with Wal-Mart and J C Penney. And Victoria Beckham has achieved something approaching fashion credibility with her eponymous brand.

It's not always easy to tell whether these projects spring out of a star's desire to further monetize their fame, or a genuine interest in fashion. Accordingly, some celebrity brands are taken more seriously by the style establishment than others. As Suzy Menkes wrote in *The New York Times*: 'Now, it's possible for a star and a stylist to drag a brand in to the 21st century. But as a fashion editor, I have to ask myself whether taste and style are really a match for creativity and experience? Sometimes I get mad thinking how tough it is for talented young creatives to get financing while stars are lavished because they're already famous.' ('Red carpet baggers', 14 February 2012.)

Celebrities are certainly not immune to a tongue-lashing from the notoriously bitchy fashion press. When rapper and singer Kanye West launched his fashion line with a Paris catwalk show in 2011, the reviews ranged from indifferent to openly mocking. *The Guardian* gleefully summed up some of the most scathing comments: 'Next season Kanye should get a tailor so his clothes might fit' (Cathy Horyn, *The New York Times*); 'A celebrity tag and a lively audience filled with music business friends does not cut it in Paris' (Suzy Menkes, *International Herald Tribune*); 'Kanye West's fashion show was like being subjected to an hour-long MRI scan – but not as much fun (Lisa Armstrong, *Daily Telegraph*). ('Proof that Kanye can't cut it on the catwalk', 3 October 2011.)

The irony is that West seems genuinely passionate about fashion – at previous Paris fashion weeks he scrutinized the shows with more than mild interest and mingled joyously with bloggers and fashion moguls alike – and did not hide his frustration at the fact that the establishment seemed determined to shut him out. Undaunted, he returned to Paris the following year, where the press praised his pluck and even allowed that his designs had improved. 'These were video clothes, perfect for on-camera dry humping,' wrote Luke Leitch of *The Telegraph*, with somewhat faint praise. ('Kanye West samples Givenchy, and Kim Kardashian will want to wear it', 6 March 2012.) At the time of writing, it seems that Kanye is willing to keep on taking it until they take him seriously.

Whether embraced by the fashion press firmament or not, the high media profile of VIP-designed fashion has driven another evolution in the relationship between clothes and celebrities: the recruitment of stars by existing brands. This trend led Ungaro to recruit Lindsay Lohan as a designer, while Halston turned to Sarah Jessica Parker. Both collaborations were short-lived. In a variation on the theme, the designer Nicola Formichetti, who is trying to revive the Thierry Mugler label, appears to form a tandem with Lady Gaga.

By far the most widely reported example to date was the partnership between Britain's Topshop and one of the country's most visible exports, Kate Moss. The selling point here was that the collection with Moss's name on it was co-designed by the model, based on favourite items from her wardrobe. It was also extremely accessibly priced, so her young fans could dress up as their heroine for as little as £45 (around US$80): the cost of a slinky black dress. Importantly, for marketing-savvy consumers, the alliance felt honest. 'Moss is a long-time fan of the store and has always shopped there, mixing in cheap pieces with her ultra-fashionable wardrobe.' ('Kate Moss: Topshop's new muse', Telegraph.co.uk, 20 September 2006.) The deal with Moss was said to have cost Topshop parent company Arcadia around £3 million (US$5.4 million). The not entirely surprising results of the partnership were straggling queues outside Topshop in Oxford Street and Barney's in New York, where the 80-piece collection also went on sale.

Commenting on the relationship in MSN Money, Verdict Research director Neil Saunders said: 'It is increasingly difficult to drive volume on [women's] clothing. The number of clothing items a woman buys each year has doubled over the last 10 years, and that can't continue. That's why retailers can add value by model association.'

But associations with top models may not be enough. How about teaming up with a global superstar? Having already supplied an 'off-stage wardrobe' for Madonna and her stage crew during a 2006 tour, the following year H&M asked the singer to design a collection under the name M by Madonna. Consumers were informed that the star 'worked closely' with the company's head of design Margareta van den Bosch to come up with the resulting clothes. And Ms van den Bosch herself was on hand to assure us that '[Madonna] was extraordinarily style conscious, passionate and involved in even the smallest details.' ('Madonna becomes H&M's material girl', Evening Standard, 12 February 2007.)

It is reasonable to assume that most celebrity-driven collections are either one-offs, or fragile structures that are unlikely to stand the test of time. Those that emerge from the spin cycle will be the most sincere and the most qualitative: in other words, striking, good-value products that are the result of a genuine collaboration between a star with a vision and a designer who knows how to interpret it.

Further down the line, with fame fatigue continuing to spread, many consumers may yearn for the return of genuine brands created by real designers. The presence of a celebrity in the strategy may soon be read as a signal that the marketing budget has taken precedence over the quality of the product.

Press to impress

11

Fashion magazines are an extension of the marketing departments of large fashion companies.

Marching down a steel-cold street in central Stockholm with about an hour to kill before my appointment at H&M, I end up doing what I always do in these circumstances: I find a store selling magazines. But this time, rather than simply catching up on the news and topping up my pop culture references while thawing my hands and feet, I decide to write down the names of all the fashion and style magazines on the shelf. I'm looking at the list now, scrawled in my notebook. Alongside local-language magazines and the heavyweight bibles that can be found almost everywhere – *Vogue*, *GQ*, *Elle*, *Marie-Claire* – there are lots of cultish titles that none the less strive to be 'international': *Zink*, *V*, *Nylon*, *Oyster*, *Pap*, *Citizen K*, *WAD*, *Plaza*, *Squint*, *Rebel*, *Black Book*, *Dazed & Confused*, *Tank*, *Flaunt*, *Surface*. There is even a magazine called *Shoo*, devoted entirely to accessories. And this is a relatively small shop in Stockholm, not a giant media emporium like Borders in Oxford Street or the magazine kiosk at Grand Central Station in New York.

Whether all these magazines will still exist by the time this book comes out is open to question. *The Face*, the style magazine of my youth, closed down long ago, having failed to age gracefully with its audience, while simultaneously losing touch with its target market of suburban hipsters. Nevertheless, my little experiment shows that despite the web, fashion consumers are still addicted to those glossy pages; and fashion advertisers, too.

What I'm really interested in here, of course, is the relationship between fashion magazines and advertisers. The situation warrants scrutiny. While fashion is often presented as an art form, or at least a form of entertainment, it almost entirely lacks a critical press. Movies and books are regularly disembowelled with a few strokes of the pen, but the vast percentage of fashion journalism is at best effervescent, at worst fawning. Could it possibly be because magazines need to keep their advertisers sweet? After all, following the frenzied consolidation of the last few years, which saw most of the luxury brands swallowed up by a handful of conglomerates – LVMH, Gucci Group and Richemont – fashion advertisers are wealthier and more powerful than ever.

A few days after my return from Stockholm, during fashion week in Paris, I manage to grab a few moments with Masoud Golsorkhi, the founder and editor of a magazine called *Tank*, one of the edgier and more intelligent style magazines. Golsorkhi says, '*Tank* strives to provide an alternative perspective, and as such it is far more critically engaged than many of its competitors. Most fashion magazines are an extension of the marketing departments of large fashion companies. Our approach isn't about buying the complete marketing message; although we don't entirely reject it, either. We accept that fashion is not essential, but as there's clearly a sociological and psychological desire for its existence, it's a subject that merits intelligent coverage.'

So why don't other magazines have a similar outlook? Golsorkhi seems almost shocked by my naivety. 'The fashion press is very much gagged,' he says. 'This is not just about advertising cash – it's also about gifts and holidays. The connection between fashion brands and the media is based on relationships, and fashion PR people work very hard to stimulate friendships with journalists. It's very difficult to write nasty things about your friends.'

A press relations executive working for a designer label tells me a story about a training event for young PR people hosted by a leading UK fashion journalist. 'We'd all been summoned to hear this journalist tell us how we could best convince her to write about our brands. She had a list of 10 do's and don'ts. The only one I remember is this: "If you must give us free gifts, give us vouchers instead".'

Golsorkhi says that *Tank*'s comparatively high cover price – an issue costs just over £10 – is designed to guarantee its independence. 'The idea is that the magazine survives on sales rather than advertising sponsorship. Of course we carry advertising, but we maintain the right to say what we like. And the magazine's balance is far more in favour of editorial than advertising.'

Golsorkhi believes that fashion brands are over-protected by the media, which can lead to marketing errors and ruined businesses. 'The clothes go straight out there to the biggest focus group in the world – the consumers, who have a nasty habit of rejecting a brand whose designs they don't like, even if it has spent a fortune on advertising and thus been given the stamp of approval by the fashion press. A more critical press would ultimately benefit the industry.'

Perhaps it's wrong to try and separate fashion magazines from the industry they cover. Fashion is not politics, after all. It's a relatively small and self-contained community in which stylists, art directors, photographers and editors flit from magazines to advertising campaigns and back again. (This explains the common complaint that it's often difficult to tell a fashion spread from an advertisement: the same team may have created both.) Fashion editors and stylists also offer their services directly to designers at the start of the creative process, which handily enables everyone to come to an agreement on prevailing trends.

Nicholas Coleridge, managing director of Condé Nast in the UK – home to *Vogue*, *Glamour*, *Tatler*, *Vanity Fair* and *GQ*, among others – says, '*Vogue* and other fashion magazines don't exist to be overly critical; although they can criticize by exclusion. Our job is to cover trends. The editors themselves choose the clothes they want to present on the editorial pages, and the stylists have considerable room for manoeuvre. There is no pre-arranged deal in terms of editorial space in return for advertising support. The editors are as keen to show little-known designers as they are to cover the big brands. Having said that, it would look pretty strange if we didn't cover the major designers – it's what our readers expect of us.'

Xavier Romatet, president of Condé Nast France, confirms this opinion: 'We are 70 per cent funded by advertising, but we are not enslaved to our advertisers. If our editorial was purely driven by our advertising you would see as much [of mid-market brands] Maje and Zadig & Voltaire as you do Dior and Chanel. Our editorial reflects what we consider to be right for the magazine and for our readers.'

He admits, however, that fashion journalists have a close relationship with brands. 'Naturally, both sides are passionate about the business. If [LVMH boss] Bernard Arnault calls me to say he's unhappy about something, I'm glad – it means we count... Of course both sides socialize and of course journalists wear designers' clothes – just as journalists who write about cars road test cars.'

But with many journalists accepting positions as part-time consultants and stylists to brands, the sphere for objective reporting seems severely limited. This situation may have been curtailed at *Vogue*: incoming editor Emmanuelle Alt was widely reported to have dropped a consulting role at Balmain when she moved up from the second slot to take over from Carine Roitfeld in 2011.

The methods fashion editors use to choose the clothes they feature merit a brief explanation. Aside from catwalk shows and presentations, they can turn to 'look books' – essentially catalogues sent to them by the fashion brands to present each season's collection. But former French *Vogue* editor Roitfeld believes upcoming young designers can break through simply by being pushy. 'In my experience, American designers are far more confident and ambitious than their European counterparts. In New York, people will approach me and talk to me about their work. It happens much less over here.'

Her successor, too, has claimed that it is her duty to promote up-and-coming designers. Emmanuelle Alt told *The Telegraph*'s Hilary Alexander: 'I will try even more to support young designers. I like to keep my curiosity up. The industry is always waiting, begging for a name. But it is rare to find a big "trésor", so you must keep looking.' ('Emmanuelle Alt interview', 7 March 2011). Indeed, Alexander reports, one of her first moves on being appointed editor was to host 'the first French Vogue platform for 10 new talents, with an exhibition at The Crillon Hotel, which opened last week, with Kate Winslet as a guest of honour'.

Nevertheless, small and mid-range designers with severely limited or non-existent advertising budgets complain that they feel excluded from glossy magazines. The French designer Isabel Marant once stated bluntly, 'To be well known in fashion today, you have to appear in the women's press. But, without buying advertising, it's almost impossible. The relationship within the fashion business is one of give-and-give: "You pay, and I'll give you some editorial. You don't pay, and I'll write about you when I have the room." Fashion journalists, rain or shine, are in the grip of their advertising departments. Advertising is a very heavy burden for a small fashion house like mine.' ('Isabel Marant: Un bon vêtement raconte une histoire', *L'Express*, 6 September 2004.)

There is no doubt that glossy magazines wield tremendous marketing clout. Over the years the fashion press has handed many designers a place in history. It was Carmel Snow, the editor of American *Vogue*, who wrote of Christian Dior's designs in 1947: 'This is a new look!' And the support of Hélène Lazareff, the founder of *Elle*, was fundamental to Gabrielle Chanel's comeback in 1954, when the designer was severely out of favour – having ill-advisedly spent the Occupation shacked up in the Ritz with a German officer.

Today, fashion fans continue to base buying decisions on what they see in the glossies. April Glassborow at Harvey Nichols says, '*Vogue* is still very influential – the photography remains beautiful. I think readers make the separation between the editorial and the advertising; but at the same time they accept that advertising is part of the package.' Glassborow adds that some of the best fashion coverage can be found in newspapers. She cites the *Style* supplement of *The Times* as particularly effective. And, indeed, it would be churlish not to mention Suzy Menkes, the *International Herald Tribune*'s redoubtable fashion journalist, who is by no means afraid of crossing swords with designers. Cathy Horin at *The New York Times* frequently dips her pen in acid, too.

But even some mainstream reporters don't feel entirely free of the yoke of advertising. Janie Samet, who has been writing about fashion in *Le Figaro* for many years, tells me, 'My first newspaper, *L'Aurore*, was actually owned by Marcel Boussac, the then owner of Dior. Newspapers can't survive without advertising, of course, and it's worth noting that today luxury companies are their largest advertisers, alongside automobiles. [Luxury brands] use us as auxiliaries of their advertising, in order to promote new shops and so on. Designers measure their column inches to see how much the same space would have cost them in advertising.'

A familiar criticism of the glossies is that the advertising threatens to obscure the editorial, particularly in the early sections of the magazine. In reality, there is a fairly even balance between editorial and ad pages, but the major brands all insist on prime up-front positions. A healthy advertising market also means a top-heavy product.

Nicholas Coleridge comments: 'The good thing for us is that the big fashion companies believe strongly in the power of advertising. As the likes of LVMH and Gucci have acquired more brands, they've been keen to market them. Their system is to buy a fashion or luxury business, improve the product, and then tell lots of people about it very quickly. And they've tended to do this through the pages of *Vogue* and the other glossies. At the same time, because their total advertising spend has risen, their negotiating power has increased. Related to this is the way that the competition for good positions, ie as close to the front as possible, has become intense.'

I wonder aloud whether this insistence on being 'at the front of the book' isn't indicative of a lack of imagination or advertising strategy within fashion companies. Coleridge says, 'Publishing companies are forced to perform a delicate balancing act, juggling what you might call the best seats in the house among big advertisers. You might have expected that, as media buying became more sophisticated, advertisers would begin to take up other positions – but that hasn't happened at all; rather the reverse. For example,

Chanel used not to mind where it was; it minded more about price than about position. Now it cares about position. Dior cares passionately about position, so do Louis Vuitton and Gucci. Dolce & Gabbana has become very prominent. Armani is pushing for better and better positions. Ralph Lauren and Ferragamo "own" historic positions within glossy magazines and will not let them go.'

He confirms that many brands simply refuse to advertise unless they're given an up-front position. And as fashion houses have bought one another, they've tried to move their subsidiary brands into better positions on the back of the big spenders. For example, if Gucci has an advertising spread in *Vogue*, it can argue that its sister brand Yves Saint Laurent should run alongside it. 'The most striking trend [in advertising sales] is the desire to upgrade positions. And now the jewellery companies want to push forward too. All this is exacerbated by the luxury companies' increasing use of media-buying and planning agencies, which sometimes imply that they can negotiate better positions. This can lead to short-term unpleasantness. The fact is of course that a magazine is a 3-D object, so not everyone can be first.' So what can the magazines do? Coleridge smiles mischievously: 'They pay smooth-tongued publishers to instil a sense of fairness and balance into proceedings.'

Although the clamour for high-profile positions can cause headaches for advertising sales executives, it is a sign that fashion companies still rate glossy magazines as the best way of reaching their target markets. Upmarket fashion brands have little use for television. 'Television advertising is expensive, and there is colossal waste,' observes Coleridge. 'If you take a brand like Saint Laurent, it probably has something like 80,000 potential customers in the whole of the UK. And I would suggest that the most efficient way of reaching them is through one of our magazines. Advertising on, say, Channel 4 would cost many times more, and they would be communicating pointlessly to a large percentage of people who, frankly, would not be interested.'

For a designer, the fashion show is a way to broadcast ideas. It is a medium.

Watching a fashion show can be an exhilarating experience. Watching 50 in a week is an exquisite form of torture. At least, that seems to be the opinion shared by many of the people filing into the Chanel show at the Grand Palais. Some of them have been on the road for nearly a month, starting with New York fashion week before moving on to London, Milan – and now Paris. With their bright plumage and malicious eyes, they look like waterfowl descending on a marsh.

I am not an accredited fashion journalist – I am, as always, an interloper in their world – so I wait outside, observing the comings and goings. The show is due to start in about half an hour. Everybody knows it will not begin on time. That would be unfashionable.

The bi-annual women's prêt-à-porter collections in Paris, which take place in March and October, are among the most important events (some would say they are *the* most important events) in the fashion calendar. There are other fashion weeks around the world – in Miami, Barcelona, Sydney and Hong Kong, to name a few – but they lack the prestige of the four major spectaculars. There's a whole raft of trade shows and expos that attract little attention outside the textile industry. And then there are the haute couture shows, which these days have taken on the air of performance art. But we'll return to those later. For the moment, the circus surrounding the spring/ summer prêt-à-porter collections is in full swing. This week, as many as 2,000 journalists and 800 buyers are in town.

People arrive and kiss one another on both cheeks, then stand around ostentatiously fanning themselves with their gold-dust invitations. Suzy Menkes of the *International Herald Tribune* sweeps regally past, unmistakable with her cresting-wave hair-do. A parasitical gaggle of hangers-on – a large percentage of them young bloggers – take photographs of everything that moves. Although I, too, am a hanger-on, a residue of pride prevents me from doing the same. I already know that I don't have a chance in hell of getting in to the Chanel show.

And yet, on a couple of occasions now, I've interviewed the most important figure on the Paris fashion circuit.

The power behind the shows

Didier Grumbach is president of the Fédération Française de la Couture, du Prêt-à-Porter des Couturiers et des Créateurs de Mode. In other words, he runs the organization that runs the Paris collections. His office is located in a discreetly elegant building on the Rue du Faubourg Saint Honoré, not far from the French headquarters of *Vogue*, as well as those of many of the fashion houses that his organization represents. Grumbach himself is not a designer, but a businessman. He helped Yves Saint Laurent and Pierre Bergé found Yves Saint Laurent Rive Gauche, and he ran Thierry Mugler until 1997, when he was elected president of the federation. He is, he says, 'completely impartial' in matters of design; which is just as well, because becoming a member of his organization – and thus gaining permission to show in Paris – is moderately harder than joining a secret society.

Although the federation is best known – to outsiders, at least – for organizing the Paris shows, it has a number of other functions, including teaching and encouraging aspiring designers; representing French fashion abroad; and combating the theft of intellectual property. It is divided into three sections, or *chambres syndicales*: haute couture and men's and women's prêt-à-porter. The Chambre Syndicale de la Haute Couture (of which Grumbach is also president) was created in 1868; the spin-off prêt-à-porter bodies as recently as 1973. Grumbach's umbrella organization oversees all three of them.

He is well aware of his privileged position. 'I could name all my predecessors stretching back to the very beginning,' he says. 'My immediate predecessor stayed for 26 years. The gentleman before him occupied the post from 1937 until 1972. I imagine this demonstrates that they were excellent politicians.' What Grumbach means is that his is an elected position, and that, 'like any president', he could be deposed at any moment. At the time of our meeting, however, he rests comfortable in the knowledge that he was unanimously re-elected in November 2003.

As far as the Paris collections are concerned, the federation's power is absolute. For one thing, it decides which journalists will be admitted. Editors must submit forms providing the circulation figures of their magazines and specifying the names of the reporters and photographers who will be covering the event. Their requests can be rejected. The final list is sent to the fashion designers and their PR representatives, who then choose which journalists they wish to invite.

Even more crucially, the organization draws up the schedule of shows and assigns locations. This dates back to the 1970s, when it was decided that all designers should show their collections in close proximity, 'in order to present the public with a general outlook of the fashion designers' creations and facilitate the work of French and foreign journalists', to quote its website (**www.modeaparis.com**). (Note here the rather ironic use of the word 'public', when in fact the collections are strictly off-limits to mere mortals.)

'The timetable is more or less the same each year,' Grumbach explains. 'Each member [of the *chambre syndicale*] has a specific slot, and no member can take the place of another. Generally, we reserve the first day for young brands that have begun exporting to Asia and America, meaning that they have potential. We have to place certain major designers in specific locations, because there are not many spaces in Paris that can accommodate up to 1,500 people, with all the security and organizational problems that entails.'

Until recently the Carrousel du Louvre – basically a rather bland conference facility hiding beneath the legendary art museum – was the heartland of the shows, but gradually they began to move into more opulent spaces, and now it has been abandoned altogether. Venues can range from a marquee erected for the occasion in the Tuileries gardens, to the Rodin museum.

'There are 11 shows a day,' Grumbach explains, 'which is an enormous figure, embracing all nationalities: not just French, but English, American, Japanese, Belgian, Italian... Paris remains the international window for fashion design. You can be a genius in London, but to gain true international status, you must eventually show in Paris.'

Like most decisions in the surprisingly conservative world of high fashion, membership of the *chambres syndicales* is based firmly on business performance. Those elected to the clan are judged in terms of potential or existing international sales. As Grumbach points out, 'A buyer from America doesn't travel all the way to Paris to buy something that already exists in America. So they are looking for something truly innovative. Interest from abroad is one of the key things we look for when we are considering applications for membership.'

Prospective members send a letter to the *chambre syndicale*, which then dispatches an application form. The designer must return it, along with a hefty press portfolio. 'And while a good review from Suzy Menkes helps,' Grumbach says, 'we're particularly interested in the international spread of the coverage.'

Grumbach also stresses the importance of what he calls 'the godfather figure'. Prospective members must secure the support of an established name in fashion who can state their case before the election committee. 'It is necessary to have a sponsor who can speak on your behalf, and explain why you should be admitted. This is, never forget, a club. If Christian Lacroix sends a letter insisting that you are the next big thing, it helps. And if Jean-Paul Gaultier is advising your company – bearing in mind that you are, in some ways, his competitor – we generally respect that.'

He adds that the sponsor should be the president or CEO of a fashion brand, not just a designer. Once again, although fashion is a creative industry, executives have the greatest influence.

Communication via catwalk

It's not just the brazenly clubby nature of the Paris collections that might dissuade a designer from showing in the French capital. In fact, a number of developments have placed a question mark over the wisdom of holding fashion shows at all – not just in Paris, but in all the main markets.

The most obvious is the availability on the web of images from a show less than an hour after the designer has taken a bow. Extensive web coverage means that buyers from stores are no longer obliged to attend shows. It also plays into the hands of counterfeiters and copyists, who can have knocked-off versions of the clothes on sale before the original designers have finished taking orders from buyers. Grumbach says this is 'not just a concern – it is collective suicide'. He tempers this by adding, 'Of course, there is no rule that says designers must show in public. But they want to maintain visibility, and there is nothing like a fashion show to display their art. It is a way to broadcast their ideas. It is a medium.'

These days, most buyers place orders at private 'pre-collection' gatherings in showrooms, during which the designers present straightforward commercial versions of the garments they will later send out on to the catwalks. Matthew Williamson, for instance, holds two pre-collection events, in January and June. The brand's managing director, Joseph Velosa, says,

'The pre-collection is usually unashamedly commercial: the essence of your signature without the £3,000 dress or the £6,000 coat. The overheads and the razzamatazz aren't there, so people like me approve of it because there are no up-front costs. It's just about product, in a room, that buyers respond to. Some of the brands sell as much as 70 per cent of their wholesale stock at pre-collection. So by the time the catwalk collection comes around, if the pre-collection was received positively, the designer feels much more confident and free to experiment. Shows are therefore becoming less commercial and more theatrical. They are less and less a direct selling tool.'

April Glassborow, senior buyer for international designer collections at Harvey Nichols, agrees that attending fashion shows is no longer an essential part of her job. 'It's true that we do a large percentage of our work at pre-collection stage. You see things that are less expensive, more basic, and clearly indicative of key styles and colours. And you struggle to justify going to the collections when you can see everything on Vogue.com from your own desk. There's a lot to be said for the lights, the music, the sheer drama of the shows – but the fact is that they are more important for the media than for buyers.'

Fashion shows are, in fact, live advertisements. They are expensive and extravagant but, according to Velosa, very effective. He says, 'People outside the industry think it's crazy: "You work for six months for something that lasts for 10 minutes?" But actually those 10 minutes are vital, because everyone is hyper-sensitive to what you're saying. They're all looking at your stage sets, the models you've been able to pull in, your front-row celebrities, whether [US *Vogue* editor] Anna Wintour has turned up... You are gauged hot or not every six months. And of course the product is out there on the biggest pedestal you could imagine. The product has to be right, of course, that's the cornerstone. But if you get everything around it right too, you can change it from being merely a good product into a hot product. The press write about you, the buyers see your name in magazines and, because they're like vacuum cleaners sucking up everything new, when the next collection comes around they want to come and see you.'

Needless to say, fashion designers don't design fashion shows – not entirely, anyway. In Paris alone, a directory's worth of event organizers and set designers are on hand to help them create their spectacular showcases. Thierry Dreyfus is a freelance lighting designer and show director working regularly with a company called Eyesight, whose past clients have included Cacharel, Chloé, Dior Homme, Paul & Joe, Sonia Rykiel and Yves Saint Laurent. In his view, 'The fashion show is not an art – it is an element of marketing. For the amount you invest in a show, you can generate between 10 and a hundred times the cost in free advertising, in terms of photos in magazines and newspapers, television coverage and so forth. One designer told me that if he does a good show he doesn't have to buy advertising space for a year.'

Companies such as Eyesight and their associates have a lot on their plate. Selecting the models, organizing fittings, devising the running order, coordinating accessories, liaising with stylists, hairdressers and make-up artists, arranging sound, lighting, security, catering and seating plans are just a few of the things that must be taken care of. Occasionally, the event organizer is responsible for luring celebrities to events. 'Sometimes they want to come, sometimes they are invited, and sometimes they are paid,' Dreyfus reveals.

Perhaps the greatest of their challenges is creating the 'mood' of the show. People like Dreyfus are paid to ensure that the message the designer wants to get across is evident not just to the people sitting in the room, but also in the resulting media coverage. 'Every detail is important. For instance, because of digital photography, the way photographs are taken is changing, so we have to take account of that in the lighting. It's sort of a magic trick. Each designer wants to ensure that when you see an image from his show, you can immediately identify his particular look. The show has to illustrate the brand.'

Given the importance of accessories, runway shows are likely to have an increasingly close connection with a brand's advertising strategy. For example, Louis Vuitton's autumn/winter 2012 show featured not only a real live steam engine, but porters toting the luggage that is an essential part of the LV heritage. (Not remotely by coincidence, the Musée des Arts Décoratifs had just unveiled an exhibition devoted to the work of trunk-maker Louis Vuitton and fashion designer Marc Jacobs, synthesizing the two sides of the rather schizophrenic brand in the same manner as the show.)

Dreyfus denies that fashion shows have become more about special effects than clothes – 'their main goal is still to show the way fabric moves on a human body' – but he admits that designers are under increasing pressure to make an impact. An important journalist like Emmanuelle Alt or Suzy Menkes, assuming they've already been to the collections in New York and Milan by the time they arrive in Paris, could end up seeing 40 or 50 shows by the end of a season. So the trick is to be remembered.

Dreyfus is unwilling to reveal the cost of staging a fashion show, but estimates range from £20,000 to well over £100,000. Dreyfus says, 'Certainly, if you're a young designer, my advice would be not to show. Rent a showroom, ask a couple of friends to model your clothes, try to develop personal relationships with the press. Because even if you can get a model agency to lower their price to €800 a girl, even if you can get sponsorship from hair and make-up companies, and even if you can find a cheap venue, it's still going to be less than professional and cost a fortune. Better to wait until you can afford to do it properly.'

Back in Didier Grumbach's office, I'm now dying to see my first show. But how do I get in? 'Well, you can't,' he says, with a laugh that may either be sympathetic, embarrassed, or merely incredulous. Perhaps registering my crestfallen expression, he adds, 'Look, you've got a press card, haven't you? Why don't you come along, and we'll see what we can do.'

And so, on the first day of the Paris collections, I stroll in to the media centre and explain the situation to the beautiful girl on the front desk. I tell her that I'm writing a book about fashion, that I recently interviewed Didier Grumbach, and that the great man hinted that I might be able to get in to a show or two. She is just about to reply when a young, thrusting type with fashionably dishevelled hair appears at her side. 'Certainly not,' he says, in his clipped French accent. 'I can assure you, monsieur, that if you do not have the correct accreditation, there is nothing we can do for you.'

My fist involuntarily curls in my pocket, but I smile politely and apologize for wasting his time. Clearly I will have to resort to what the French call 'System D': the system for getting around the system.

Haute couture laid low

I dread to imagine what it might have been like if I'd tried to talk my way into a haute couture show. As you know, haute couture has its roots in the origins of fashion, when wealthy women had dresses made to measure. There were interminable fittings, and clothes were painstakingly stitched by hand. Prêt-à-porter – or ready-to-wear, to give it its more egalitarian appellation – came along much later, driven by 20th-century technology and the democratization of dress. But as ready-to-wear increased in sophistication, price and marketing support, taking on the names of designers that might previously have been associated only with couture (Yves Saint Laurent Rive Gauche was the pioneer in this field), it nudged haute couture slowly towards irrelevancy.

The haute couture shows are held in January and July. According to the rules of the Chambre Syndicale de la Haute Couture, a fashion house can only use the term if it has 'made-to-measure dressmaking activity in the Paris area'. But this humble phrase disguises the true nature of an haute couture dress, which is to fashion what a Lamborghini is to the automobile industry or a newly discovered Van Gogh to the art world. Hand-made in every detail, fused to the body of the model who displays it (and later, perhaps, to the fabulously wealthy customer who acquires it), a haute couture dress is wearable sculpture. One legendary Chanel creation, hand-embroidered by the celebrated Maison Lesage, is said to have sold for €230,000.

And there's the rub. That item may have been exceptional, but haute couture dresses, being one-offs, are worth tens of thousands of pounds. Didier Grumbach himself admits that there are perhaps only 1,000 haute couture customers in the entire world. I have heard estimates as low as 300. In Paris today the official list of permanent haute couture designers stands at 11: Adeline André, Atelier Gustavolins, Chanel, Christian Dior, Maurizio Galante, Jean-Paul Gaultier, Givenchy, Christophe Josse, Stéphane Rolland, Franck Sorbier and Giambattista Valli. This schedule is completed with respected overseas names – Armani, Valentino and Versace – and padded out with young guest designers, as well as jewellery collections. Even Gaultier, who started out in ready-to-wear and joined the haute couture clan in 1997, admits that he does it for love rather than money.

Lately, the French media have begun loudly wondering whether haute couture is on its last legs. Yet there are a number of fairly good reasons for keeping haute couture alive. The first is, as ever, marketing. If a fashion show is little more than a live advertisement, then haute couture is the most spectacular commercial break of all. Say what you like about John Galliano, but his sumptuous creations for Dior were worth their weight in sunglasses and handbags.

Bernard Arnault, chairman of LVMH – which owns the house of Dior – said recently, '[Haute couture] is a fantastic tool to demonstrate the prestige of the house. Its impact on all the other lines – clothes, accessories, and cosmetics – is enormous. Of course it's very costly, but it's not our intention to cover the cost through sales.'

The second reason for the existence of haute couture is simply to push the limits of fashion. While prêt-à-porter has become increasingly commercial, fashion still wishes to maintain a shred of credibility as an art form. Haute couture is its laboratory, encouraging experimentation and generating ideas that may, one day, change the way people dress. According to Bernard Arnault, 'It is the domain in which the designer can go to an extreme...

express the ultimate in quality and creativity. And this link is present in the consumer's mind when they buy prêt-à-porter.' This may explain Giorgio Armani's decision in 2005 to begin showing haute couture for the first time.

The third reason – and the most humane – is simply to preserve the crafts-manship that goes into haute couture. As well as the people who work in the designer's atelier, there are a number of cottage industries adding the luxurious touches that give these outfits their appeal. The embroidery house Lesage, the glove-maker Millau, the milliner Maison Michel, exquisite feather creations from André Lemarié and lace from Puy-en-Velay – all these traditions might be lost if haute couture were to vanish for ever.

Front-row fever

The seating arrangements at Paris fashion shows are clearly defined and almost invariable. On either side of the runway there are separate blocks of seating for VIPs, magazine journalists and buyers. French journalists get a block to themselves. The UK is lumped in with the United States. Japan is seated, inexplicably, with Italy; the rest of Europe peers out from behind the battery of TV cameras. The buyers get a block of their own. The daily news-papers, which provide the swiftest exposure to the largest audience, are given the best vantage point at the front of the room, close to Didier Grumbach. The seating plan strives to observe political sensitivities: for in-stance, US *Vogue* must not be placed next to either UK *Vogue* or *Harper's Bazaar*. Certain journalists – notably Anna Wintour of US *Vogue* and Suzy Menkes of the *International Herald Tribune* – automatically get the best seats.

The entire front-row phenomenon is fascinating. Fashion journalists will tell you that it is vital that they sit in the front row because it enables them to see the clothes properly – including the shoes. But, off the record, they admit that it is as much about status as it is about professionalism. The further back you are, the less important you (and, by extension, your publication) are perceived to be. And if you receive one of the dreaded 'standing' invitations, reserved mainly for students, it might be better not to turn up at all.

Personally, I would be happy to stand. After my brush with the bouncer at the media centre, I return to my office and start phoning PR people. I eventually make contact with a small brand called Impasse de la Défense, created by the designer Karim Bonnet. Based on a back street of the lively

18th *arrondissement* – from which his brand gets its name – he fuses fashion with art, producing bohemian hand-painted dresses. As I live nearby, I'll effectively be supporting my local designer. I get through to a young woman and explain why I want to see the show. 'Sure,' she says, brightly. 'We'll send you an invitation right away.'

It arrives the very next morning, and I note with considerable pleasure that the show will be held at the Salle Wagram, an ancient ballroom notable for its brief appearance in the film *Last Tango in Paris*. When I turn up, there are plenty of people milling around outside. I even spot the requisite fashion students begging for invitations. Clutching mine, I feel an uncharacteristic surge of condescension.

Finally the doors open, and we can escape the late-October drizzle. The theme of the show is 1960s pop music, and a psychedelic sitar band twangs merrily away in the lobby. There is a vague whiff of incense. I hand my invitation nervously to one of the two pretty young women standing at the entrance to the hall, casually mentioning that I'm a journalist.

'Oh,' she says, beaming. 'In that case, you'd better sit in the front row.'

With a sense of triumph that is utterly misplaced, I settle into my seat. I have been there for approximately five minutes when another young woman approaches.

'I'm terribly sorry,' she says. 'But I'm afraid you'll have to move back a row. These seats are reserved for the journalists from *Madame Figaro*.'

Any trace of superiority I might have felt drifts away like chiffon in a cold draught. As I get to my feet, a perfumed gaggle of 40-something ladies bears down on me. These are the representatives of *Madame Figaro*, the venerable French women's magazine. I may be supporting my local designer, but during the collections those with a short-cut to the buying public will always have the upper hand.

Accessorize all areas

13

The handbag is killing fashion.

Today, if you really like a fashion brand, you needn't just wear it or spray it on – you can move in. Take Giorgio Armani's giant lifestyle space at Via Manzoni 31 in Milan. It's the perfect example of brand extensions run riot. Sip coffee in the Emporio Armani Caffè. Have your feet rubbed in the Armani Spa. Shop at Armani Libri (books), Armani Fiori (flowers) or Armani Dolci (chocolates). Pick up your key to the Armani hotel and wallow in the pale, sleek and discreetly modern room furnished by Armani Casa. A little later, pop down for cocktails at the exclusive Armani Privé bar, named after the maestro's haute couture collection. I'm told that if you look at the entire complex from above, it resembles a giant A.

A brand is able to extend itself with a modicum of risk if it has a clear perception of what its name means to consumers. Armani is Italian, casually elegant, contemporary but understated. That concept extends very smoothly into lifestyle products, thus the launch of Armani Casa in 2000.

Unlike the Gucci and LVMH groups, which have expanded by acquiring existing brands, Armani has created its own sub-brands and diversified into new product categories, creating a coherent 'branded environment'. The group is built like a pyramid, with the signature Giorgio Armani brand at the top setting the tone and style for everything it does. When the company moves into a new market, it always opens a Giorgio Armani boutique first, to set the standard, before any of the other brands follow. Beneath the signature brand is Armani Collezioni, a slightly more accessible diffusion line predominantly distributed through department stores; it is followed, in descending order, by Emporio Armani, Armani Jeans, and A/X Armani Exchange, a series of licensed casual-wear stores not a million miles from Gap in style. Each of these labels also markets accessories such as eyewear, watches and fragrances, produced through licensing arrangements. Although licensing was once deemed unfashionable – in the 1990s many luxury companies spent a fortune buying back licences, feeling that over-extension had corrupted the integrity of their brands – it is now sneaking back into favour.

Armani is not the first brand to move into interiors – Ralph Lauren, the king of 'lifestyle' marketing, got in on the act around 20 years ago. Rosita Missoni, having decided to leave fashion to the younger designers in her company, launched a range of home products. Pucci, the Florentine fashion house majority-owned by the LVMH group, has produced winter sportswear in partnership with Rossignol. Pucci's daughter Laudomia is the brand's 'image director'. Pucci was well known for putting his trademark print on everything from curtains to carpets (the Apollo 15 crew carried a Pucci-designed flag to the moon), and in 2001 the label launched a range of furniture in association with Cappellini. But while a Pucci ski jacket certainly stands out on the slopes, isn't it moving beyond the logic of the brand?

Certainly not, says Laudomia. She points out that her father 'lived on the slopes' (he was a member of the Italian skiing team), adding that his very first designs were skiing outfits. 'Pucci comes from a sportswear background, which is very important to point out in terms of legitimacy. We are merely going back to our roots. We have always been a lifestyle company.' Pucci even created a one-off 300-square-metre sail for a racing yacht, perfectly underlining, says Laudomia, 'that we're Mediterranean and we're all about colour'.

Sportswear seems to be a legitimate arena for high-fashion brands, with Céline, Chanel, Dior, Hugo Boss, Prada Sport and Versace Sport all venturing onto the ski slopes and beyond (Chanel has even made a branded snowboard). The lure of brand extensions for fashion labels is obvious, given the many purposes they serve. They can be money-spinners in their own right, public relations tools for drawing attention to the brand (I mean, really, a Chanel snowboard?), or part of an overall branding strategy – another molecule in the brand universe. But what happens when the relationship between clothing and accessories is reversed? Have clothes simply become promotional tools for branded goods?

Emotional baggage

French fashion journalist Janie Samet believes designers' insistence on brand extensions has led to a declining interest in their clothes, and fuelled the success of affordable fashion brands like Zara, H&M and Topshop.

'Naturally, [the designer labels] are keen on accessories because they provide greater profit margins,' she says. 'And customers like them because no matter what else you are wearing, if you have the right bag, you are immediately placed in a certain social context. The problem is that if you have the right bag, the right shoes and the right belt, you may decide that you no longer need the right dress. In this way, the success of bags is killing fashion.'

But fashion and handbags lead a symbiotic existence. While Dior stages fashion shows that are arguably advertising campaigns for its accessories, brands such as Hermès, Prada and Louis Vuitton began making luxury accessories, and then moved into fashion. The clothes that Marc Jacobs creates for Louis Vuitton are – like Armani's flowers and chocolates – part of a branded world. From Bottega Veneta to Loewe via Dunhill, ST Dupont and Asprey, selling accessories is no longer enough – a designer brand must touch every aspect of its customers' lives.

When you're talking about bags, there's no getting around Louis Vuitton. Hours before the opening of its flagship store on the Champs-Elysées, dozens of tourists stand in line to experience the Coca-Cola of luxury brands. Louis Vuitton himself was born in 1821 in a small French village not far from the border with Switzerland. He grew into a natural craftsman, skilfully handling the tools of his father, a joiner. Legend has it that the ambitious young Louis walked 250 miles from his home to Paris, where he became an apprentice at a packing-case maker near the Madeleine. The age of international travel was dawning, with railway lines extending their steel fingers across France and the first steamers traversing the Atlantic. Their wealthy passengers required a great deal of luggage – the more elegant the better. Spying a growing market, Louis Vuitton decided to start his own business.

Vuitton's first commercial premises opened in 1854 on the Rue Neuve-des-Capucines, not far from the Place Vendôme – and thus close to a steady influx of rich clients. His stroke of genius was to upholster his cases not in leather, but in durable waterproofed canvas. The classic Vuitton trunk was a glamorous monster. Made of poplar, encased in canvas, strengthened with black lacquered metal corners, it bristled with brackets, handles and crosspieces, and contained myriad trays, compartments and drawers. It was a portable wardrobe, and it was a big hit. By 1888 the design had become so widely copied that Vuitton was forced to print his surname on the canvas at regular intervals. From then on, the name Louis Vuitton was indivisibly associated with stylish travel.

Vuitton was undoubtedly an innovator (his inventions included the round 'chauffeur bag', which fitted into the centre of a pile of spare tyres; the 'aero trunk', which floated in the event of a landing on water; and the 'secretaire trunk', a mobile writing desk), but it was his son Georges who contributed the logo that still causes all the fuss today. He designed a monogram pattern consisting of an encircled four-petal flower, a lozenge containing a four-pointed star, the same star in negative, and the initials LV, in homage to his father. The pattern is said to have been inspired by Japanese prints, which perhaps in part explains the brand's immense appeal in that market today.

Georges also created the 'Keep-all', a light canvas bag that was originally designed to contain dirty linen, and to be packed into the trunk. But it was adopted as an accessory in its own right – the first Louis Vuitton bag that voyagers kept by their side. As the years rolled on and new generations of Vuittons headed the company, its bags grew smaller and softer. At first, the family struggled to find ways of printing the monogram logo on flexible surfaces. The arrival of plastic in the late 1950s changed all that, and Louis Vuitton bags became available in all shapes and sizes. Now the iconic logo remains, and the old, original steamer trunks are collectors' items that occasionally double as coffee tables.

In 1987, Louis Vuitton merged with Moët and Hennessy. Enter Bernard Arnault, who would equip LVMH for the 21st century. Born in 1949 in Roubaix, France, Arnault was a graduate of the elite École Polytechnique in Paris. After pursuing a successful career in real estate in New York, he returned to France to apply his US-style business savvy to the country's oldest and most conservative industries: couture, Champagne and luxury goods. Arnault and a business partner from the French bank Lazard Frères and Co raised US$80 million to buy Boussac, the textile firm that owned the Christian Dior fashion house. In 1987, Arnault was invited by Henri Recamier, the chairman of LVMH, to invest in the company. Two years later, Arnault took full control; becoming the holder of the key to what would become the world's largest luxury conglomerate.

According to Arnault's communications adviser, Jean-Jacques Picart, the secret of Louis Vuitton's continuing success was the fusion of luxury goods with fashion: 'Monsieur Arnault invented what might be called "*luxe-mode*". He devised a way of persuading customers that a luxury item was a fashion statement, and therefore needed to be renewed or replaced. In effect, he introduced the concepts of experimentation, fluidity and renewal that characterize fashion into the world of luxury products, which are by nature timeless and long-lasting.'

Arnault did this in 1997 by appointing Marc Jacobs as Louis Vuitton's artistic director. A young, acclaimed American fashion designer (he had already been named Women's Designer of the Year three times by the Council of Fashion Designers of America), Jacobs was about to open his own store in New York. Hiring a hip New Yorker to pump fresh blood into a venerable Parisian luggage firm was a typically audacious Arnault gamble. A year later, Louis Vuitton launched a range of clothing, shoes and jewellery. That same year, not at all coincidentally, it opened the first of its 'global stores' on the Champs-Elysées. Although it had existing retail outlets (more than 300 around the world), the Champs-Elysées store was the blueprint for a series of giant spaces, from New York to Ulan Bator. In 1912, the very first Louis Vuitton store in Paris covered some 500 square metres. The New York store offers 1,200 square metres of floor space.

Under Jacobs, the monogram pattern was transformed into graffiti (in 2001) and became multi-coloured (in 2003) thanks to collaborations with artists Stephen Sprouse and Takashi Murakami. Jacobs also deployed print advertising to modernize Louis Vuitton's image: first by using well-known models such as Eva Herzigova and Naomi Campbell; later by recruiting popular-culture celebrities such as Jennifer Lopez, Scarlett Johansson, Uma Thurman and Madonna. The images themselves have the gloss, superficiality and sexuality of contemporary fashion photography, owing little or nothing to Louis Vuitton's 'luxury travel' heritage.

Since Jacobs' arrival, Louis Vuitton has also moved into menswear and launched a range of watches. But alongside its more fashionable endeavours, it quietly maintains a series of branding initiatives that lie closer to its roots: the Louis Vuitton Classic car rally; the Louis Vuitton Cup yacht race; and a series of upmarket city guides and travel books. More recently, it hired the agency Ogilvy & Mather to create a series of advertisements designed to remind consumers about the more traditional aspects of the brand. The first print ads featuring Mikhail Gorbachev, Catherine Deneuve and Sean Connery – among others – alongside their Vuitton luggage in exotic settings, were backed up by web films in which they described their favourite journeys. Even if Jacobs sends eccentric items on to the catwalk or creates blatantly youth-oriented advertising campaigns, Vuitton keeps its original values polished.

There is a certain similarity between Louis Vuitton and that other Parisian luxury-goods house, Hermès. Indeed, LVMH slowly built up a 20 per cent stake in Hermès in what was seen by many as a bid to take over the company. This was blocked by the creation of a holding company that would enable it to remain a family-owned business. Hermès wishes to retain the air of unabashed elitism that Vuitton has played down in favour of seducing the mass market. Hermès is refined and more than a little haughty. It pushes hard on terms such as 'hand-crafted' and 'artisans'.

Hermès started out as a saddler in 1837, and still uses equine imagery in its branding. Thierry Hermès made harnesses and saddles for the fashionable horse-drawn buggies (*calèches* and *fiacres*) that clopped along the boulevards of 19th-century Paris. Fortunately for the company, future generations of the Hermès family saw the automobile coming. Emile-Maurice Hermès diversified into luggage, hand-stitched leather goods, gloves and silk scarves. (The world-famous Hermès Carré silk scarf was said to have derived from the fabric used for jockeys' caps.) Watchbands and jewellery followed. In 1951, Robert Dumas took over from his father-in-law, and proved to have a strong grasp of marketing techniques. It was during this era that the brand launched its logo (a *calèche*, naturally) and its signature orange colour, while the window displays at its headquarters in Rue du Faubourg Saint-Honoré became increasingly opulent. Hermès goods were sought after by celebrities; something that the house encouraged by naming a bag after the actress Grace Kelly. The Kelly bag became a cult object.

Robert's son, the late Jean-Louis Dumas, took over in 1978 and presided over the modern era until his death in 2010. His highly successful transition of the brand into the hyper-competitive luxury world of the late 20th and early 21st century included design partnerships with Martin Margiela and Jean-Paul Gaultier and the opening of dozens of new stores. He reigned in franchises and took tighter control of the brand's image, instead investing in French artisanal manufacturers of silverware, glassware and tableware. A chance meeting on a plane with actress and singer Jane Birkin – an icon in France – led to the immensely successful sequel to the Kelly bag, the Birkin.

The company now has more than 200 boutiques around the world, including a glass tower in Tokyo that offers not only the full range of Hermès goods, but also regular screenings of French films. But Jean-Louis Dumas once insisted that 'Hermès is not a fashion house. It preserves a certain distance while at the same time being determined to remain contemporary. The notion of permanence gives us an aristocratic distinction which has, we must admit, an intimidating side.' (Hermès: L'oeil du maître, *Le Point*, 8 April 2004.)

Nevertheless, Hermès has plenty of the attributes of a fashion business – notably an interest in fragrances. Eau d'Hermès in 1951 was followed by Calèche, Equipage, Amazone, Bel Ami, Eau d'Orange Verte and 24 Faubourg, among others. Janie Samet, who is as realistic about fragrances as she is about bags, comments, 'Perfumes are the heart of the luxury war. Scent makes the cash registers ring.'

A brand in a bottle

Fragrances are the interface between the general public and the world of luxury. Even the most expensive scent is well within the reach of the average consumer, who, while baulking at the cost of a Chanel evening dress, may decide to splash out on a bottle of No. 5.

Michael D'Arminio, a marketing consultant who has worked on beauty products and fragrances within the Unilever group, says, 'I've been in this field for nearly 12 years, and I have never worked with a designer who said they were just in it for the cash. However, it is 100 per cent about building the brand, communicating its values, and opening up that brand to a larger customer base. The price points within the designer fashion market continue to increase, so fragrances and cosmetics make those brands more accessible and help to build a designer's business. Clearly there are royalties at the end of it, but the process is much more subtle than "take the money and run".'

Fragrances are rarely, if ever, developed by designers alone. Instead, they are produced under licence by large beauty companies such as L'Oreal or Unilever. Designers have neither the expertise nor the budgets to create, manufacture, distribute and market perfumes.

D'Arminio suggests that the gestation period for a fragrance is between 15 months and two years. 'Developing a fragrance and bringing it to market is a lengthy and incredibly expensive task,' he stresses. 'Normally you look to turn a profit two or three years out. Up until that time, you're still paying for the groundwork. In the United States, if you want to go into the department store market and be a top-15 player, you're looking at spending between eight and 15 million dollars on a launch. Then you can add another eight or 10 million for Europe. And the figures I've just given you are purely for media spend – I haven't included all the development costs.'

For this reason, creating a fragrance is a delicate business. The result has to be fashionable but not a flash in the pan. It should reflect the brand's values without being overly complex. Ultimately, no matter whose name is on the bottle, it's the juice that's being judged. And as an unsuccessful fragrance can be de-listed, ultimately damaging the parent brand, designers tend to monitor the development of their perfumes very carefully. 'In my experience,' says D'Arminio, 'the designer is involved at every stage, from beginning to end. It's like a marriage.'

This is confirmed by Valérie Sanchez, who has worked on fragrance brands for Rochas, Cacharel and, most recently, Giorgio Armani. At the time I met her, she had just helped Armani launch his male fragrance, Black

Code. She says, 'Our job is to translate the spirit of a brand into a fragrance, so it's essential that we work hand-in-hand with the designer. Working on projects for Armani, we would travel to Milan to meet with him at least once a month. The designer respects the fact that perfume is our métier and not his, but he still demands, and gets, full control.'

Before the odour comes the name. Both D'Arminio and Sanchez confirm that this is chosen at the very beginning of the process. Devising a name for a perfume is increasingly troublesome, because many of the most poetic words and phrases in English, French and Italian are already owned by somebody. This is another incentive to work with a large company such as L'Oreal to develop a perfume – as the leading company in the worldwide beauty market it has the firepower to purchase almost any name. Another alternative is to register a combination name, like Flower By Kenzo or Cerruti Sí, for instance.

Often, designers are asked to provide lists of potential names. But Sanchez says that Black Code came out of a brainstorming process at L'Oreal. 'The concept for the fragrance was inspired by a midnight-blue Armani tuxedo that Denzel Washington wore to the Oscars. So we were looking for words around "ceremony", "black tie" and "dress code". "Black Tie" was not international enough: although English is now regarded as the international language of marketing, we felt some nationalities might have problem with the word "tie". So we shuffled things around a bit and ended up with Black Code.'

The fragrance itself is a team effort involving the designer, the licensing company, and a fragrance house. There are only a handful of fragrance houses in the world, and every scent on the market has been designed by one of them. The most famous are IFF (International Flavours & Fragrances), Firmenich, Givaudan, Haarman & Reimer, Takasago, Quest International and Sensient Technologies. As well as fragrances, they conjure up aromas for food companies (yes, your yoghurt smells of strawberries because somebody has perfumed it). The people who work at these houses combine the talents of chemist, musician and wine-taster.

Valérie Sanchez explains, 'Contrary to what you might have read in Patrick Suskind's novel *Perfume, les nez* [the "noses"] are not born with their talent. They may have an interest or an aptitude, but, like musicians, they are educated in their art. Odours are like musical notes – but they are also like molecules, which work together in different ways. Perfume is a science as much as it is an art. Each "nose" works with a palette of between 300 and 500 scents, which they constantly smell to keep the odours fresh in their memory. The variations are infinite. We know that certain "noses" have a particular signature, and we can ask for them by name if we have a specific type of scent in mind. But generally we brief two or three different houses, which compete for the task. Until we make a decision, they are paid nothing. But they are aware that, if their fragrance is selected, they've hit the jackpot.'

The fragrances that the houses put forward are tested by L'Oreal's in-house 'nose', as well as by the designer. As Sanchez says, 'After a while, we know what kind of scents a designer likes and dislikes; or which best reflect the brand. There is also an educational process as a designer's olfactory skills evolve. At the end of the day, although we can make suggestions or nudge a designer away from a direction that may not be commercial, they have the final say.'

Once the fragrance has been selected, there is the all-important matter of designing the bottle. A perfume bottle represents a subtle form of brand communication as well as being a beautiful object in its own right, proudly displayed on a dressing table or bathroom shelf. Again, the designer has a strong influence here; but a specialist can also be called in. The bottle for Black Code was created by New York-based art director Fabien Baron, who has collaborated with Armani on a number of projects.

The manufacturing of perfume bottles is also a specialized industry. Three-quarters of the world's perfume bottles are produced by some 60 enterprises and 7,000 workers in the Vallée de la Bresle, not far from Dieppe in northern France. The largest, Saverglass, produces a million bottles a day. (It's worth observing at this point that the production of essential oils is no longer associated with France, despite romantic images of white jasmine flowers picked and crushed in Grasse and elsewhere in Provence. Fragrances are just as likely to be constructed from Turkish roses, Madagascan vanilla or, more often than not, synthetic substances.)

The final stage is, of course, the marketing. Increasingly, to ensure that the perfume slots neatly into the label's overall brand strategy, the designer tends to turn again to his or her regular advertising collaborators. This makes sense, as the imagery utilized to promote the fragrance, whether in the media or at point of sale, may eventually lead customers to clothes, bags, sunglasses, and other products. Sanchez says that, as well as designing the bottle for Black Code, Fabien Baron also oversaw the advertising imagery for the fragrance. And when Chanel re-launched No 5 with a campaign starring Nicole Kidman, the actress also appeared alongside designer Karl Lagerfeld on the catwalk. The art director Thomas Lenthal, who works for YSL Beauty, observes, 'The big difference is that when you are selling a dress, you're perhaps talking to thousands of people. But when you're working on a perfume, you're talking to millions of people. So the imagery is different – smoother, more conceptual.'

Sanchez points out that marketing a fragrance is challenging because it centres on an atmosphere rather than a visible product. She says, 'Often the psychology behind the images is quite complex, because it must tempt the customer to try the scent, as well as capturing the overall philosophy of the brand. A perfume may be a product – but it's not a detergent.'

Be that as it may, the commoditization of perfume is leading some discerning (and wealthy) customers away from mainstream brands. Just as in fashion there is a move towards limited editions, vintage finds and general exclusivity, so there is a growing market for made-to-measure fragrances. In Paris, both Guerlain and Jean Patou offer 'olfactory education' courses, followed by the chance for the individual to create a unique perfume from a range of aromas. Patou customers can even spend the day with the perfumer's resident 'nose', who will lead them to chocolate shops and markets to find out exactly which smells they prefer. He can then concoct an entirely idiosyncratic fragrance based on the results. But, as usual, individuality comes at a price – in this case, between €20,000 and €50,000.

Retro brands retooled

14

"With these brands you have to feel as passionate about the heritage as about the future.

When you stand before the urbane façade of the Gucci store in Milan's Galleria Vittorio Emanuele II – a 19th-century shopping arcade that is as far from a suburban mall as it is possible to imagine – words like 'melodrama' and 'bloodshed' don't exactly leap to mind. But as part of the brand royal family, Gucci has grabbed more than its fair share of headlines.

Along with Burberry, Gucci is probably the finest example of image turn-around in the history of fashion. So revered is the story of its reinvention that 'doing a Gucci' has become a stock phrase, whispered like a mantra by all those trying to resurrect a designer relic. After Gucci's success, everyone assumes they can take a half-forgotten label and bring it up to date in a cool, iconoclastic kind of way. Unfortunately, not everyone is Tom Ford.

The story began in 1922, when Guccio Gucci opened a company making upmarket baggage in Florence. Legend has it that the young Gucci had spent several months working at the Savoy hotel in London, where he noticed a nascent market of rich globetrotters and correctly assumed they would be keen purchasers of luxury luggage and accessories. Italy's leather-goods savoir-faire and its instinctive adoption of family businesses favoured the growth of Gucci's empire, and Guccio soon had outposts in Rome and Milan.

In the 1950s, Guccio's son Aldo opened a boutique in New York – which was to be followed over time by branches in London, Tokyo, Hong Kong, and Paris. Rather like Hermès, Gucci profited from post-war consumer culture and the new marketing techniques that were being developed alongside it. The brand's iconic bamboo-handled bag, the 0063, appeared in 1957 and was quickly adopted by the likes of Jackie Kennedy and Liz Taylor. Gucci loafers found their way on to the feet of John Wayne. In 1964, the company produced a silk scarf in homage to Grace Kelly, which she wore in the presence of the paparazzi.

By the 1970s the brand's distinctive interlocking double-G logo could be seen everywhere, from key-rings and T-shirts to bottles of whisky. But that was just the problem: the enterprise had split into a number of separate fiefdoms, each managed by a Gucci family member. With no logical strategy, licences were signed this way and that, and over the next decade the brand lost direction and prestige. Meanwhile, to the delight of the tabloid newspapers, the internal struggle to wrest control of the business had turned into a thriller, featuring financial mismanagement, denunciations in court and finally murder, when Maurizio Gucci – the last member of the family to run the company – was killed by a hit-man in 1995. His widow, Patrizia Reggiani Martinelli, was convicted of organizing the murder and sentenced to 26 years in prison. History will remember that the scandal almost finished off the Gucci brand for good.

Shortly afterwards, the business was fully acquired by a Bahrain-based investment company called Investcorp, which had already held a 50 per cent stake. At that stage, Tom Ford had already been working as the company's in-house designer for five years, having been hired in 1990 by Dawn Mello, then Gucci's creative director. Born in Texas in 1962, Ford had graduated from Parsons School of Design with a degree in interior architecture. But the subject was not quite to his taste. In the book *Visionaries*, he tells Susannah Frankel, 'Architecture was just way too... it was just so serious. Oh my god, the pretentiousness of architecture! So I realized that I was getting more excited every month buying *Vogue* and I thought, you know, this is what I love, this is what I seem to be drawn to the whole time.'

Following his instincts, Ford worked with the New York fashion houses Perry Ellis and Cathy Hardwick before joining Gucci. It took some time for him to make his mark, but gradually his contemporary twist on 1970s designs began attracting critical attention. Ford's interpretation pushed the glitzy, logo-heavy side of Gucci into the background and favoured sophistication, sex and gloss. Crucially, he understood that a brand had to have a singular vision. As well as designing clothes for men and women, he took responsibility for handbags, shoes, accessories and two new Gucci scents: Envy and Rush. Nothing that the company produced, from an advertising campaign to a store design, went ahead without Ford's approval. 'His great genius was to reconcile creativity with coherence,' says fashion consultant Jean-Jacques Picart.

In 1995 Ford hired French stylist Carine Roitfeld and photographer Mario Testino to overhaul Gucci's advertising. It became brazen, sexual, even shocking. Celebrities and opinion-formers noticed the change and adopted the brand – and with them, of course, came the wider public. Almost bankrupt when Ford came on board, Gucci became the lynchpin of a giant luxury group.

Climbing out of a trench

One of the British companies that has 'done a Gucci' most successfully is Burberry. Although it has experienced image problems in the UK (see Chapter 2: Fashioning an identity), its achievements should not be underestimated.

The history of Burberry is fairly well known. Thomas Burberry opened his outfitters in Basingstoke, Hampshire, in 1856. It was a modest concern until his sons joined the business in the 1880s, when it opened a second store, in London, in partnership with a company called RB Rolls. During this period, Burberry perfected the woven waterproofed yarn known as 'gabardine', which proved perfect for rainwear. The fabric caught on, and Burberry was soon exporting to the rest of Europe, as well as North and Latin America. An outlet in Paris opened as early as 1909.

The company's most significant breakthrough came when it was asked to provide rainwear for officers during the First World War; the item it came up with became known as the 'trench coat'. If anything, this iconic garment became even more popular after the war, sported by explorers, plain-clothes policemen and members of the public with secret dreams of heroism. Thomas Burberry & Sons was floated on the London Stock Exchange in 1920. Four years later, the famous black, white and red check made its first appearance as a raincoat lining.

When Thomas Burberry died, in 1926, his second son Arthur Michael Burberry continued to run the business, remaining at its helm until the early 1950s. By the time the company was acquired by Great Universal Stores (GUS) in 1955, its raincoats were considered classics, having been worn by Humphrey Bogart and Ingrid Bergman in *Casablanca*. (It's hard to reconcile Bogart's hard-bitten screen persona with an interest in fashion, but there you go.) Audrey Hepburn later wore one in *Breakfast at Tiffany's*. The brand rumbled along through the 1960s and 70s. In the 1980s, under chief executive Stanley Peacock, the company multiplied its licences. This had the old, all-too-familiar effect of increased sales in the mid-term, but a long-term degenerative impact on the brand.

The 1990s began badly for a weary and outmoded Burberry. Its umbrellas and raincoats did well with Japanese businessmen who admired British style, but elsewhere its trademark check was no longer considered a guarantee of quality. More than 30 licensees worldwide had plastered the Burberry name on everything from watches (in Switzerland) to whisky (in Korea). To boost profits the company was selling its goods in bulk to cut-price Japanese 'grey-market' retailers, who undercut the prices charged by classier outlets. When the economic crisis in Asia robbed Burberry of its most lucrative market, its finances plunged into turmoil.

Stanley Peacock retired as chief executive of Burberry in 1996. A year later, GUS recruited Rose Marie Bravo from Saks Fifth Avenue as Burberry's new CEO, hoping she would be able to breathe life into the ailing brand. Briskly, controversially but effectively, Bravo took the matter in hand. She cut off the supply to the Japanese grey market, which had the immediate effect of causing Burberry's sales to slump even further. GUS was advised by analysts to sell the brand – but its management bravely waited to see what Bravo could achieve. She reined in distribution, renegotiated licences, closed a number of small stores and gave the important ones a spiffing Britpop makeover. In the meantime she recruited a new design team, headed by Roberto Menichetti (he was succeeded by Christopher Bailey in 2001). Menichetti launched the upmarket Prorsum range of womenswear (the name derives from the company's Latin motto, and means 'forwards'), which soon garnered positive reviews.

Through print advertising, Kate Moss and a host of other fresh British faces brought an unexpectedly rebellious, streetwise image to the brand. Consumers were intrigued – and what the advertising promised the stores and the designs delivered. Burberry had not just been repositioned, but 're-imagined'. Alongside men's and women's apparel, its range now includes accessories, fragrances, children's clothing and household objects. Burberry had shown, once again, that it was possible to bring a brand back from the brink.

The art of plundering the past

That was just the beginning. Following in the slipstream of Burberry and Gucci, a whole host of brands emerged from the cobwebs of history. Almost every week, it seems, we hear of another venerable label that has been given a facelift and a new suit of clothes, and then wheeled out to meet the shopping public. And the strategies are eerily similar.

Take Mulberry, for instance. The accessories and clothing brand is unusual in that, even though it was founded in 1971, it seemed superannuated almost from the start. It was only in 2002 that CEO Lisa Montague finally decided that the doddery granny drastically needed a Burberry-style makeover. She hired designer Nicholas Knightly (who had previously worked at Ghost), and he proceeded to knock Mulberry into shape by eliminating frumpiness and adding British eccentricity. The result was an odd but alluring blend of vintage and modern, as if Quentin Tarantino had decided to film an Agatha Christie novel. 'I think of a big house in the country with chests of overflowing drawers,' Knightly said. 'You may not have the house in the country, but you can have the dress to swan about in it.' ('A very British coup', *The Guardian*, 23 October 2004.) Perhaps not surprisingly, Knightly was later lured away to design leather goods at Louis Vuitton.

An equally successful transition was managed by Scottish knitwear company Pringle, for ever associated with diamond-patterned sweaters and golfers. The brand's adoption by soccer 'casuals' (read: 'thugs') had edged its status further down the road to decline. Almost bankrupt under its previous owner, Dawson International, Pringle was bought by Hong Kong millionaire Kenneth Fang for just £5 million in 2000. By 2003, sales were running at more than £100 million. 'Pringle is the new Burberry', raved *The Guardian* (24 September 2003), as the brand took the previously unimaginable step of rolling out a collection during London Fashion Week.

The turnaround was attributed to the skill of chief executive Kim Winser, previously the only female director of Marks & Spencer. Winser observed that in the 1950s and 60s Pringle had been 'an amazing, glamorous brand', and noted that advertising images from the period featured curvaceous 'sweater girls' in Pringle jumpers. In a stroke of genius, the sexy British model Sophie Dahl was recruited as a modern-day sweater girl for an advertising campaign. A revamped store in London's Sloane Street was opened by the actor Ewan MacGregor, cleverly summing up the brand's new formula of Scottish roots meets contemporary glamour.

Winser also had an incredible advantage in the shape of designer Stuart Stockdale, who had worked with the likes of Jasper Conran, upmarket US retailer J Crew and Romeo Gigli. Stockdale's collections enhanced positive elements like the diamond motif and the brand's association with luxury cashmere, while running roughshod over its dullsville recent past. He showed items such as cashmere twinsets in searing fuchsia pink, strapless lemon yellow vests worn with bikini bottoms, pastel-coloured coats, sweaters made of chiffon, and cashmere knickers with buttons up the front.

Pringle's return to grace was so remarkable that in 2003 Winser was voted Europe's third most successful businesswoman by *The Wall Street Journal*. Helpfully, she later shared some rebranding tips with the *Financial Times*. 'I think probably the most important thing is to understand the brand's personality,' she explained. 'With these brands you have to feel as passionate about the heritage as about the future. Secondly, you have to decide what is at the heart of the brand: Burberry has the raincoat, we at Pringle have our cashmere and knitwear... I also think it's absolutely fundamental at the early stages of taking on a brand to involve all your team – your immediate senior team, your management... suppliers... If they totally understand the vision they'll help you to achieve it. Obviously, you also have to focus on what people are spending their money on, and you have to work on your PR: if you're going to be making changes, people have to understand your changes.' ('Textbook changes', 7 May 2004.)

Back in Paris, the name of the game seems to be to take legendary names from the history of haute couture and transform them into thriving ready-to-wear businesses. Nicolas Ghesquière has done so very successfully at Balenciaga, balancing nods to Cristobal Balenciaga's original vision with his own science fiction-infused creativity.

And a ghostly parade of names has emerged in Cristobal's wake. Paquin, created by Jeanne Paquin in 1891 with her husband Isidore, had lain dormant since 1956 until Antwerp-born perfumer Louison Libertin came on board in 2010 to launch a new fragrance line and steer its re-emergence as a fashion label. A discreet 'Anglo-French' group owns the brand. Jeanne Paquin was among the first designers to organize fashion shows and to ensure that her models attended fashionable operas dressed in her pieces. She also designed for theatre productions and collaborated with artists. In other words, a thoroughly modern luxury brand lurks within the Paquin DNA.

In 2009, visitors to the fashion wing of Les Arts Décoratifs in Paris were enthralled by an exhibition devoted to the designer Madeleine Vionnet, whose career stretched from 1912 until 1939. Vionnet's clothes were inspired by classical antiquity, and their sleek minimalism makes them remarkably relevant today. Greek designer Sophia Kokosalaki was tasked in 2006 with re-launching the brand, then owned by the de Lummen family. Kokosalaki left a year later to concentrate on her own label, but was replaced by former Prada designer Marc Audibet. Although both designers were praised by fashion writers, the label refused to take off. It has since been acquired by the Milanese luxury goods tycoon Matteo Marzotto. Another Prada alumni, Rodolfo Paglialunga, stayed in the designer hot seat for 10 collections before, again, moving on. He was replaced by Italian-born sisters Barbara and Lucia Croce, who worked at Prada, Miu Miu, Gucci and Valentino. For now, Vionnet is alive, but hardly kicking.

Moving even further back in time, the spirit of 'the father of haute couture' – Charles Frederick Worth – has been summoned with a line of boudoir-style garments and a revival, appropriately enough, of his fragrance, Je Reviens.

The challenge in all these cases, of course, is to update the brand while remaining respectful: betray its memory and you could get slated. This may be why Diego Della Valle, the owner of Tod's, has hesitated so long over Schiaparelli – a brand he acquired in 2007. Schiaparelli's 'shocking pink' universe certainly offers rich potential for reinterpretation. Designers such as Giles Deacon, Olivier Theyskens and even John Galliano have been linked to a potential revival, although nothing is clear at the time of writing.

A more concrete revival has been that of swinging 60s brand Courrèges, which was resurrected by a pair of French former advertising executives. Previously co-presidents of the Paris branch of Young & Rubicam, Frédéric Torloting and Jacques Bungert acquired Courrèges at the beginning of 2011 with borrowed capital. They say they paid 'between €10 million and €50 million', hinting that the price was closer to the latter.

Founded in 1961 by André Courrèges and his wife Coqueline, the brand is famous for launching the mini skirt – a claim it shares with Mary Quant. Offering a groovy, space-age vision of geometric shapes and synthetic materials, it was one of the first Paris couture houses to open ready-to-wear boutiques. At the time of writing only the flagship remains, in rue François Ier, a short stroll from the Champs-Elysées.

Coqueline, 77, still has an office above the store. Although she remains an unofficial mentor, she no longer has any financial connection with the brand, which she managed alone as André's health declined. She met several potential buyers, but came across the advertising duo by chance. 'She read an article we'd written about the power of brands,' confirms Torloting. 'She was inspired by it and got in touch. We found her to be an incredible, energetic, visionary person. After a few meetings we formed a mutual fan club. She told us, "I'd like you to buy Courrèges. If you're as passionate about it as I think you are, you'll find a way." It was an ambition of ours to run a company that actually made something.'

Having taken over the fashion house, the pair set about updating it. Torloting says: 'That was easier than you might imagine, because Courrèges was conceived as a futuristic brand. Now it simply feels contemporary. The pure lines and simple silhouettes are timeless.' He describes Courrèges as 'elegant, colourful, fun and optimistic'. Although white remains its signature, primary and fluorescent colours also pop out of the collection. 'There's something quirky and sociable about the label. Strangers ask you where you got the clothes.'

Contrary to resurgent labels such as Paco Rabanne and Thierry Mugler, the duo broke the conventions of high-end fashion in a number of ways. They disdain seasonal collections and runway shows. 'The built-in obsolescence of fashion is out of tune with the 21st century. Everyone's talking about over-consumption, yet we're asked to constantly reject our clothing. We want to design pieces that we'll still be selling in 20 years' time. The label's consistent bestseller is a vinyl blouson from 1972.'

Nor did they bring in a hip young designer. A creative team of 10, a mixture of youth and experience, reports to Lionel Giraud, formerly vice-president and artistic director of jewellery brand Chaumet. He plays the role of 'creative coordinator' and day-to-day manager. 'We were very clear that we wanted a manager and not a star designer,' says Torloting. 'Courrèges has never been celebrity-driven.'

Torloting and Bungert expanded the label's distribution network: Courrèges can now be found in Selfridges in London, Jeffrey in New York and 10 Corso Como in both Milan and Seoul. The brand's e-commerce site opened for business in spring 2012. It features models reflected in the mirrors that are another element of the brand's visual identity. 'Real women in real dresses, shot in a way that lets users see the entire garment,' says Torloting.

All the clothes are made in France, and they don't come cheap at between €1,500 and €1,800 a dress. But the success of fashion brands depends on accessories sales, so the new owners have re-launched two historic perfumes, Empreinte and Eau de Courrèges, alongside a new fragrance called Blanc de Courrèges. More unexpectedly, Torloting and Bungert want to launch a limited edition electric car. Coqueline and André Courrèges – who studied engineering – worked on prototypes as early as 1968. 'It's just another way they were ahead of their time,' says Torloting. 'Imagine a little fleet of Courrèges vehicles tooling around Paris? That's better than any ad campaign.'

15

> *Men don't buy fashion – they buy clothes.*

Sean Connery, Michael Caine and Steve McQueen. Cary Grant and Humphrey Bogart. Maybe a hint of James Dean and early Brando. Sinatra when he was recording for Capitol. Al Pacino in *Scarface*. The guys from *Reservoir Dogs* and *Pulp Fiction*. These are the sort of men we would like to emulate, if we had the looks or the charisma. We can, at least, aspire to the clothes – which is why adult men's fashion tends towards the conservative. Most of us don't care what the male models on the catwalks are wearing; we'd much rather resemble our icons. And so, in offices and on the streets, men's fashion barely changes from season to season. A button more or less, double- or single-breasted, the colour of a shirt, the width of a tie or a trouser-leg – but that's about it. We wear suits and coats and jeans and T-shirts.

In terms of distribution, women have a choice of up to four times as many stores as men. Things are evolving, however – slowly and infinitesimally. At least men are paying attention to their appearance these days. They're more interested in cut and colour; they go to the gym; they buy hair gel and moisturizer. They have even been known to go shopping unaccompanied. It may sound ludicrous, but this is all quite new.

'Very GQ'

In the opinion of Dylan Jones, the editor of British *GQ*, '[Men] are certainly less sophisticated consumers of fashion than women. When you look at the menswear industry in Britain, it's only about 20 years old. And when you look at the men's magazine industry, it's about 17 years old. This generation of men is the first that has been acclimatized to spending money on fashion. It started with the rise of style magazines in the 80s, when men started seeing images of themselves projected back at them for the first time. Suddenly you were looking at pictures that resembled you, rather than a model. And this, combined with the rise of menswear in Britain – which was basically kick-started by Paul Smith – made it a very exciting period for men's fashion.'

Jones speaks from experience, having edited the influential men's magazine *Arena* in the 1980s. *Arena*, a deeply stylish publication showcasing the organic graphic design of Neville Brody, was the first men's style magazine I ever saw. It was also the first time that I became aware of brands like Armani, Cerruti and, yes, Paul Smith. (But my favourite cover was still the one of Michael Caine, shot by David Bailey back in the 1960s.)

The men's magazine market has evolved considerably since then, and there are now titles serving almost every sector, from the blue-collar publications once known as 'lad mags' to the niche and sophisticated *GQ*. Jones notes with humorous pride that *GQ* has been pegged as one of the few magazines serving the 'metrosexual' market – a faintly derogatory term covering men who have more in their bathroom cabinets than a Bic razor, Gillette shaving cream, cheap aftershave and deodorant.

'Men who buy *GQ* are buying into a certain world, just as the women who buy *Vogue* are buying into that world,' Jones observes. 'Fashion is part of it, but we're also covering cars, sex, food, travel... In any case, it's fair to say that men don't buy fashion, they buy clothes. If you go to the collections twice a year to see what the men's fashion designers are up to, it's really just a question of tweaking. One year sportswear might be more prominent, the next tailoring. It's very difficult to reinvent the wheel every six months with menswear. *GQ* readers are probably more interested in fashion than the readers of any other men's magazine, but men in general are not as obsessive about the changing nature of fashion as women can be.'

Paradoxically, this opens a window of opportunity for fashion brands, which – if they prove their worth – can land very loyal male consumers. Jones observes, 'Men are concerned about status and they like to be confident. So if they feel good in a certain item, if their wife or girlfriend approves, and it gets a nod of appreciation from their colleagues, they're likely to go back for more.'

This explains the continuing success of Armani and Paul Smith. One might also add Hedi Slimane, formerly at Dior Homme, to the small pantheon of designers who have been enthusiastically embraced by men. With his sleek, skinny black suits that armour the body like a carapace, the rigorous Slimane was yang to John Galliano's yin. The svelte young designer joined Dior Homme from Yves Saint Laurent in 2001. By the time he left, in 2007, his whip-thin cuts had created an entirely new male silhouette.

A talented photographer, Slimane was known for his connections with the world of rock music. He dressed Alex Kapranos from the rock band Franz Ferdinand, Sonic Youth's Thurston Moore, and the singer Beck. In a market where consumers take their cues from their idols, the celebrity connection is perhaps even more important than it is in the women's fashion arena.

This explained the presence of Adrian Brody, the Oscar-winning actor, in a successful print and poster campaign for Ermenegildo Zegna. Although Brody was by no means an obvious choice, he incarnated a certain intellectual grace that fans of Zegna appreciated. In any case, the brand was already an established favourite among well-heeled, well-dressed males.

Michelangelo Zegna put down the roots of the business in Trivero, Italy, at the end of the 19th century. For the first few years it was a small-scale fabric producer, but then Michelangelo's son Ermenegildo began importing luxurious wools – fine merinos, vicuñas and cashmeres – from Asia, South America and Australia, to compete with the dominant English and Scottish textile markets. The firm established a reputation for providing the softest and most sumptuous fabrics, and by 1938 Ermenegildo Zegna was exporting to more than 40 different markets. Even today, the family continues to supply fabric to brands that it should, by rights, consider rivals.

Ermenegildo's sons, Aldo and Angelo, led the expansion into ready-to-wear in the 1960s, having understood that tailors were a vanishing breed. Today the label has nearly 400 stores around the world. As well as ready-to-wear and tailored suits, it sells accessories, a sportswear line and a fragrance. But the quality of its fabrics remains the key to its brand identity. To underline this fact, each year the company weaves its finest wools into an almost mystical yarn, with which it makes no more than 50 suits. These can be bought for €8,000 each – and there is always a waiting list. Each purchaser's name is hand-sewn into the lining. A further cry from tracksuit bottoms and football shirts is difficult to imagine.

Fine and dandy

While it's easy to portray guys as a bunch of slobs whose idea of dressing for dinner is to change their socks, there have, of course, always been trends in men's fashion – and even some people who subscribe to them. The basic form of today's suit can be traced back to the 19th century, when the English gentry were proud landowners, spending a great deal of time outdoors.

Anglo-Saxon style, therefore, was practical and pared down, and basically descended from riding gear. Simplicity was the order of the day – ostentation was considered bad form, if not downright suspect. The men's clothing of the late 19th and early 20th century was the sartorial equivalent of a stiff upper lip. Austere though this style may have been, it set the standard for the Western male, and ensured that Britain led the field in the textile sector.

Le style anglais was undermined in the 1920s by the Americans, who began experimenting with a new style of relaxed fashion. Voluminous trousers, short-sleeved tennis shirts, soft-collared shirts worn without ties, relaxed suits that could be worn all day... these developments were shockingly new. In addition, the electric razor, invented in 1928, meant that more men were shearing off their moustaches and beards. The template for the 20th-century male had been set.

US influences dominated the 1940s and 50s as well. The young *zazous* of Paris, with their over-long jackets and greased-back hair, looked like cartoon versions of Chicago gangsters. Fashion historian François Baudot observes that the scene was closely linked to jazz, swing and the jitterbug – possibly the first example of a youth trend that combined music and dress. It was taken to extremes in the various forms of dress codes associated with rock and roll, from the timeless white T-shirt, leather jacket and jeans to the Teddy Boys, those sartorial throwbacks who took their cues from Edwardian costume. For those who didn't fit into the strange new category of 'teenager' – a creation of post-war consumerism and marketing – inspiration was to be found in Italy, with its sharp suits and Vespas. The film *Roman Holiday* (1953), starring Gregory Peck and Audrey Hepburn, still looks like a fashion plate.

It is difficult to summarize the 1960s, a period in which men's fashion seemed to go into overdrive. This was the time when ready-to-wear took the high ground, and the concept of personal tailors appeared to have been relegated to the past. While some men clung doggedly to a more classic look, it was generally a time of rejection and invention – wear anything, as long as it's something your father wouldn't have been seen dead in. The experimentation continued into the following decade, an era of androgyny and excess that made the generation gap seem far wider than a mere 20 years. The growing influence of Milanese designers was apparent in the dance-floor sheen of disco, but the Brits, doing rather better out of the deal, had saved themselves by embracing punk rock.

The term 'punk' (which derived from prison slang meaning 'delinquent' or 'worthless trash', with catamite undertones) had been current since the early 1970s in the United States, where it was associated with the low-tech garage rock thrashed out by the likes of Iggy & the Stooges, the New York Dolls and, later on, The Ramones. In the UK, though, punk rock was a pure creation of marketing. It owed its genesis to Malcolm McLaren and Vivienne Westwood, who ran the Sex store in London's King's Road. McLaren was a former art student who had been inspired by 1960s radical politics, notably the Situationist movement in Paris. Westwood, meanwhile, had moved on from making clothes for die-hard Teddy Boys to something altogether more original, running up quasi-fetishist garments daubed with arcane political slogans.

Both McLaren and Westwood were well versed in subculture and understood the mechanics of the media. In order to give Sex a live, physical presence, McLaren brought together the Sex Pistols as a promotional vehicle for the store. Key to the band's runaway success was the energetic presence and aggressive sartorial style of John Lydon, with his green hair and ripped, safety-pin-adorned T-shirts. At the time, Britain wallowed in deep recession, and punk provided the perfect outlet for its unemployed, disaffected youth, who literally spat frustration. With McLaren's management, Westwood's designs and the Pistols' own anarchic enthusiasm driving it, punk rock took off. As McLaren had calculated, an outraged mainstream media was delighted to cover the phenomenon. By the time the Pistols split, in 1979, they had spawned dozens of imitators and spearheaded a movement that traversed Europe and the United States.

By the mid-80s, however, it seemed as though punk had never happened. An economic boom meant that Wall Street brokers became the new fashion avatars, with their double-breasted suits, shoulder pads and wide ties. Movies and even literature provided archetypes: Gordon Gekko, as portrayed by Michael Douglas in the movie *Wall Street* (1987); and Sherman McCoy, the callow yuppie anti-hero of Tom Wolfe's bestseller, *The Bonfire of the Vanities* (1988). Like a slightly later book, *American Psycho* (1991) – also a critique of yuppie culture – *Bonfire* obsessively cited the brand names of its characters' clothes. The conceit was designed to highlight the materialism of the age – but it also provided a handy shopping list.

The following decade saw the inevitable backlash. Sportswear, which had been gaining ground at the tail end of the 80s, thanks in part to the hip-hop community, elided almost completely with mainstream fashion – the two sectors are now virtually indistinguishable. A mass rejection of yuppie values led to an inevitable relaxation of workplace dress codes. For a while, it looked as if the suit might disappear for good. But classics are never entirely suffocated by trends: the suit not only made a return but did so in its most elitist and luxurious form.

A tailor-made opportunity

When Carlo Brandelli took over the venerable Savile Row tailor Kilgour, French & Stanbury, he already had one of the greatest fashion icons in cinematic history on his side. The tailor made the suit that Cary Grant wears throughout the Hitchcock film *North by Northwest* (1959). Whether he is being pursued by a malicious crop duster or seduced by Eva Marie Saint, Grant remains impeccably smooth; and so do his threads. Brandelli also discovered that Kilgour had made suits for Rex Harrison. Unfortunately, a fire in 1982 destroyed the patterns, almost taking the building with them. Despite this disadvantage, Kilgour is once again a reference for the sartorially discerning.

Brandelli – his heritage, as one might guess, is Italian – always had an eye for the bespoke. Growing up in Parma and Milan before moving to London, he recounts that he was surrounded by tailors and craftsmen, and learnt many of his skills directly from a generation whose lifestyle seemed to be in peril. It was almost inevitable that he would become a designer.

In 1992, at the age of 24, Brandelli launched a menswear brand called Squire, based in a former art gallery in Clifford Street, Mayfair. Working with the art director Peter Saville and the photographer Nick Knight – both legends in their own field – Brandelli invented what he terms 'a new visual identity and language for a contemporary menswear brand'. The idea was to create a world where art and fashion collided. It worked so well, he re-calls, that the brand was soon dressing celebrities in both the entertainment and design fields.

Eventually, though, the tide turned – Squire spawned too many imitators, and Brandelli grew disenchanted with the mainstream fashion business. He became a freelance designer for brands in Japan and Italy before arriving at 8 Savile Row, the home of Kilgour, French & Stanbury, in 1998: 'The move was born out of a craving to go back to my roots, to rediscover tailoring. It was only when I got here that I realized it had this chic, cinematic reputa-tion. As well as dressing stars like Cary Grant and Rex Harrison, it had worked with Tommy Nutter [the maverick tailor of the 60s and 70s], so it had always been a forward-thinking firm.'

Secretly, though, Brandelli yearned to run his own business – and to make his mark, once again, on men's fashion. He didn't know whether it would be possible to take over Kilgour but, as he says, 'I asked the question, and the answer turned out to be "yes".' He acquired the business with a group of backers in October 2003, with the ambition of creating a 'luxurious, elegant, English menswear brand'. He adds, 'I didn't want to return to the past – I wanted to bring the past back to life in a contemporary way.'

In reality, bespoke had been moving back into favour for some time, thanks to a new generation of tailors led by Timothy Everest, Ozwald Boateng, Mark Powell, John Pearse and Richard James. They had already attracted the attention of fashion editors and stars; Everest, for example, outfitted Tom Cruise for the film *Mission: Impossible* (1996). In short, through skill and luck, Brandelli found himself in the right place at the right time.

The brand name was shortened to Kilgour, and Peter Saville's design studio re-drew the logo. But this was by no means the least of the changes. The elegant 1920s Portland stone façade of the premises was renovated, while the interior was overhauled to Brandelli's specifications by interior architects Cenacchi, who had also worked on stores for Yves Saint Laurent and Chanel. 'One of my inspirations was the French architect Jean-Michel Frank. I wanted a combination of minimalism and art deco,' explains Brandelli. 'I felt that the brand identity should take its cue from the look of the store.'

So what is the brand identity? Brandelli feels that it is a contemporary look at what he calls 'correct' British style: 'I was under the impression that the traditional English look had been usurped by the French and the Italians, so to a certain extent I wanted to bring it back home.'

Just as a Scot and an Irishman provided the best incarnations of that very English agent, James Bond, perhaps it takes an Italian to show the Brits how to dress. Brandelli says his trademark suit is single-breasted and charcoal grey. 'It's a look you can wear any time. I also like the idea of a garment whose history you can trace in its design.' He adds that the 'correct' colour palette for the English male is charcoal grey, navy, white and sky-blue. Anything else smacks of the trendy. 'Men have a conservative approach to clothes. They often live difficult and complex lives, with a lot of stress, so in clothing they look for simplicity. I also think that many of them have become resistant to being spoon-fed with marketing imagery. They like to make their own choices, which is where bespoke comes in. They can be part of the process.'

Nevertheless, Kilgour was obliged to devise some marketing imagery of its own. Brandelli turned once again to Peter Saville and Nick Knight. The resulting image was a suited figure reflected in a circular mirror on a plain floor. The suit-wearer's face was not visible, but we could tell from his nonchalant pose and the way he lightly held a pair of spectacles that he was distinguished. 'Nick's idea was to play on the theme of narcissism, hence the mirror,' says Brandelli. 'We didn't want to be overt or obvious. We also wanted to avoid showing the man's face: we felt that our target customers would put themselves in the picture. Overall, we wanted an image that suited our clientele. They are well travelled and creative. They are thinkers.'

As a result, Kilgour is now considered one of the most influential British fashion brands. But quite apart from being a re-branding case study, the transformation of 8 Savile Row suggests that men's clothing is reflecting an overall trend: the search for the unique. Retaining the services of a tailor has become a statement of independence.

Groom for improvement

Even so, men who cherish the idea of a suit made by Kilgour remain rare indeed, as do those who have developed an iron resistance to marketing. When questioned by the Textile Federation in France, 46.5 per cent of male respondents listed their favourite brand as Levi's, followed by Zara, H&M and Adidas. It's certainly no coincidence that these brands are highly visible and (with the exception of Zara) have large communication budgets.

On a more upmarket level, the German brand Hugo Boss is a male fashion reference to rival Paul Smith and Armani. The original Hugo Boss founded his work-wear garment business in 1923. He died in 1948 and the company has long been out of family hands. Since 1991 the brand has been owned by the Italian group Marzotto (which also snapped up Valentino in 2002).

Boss relies heavily on marketing. Advertising images are created every season at its headquarters in Metzingen and positioned by external agencies, which place an emphasis on international business publications. Like Armani, the brand has a long-standing relationship with the film industry. In addition, since the 1970s it has sponsored a wide range of sporting events, including Formula 1, sailing, boxing, golf and tennis. These are all chosen to 'reflect the values of the core Boss brand: internationalism, perfection, and success' (**www.boss.com**). Boss has maintained its high profile in the menswear market (it launched womenswear only in 1998) by courting the business community and sticking to time-honoured male values in its communications. Hence it is seen as a 'safe bet', free of ambiguity. Even the revelation in 1997 (by the Austrian magazine *Profil* and *The Washington Post*) that Hugo Boss provided German army uniforms during the Second World War failed to dent the brand's popularity.

Creating brand imagery that appeals to men is a delicate business, according to the fashion photographer Vincent Peters: 'In men's fashion the boundaries are stricter. There's a lot of sensitivity around issues of sexuality. Many American brands, in particular, are fearful of projecting an image that might be considered too gay. The other problem for the photographer is that masculinity is a more psychological concept than femininity. I would argue that it's easier to capture femininity visually.' This explains the frequent use of established male role models as brand reference points.

One important area of male fashion is the wristwatch, a man's most prominent accessory. Watch brands have also had recourse to male icons, including the late Steve McQueen for the Tag Heuer Monaco. According to Dylan Jones, 'Watches play a similar role for men that shoes and handbags do for women; although a watch is often a much larger investment. It's obviously a status symbol. You may not have the suit you want, the car you want, the woman you want... but you can have a great watch. It says something about your taste, as well as expressing your personality and your aspirations. When you think about it, men have far fewer ways of communicating those things: we can't really do it through our hair or our shoes or our bag, so the watch becomes a communication tool.'

If men's fashion is still a growing industry, then skin products for men – often referred to as 'grooming products' – have barely registered on the radar. 'The sector is in its infancy,' confirms Dylan Jones. 'We're buying skin products, but nowhere near as many of them as we will in the future.'

Moisturized, wrinkle-free, blemishes disguised and wearing a bespoke suit – say hello to the 21st-century man.

Urban athletes

16

One of our greatest successes was to get sports shoes and apparel out of the gym and on to the street.

The obfuscation begins very soon after you have made contact with one of the sportswear brands. 'I'm not sure how much we can help you with your book,' says a European spokeswoman from Nike, with whom I am not officially having this conversation. 'You see, Nike isn't really about fashion, it's about sports. Our focus is on technology.'

The chat that isn't happening is taking place in a loft-style open-plan space called the Nike Studio, tucked away in an obscure corner of Paris. I had trouble finding it, because the exterior is discreet to the point of enigmatic. The only indication that it belongs to Nike is a single Swoosh, no bigger than the radius of your palm, beside the door. There are other outposts of the Nike Studio in Milan, London and Berlin, and similar concepts in Los Angeles and New York. They are used for product launches and achingly hip multimedia events designed to federate young opinion-leaders around the Nike brand. Nike describes them as 'a meeting point between culture and sport'. The company doesn't talk about them much, because it wants to keep them exclusive. It all sounds suspiciously like fashion branding to me.

On the other hand, it's true that most sports brands occupy a very different place in the fashion universe from, say, Yves Saint Laurent. While designer labels shy away from mass communication, brands such as Nike and Adidas retain the services of global advertising agencies and use the full gamut of promotional tools, from costly TV campaigns to guerrilla marketing. Nike has an annual revenue of US$20 billion. Sportswear is a commodity. While designer brands are keen to retain their air of elitism, it's fair to say that Nike has much more in common with McDonald's than it does with Chanel.

My friendly but anonymous spokeswoman disappears back to base, having assured me that 'a senior Nike marketing executive' will respond to my questions by e-mail. Here is my first question: 'When did sports shoes and other sportswear start crossing over to become streetwear? Did Nike and its competitors encourage this, or was it a creation of the street itself?'

And here is the answer, from Phil McAveety, then vice-president of marketing for Europe, Middle East and Africa: 'Our approach has always been based first and foremost on the product. If a product does not perform, there is a problem. Performance technologies have therefore always been at the heart of Nike, right back to when Bill Bowerman and Phil Knight founded the company, and Bill Bowerman took his wife's waffle iron and poured rubber into it to make an outsole for a running shoe... This quest for functional innovation has never stopped and the company has been synonymous with product innovations.'

The response may not be the one I was looking for, but it certainly tells us a lot about the positioning Nike has established to market its products. Tom Vanderbilt's excellent *The Sneaker Book* (1998) observes, 'Statistics routinely claim that roughly 80 per cent of athletic-shoe wearers will not use them for any kind of sporting pursuit. Still, sneaker companies strive to have top athletes as their standard-bearers and work to develop technologies that sound reasonably advanced, yet make sense to the consumer.'

Vanderbilt points out that sportswear companies have sound economic reasons for taking this approach: 'The image of athletic integrity can imbue an entire line with a positive aura; a "fashion" perception, meanwhile, can spark a trend or draw new customers, but is perceived as risky in the long term.' Nike's stance is a shining example of this philosophy. Adidas, the second-largest brand in the market, has flirted with fashion more overtly; Puma has fully embraced it.

In any case, whatever the sportswear companies might claim, their products are a key element of fashion. All of us wear sports shoes – to work, to clubs, to pubs. They are collected and cherished. They are status symbols. Their wearers have occasionally been shot dead for them. Sports shoes have become an integral part of our lives – and sportswear has developed alongside them. To find out how this happened, we need to go back more than 150 years.

Getting on track

At school, we used to call them 'plimsolls'. It was a wonderfully onomatopoeic word, evoking the squeak of rubber on a gymnasium floor. Later on, when we got older, they became 'trainers'. Americans call them 'sneakers'. In France, they're known as *baskets* (italics obligatory), because of their association with basketball. In historical terms, at least, we British kids got it right the first time. According to Vanderbilt, in 19th-century England the soft shoes used for tennis and other lawn sports were nicknamed 'plimsolls' because the line bonding sole to upper resembled the mark on a ship – named after the British parliamentarian Samuel Plimsoll – indicating correct cargo weight.

The sports shoe was made possible by the American inventor Charles Goodyear's 'vulcanization' process, patented in 1839, which involved mixing rubber with sulphur and heating it. This transformed sticky, easily malleable raw rubber into a substance that was both flexible and impervious, springing back into shape when bent. The early 20th century saw the launch of two sports-shoe brands: Reebok, produced in England by Joseph Foster from 1900, and Converse, founded by Marquis M Converse in Massachusetts in 1908. In 1923, the Converse All-Star shoe became associated with semi-professional basketball player Charles 'Chuck' Taylor. In addition, Taylor was a salesman for the company, so he was able to tour the States demonstrating the shoes and selling them at the same time. These days, sports stars are not expected to go on the road and physically sell the products they are associated with, although the principle remains the same.

Also in the 1920s, the term 'sportswear' was already beginning to enter the fashion lexicon. In the United States, items previously associated with tennis and yachting – flannel trousers, short-sleeved shirts, jerseys and caps – began to infiltrate everyday wardrobes. For the leisured classes, they expressed nonchalance and liberty. Soon they found their way into the collections of designers like Chanel and Schiaparelli. To this day, many designer brands include a 'sport' line in their range.

In general, though, sportswear brands grew out of the early sports-shoe market. The leading names have proved as resilient as the soles of their products. Adidas can trace its roots back to 1926, when the brothers Adolf and Rudi Dassler established their sports-shoe business in Herzogenaurach, Germany. In 1928, their shoes were worn by athletes at the Amsterdam Olympics. In 1936, track and field champion Jesse Owens won four gold medals in them. (The black athlete famously scuppered Hitler's plans to use the German games as a showcase for 'Aryan' superiority.)

At the outbreak of war, the brothers' factory was commandeered for the manufacturing of army boots. While Adolf Dassler struggled to keep a hold on the family business, Rudi joined the army, eventually being captured by the Allies. He was repatriated in 1947, by which time his brother was doing a brisk trade providing boots to the occupying US army. The pair's wartime experiences are said to have caused the split that pushed them to go their separate ways. Adolf (Adi) created the Adidas brand (from the first syllables of his given and family names) while Rudi founded Puma. The two brands became fierce rivals.

While Puma struggled for years, Adidas went from strength to strength, eventually dominating both soccer and the Olympics. Its success on the football field stemmed from its development of the first boots with screw-in studs, which provided better control, and were worn by the West German team during the 1954 World Cup. By the 1960s Adidas was the only global sports brand, having expanded smoothly into sports clothing, bags and equipment. In 1970, its branded football became the official ball of all international tournaments – a position it has yet to relinquish.

At around the same period, the sports shoe was continuing its slow evolution into lifestyle accessory, first as an accoutrement of rock and roll, then as a cooler alternative to stiff traditional footwear. The movie industry, as usual, helped. Tom Vanderbilt points out that the Jets and the Sharks of *West Side Story* (1961) were clad in sneakers. Later, he adds, Dustin Hoffman wore them to the office in the film *All the President's Men* (1976).

The 1970s was the decade when jogging came to the fore as a leisure activity, helping to nudge sportswear further into the mainstream. It was a market in which Puma's products proved especially popular, enabling it to gain ground on Adidas for the first time. But trouble had materialized for both brands in the form of a brash young upstart called Nike.

Phil Knight, a former member of the University of Oregon track team, started out selling Japanese Onitsuka Tiger running shoes from the back of his car. While still at university, Knight had written a paper describing how the market dominance of Adidas could be broken by importing lower-cost sports shoes from Japan. He teamed up with his former coach, Bill Bowerman, to set up Blue Ribbon sports. With the Tiger shoes selling reasonably well, the pair opened their first retail outlet in 1966. Five years later, wanting more control over his inventory, Knight paid a design student called Caroline Davidson US$35 to come up with a logo that he could put on shoe boxes. 'I don't love it, but it will grow on me,' he said of her 'swoosh' design.

However, the pair's collaboration didn't end there. Davidson continued to work for the company until it hired a full-time advertising agency. Later, she was presented with an envelope containing Nike stock.

The Swoosh would begin its rise to omnipresence when Andre Agassi won the men's tennis championship at Wimbledon in 1992. Nike had been experimenting with baseball caps and other clothing that bore the logo alone, dispensing with the brand name. Pictures of Agassi wearing just such a cap appeared on front pages around the world, creating an instant trend. Nike's designers quickly became conscious of the fact that the Swoosh transcended language barriers – it was the perfect global branding device.

Knight and Bowerman ended their deal with Tiger and began making their own trainers in 1972. Their first shoe, the Nike – named after the Greek goddess of victory – proved such a hit at the US Olympic trials that it prompted them to change the name of the company. Another early success was the waffle trainer, born out of the anecdote recounted earlier. By 1980, when Nike went public, the company had snatched more than 50 per cent of the US sports-shoe market. The strategy of delocalizing production to Asia had enabled it to undercut Adidas's prices. And in a foretaste of technological claims to come, Nike also promoted an air-cushioning system, designed by a former NASA engineer, which supposedly gave the wearer extra bounce. Nike's rivals were squeezed between the pincers of cheap labour and expensive branding – although it didn't take them long to catch on.

The market changed for good in 1984, when Nike beat Adidas to sign up basketball star Michael Jordan to wear its shoes. Tom Vanderbilt explains his appeal: 'Freshly bedecked with Olympic gold, likeable and telegenic, Jordan seemed capable of delivering basketball to the entire country. With this possibility in mind... [his agent] was able to wring from Nike the largest basketball endorsement then signed – roughly US$2.5 million over five years.'

Nike Air Jordans entered sports-shoe mythology. In 1987, Nike's advertising agency Wieden & Kennedy launched the 'Just do it' campaign. Combined with Jordan's charismatic presence and a series of high-impact TV ads – diffused by an ever-expanding international media – the slogan turned Nike into a global brand. The company was the first to blend MTV-style imagery, pop music and sport, creating a real buzz when it set a commercial to the Beatles song 'Revolution'.

Vanderbilt adds, 'From Jordan on, the creation of a persona with strong, readily identifiable characteristics would be as important to the shoe companies as it was to the NBA. Since most basketball-shoe consumers did not play basketball, the shoes clearly had an appeal beyond their functional attributes – a fact that shoe companies were slow to pick up on, but then pursued with abandon.'

The 1980s were as unkind to Adidas as they were kind to Nike. Adi Dassler had died in 1978, at the peak of his company's success, and his son Horst had taken over the running of the business. Adidas now found itself locking horns not only with Nike, but also with British outsider Reebok, which was gaining market share in giant strides. Reebok proved particularly adept at spotting and capturing the emerging aerobics market, which even Nike had failed to anticipate due to its male-oriented, sports-star culture.

Horst Dassler died in 1987 and the Adidas company was bought by French entrepreneur and politician Bernard Tapie. Tapie soon became embroiled in a corruption scandal, and he was forced to let go of the ailing sports brand. In 1993, crippled by debt, Adidas found itself in the hands of the French bank Crédit Lyonnais. It was bailed out by Robert-Louis Dreyfus, former chairman of the advertising agency Saatchi & Saatchi.

With an ad-man's flair for enhancing brands, Dreyfus slowly nursed Adidas back to health. He restructured the company, closed expensive European production plants, and placed the design emphasis back on the three-striped logo and accompanying 'trefoil' device, which had been inexplicably abandoned. Over the past few years, the brand's three-pronged strategy has focused on professional sports footwear, consumer-oriented sports heritage ('vintage'-inspired styles), and fashion, hence its partnerships with Yohji Yamamoto and Stella McCartney. While it still lags behind Nike with revenue of about US$17 billion, Adidas has none the less achieved a phenomenal comeback.

Difficult though it may be to believe, Nike has also had its share of ups and downs. The 1990s began promisingly enough, with the opening of the first Niketown superstore, selling the full range of clothing and shoes, in Portland, Oregon. It signed up an unbeatable team of celebrity endorsers – including, in 1995, Tiger Woods – and moved aggressively into soccer, a sector strongly associated with Adidas, by setting up a sponsorship deal with the Brazilian national team. Then, unexpectedly, Nike was hit by a triple whammy. In 1998, France symbolically beat Brazil in Paris in the World Cup. During the same period, the press was filled with stories criticizing labour practices in Asia, where workers in appalling conditions were paid minuscule sums to make shoes that sold for over US$100. Proof that Nike shoes were more about fashion than sport came when youngsters began abandoning them in favour of sturdy work boots. Sales in the United

States plummeted, and when the Asian economy stalled, Nike was hit by another broadside.

Nike was not prepared to lie down and die, however. It made highly publicized efforts to clean up its Asian production issues, it reshuffled its management team, and it modernized and streamlined its distribution process. When Michael Jordan retired from sport in 2000, Nike refocused on the consumer, with brand communication stressing that even an everyday slob could be a hero. This strategy also enabled the brand to place more emphasis on its apparel, something it had viewed purely as a second-string business a few years earlier. While it still retained the services of athletes such as the basketball star LeBron James (signed up in 2003 for a staggering US$90 million, according to press reports), its award-winning advertisements – 'Tag', 'Musical Chairs' and 'Hotdog' – featured ordinary people, whose Nike footwear gave them an edge in urban environments. As a key line on Nike's website reads, 'If you have a body, you are an athlete. And as long as there are athletes, there will be Nike.'

There will be Converse, too. In summer 2003, Nike snapped up the 95-year-old footwear brand for US$305 million. Converse had dominated the basketball-shoe market from the 1920s to the 70s, but by the end of the 1990s it was regarded as little more than a charming relic: low-profile ownership, zero celebrity endorsement, no flashy advertising, and minimal sales. The company filed for bankruptcy in 2001 and was briefly acquired by private investors before being sold to Nike.

The news upset remaining Converse fans, because its 'All-Stars' shoes had traditionally been seen as the footwear of the US counter-culture, having been passed down from the early rockers to The Ramones, Nirvana, and a whole new generation of black-wearing, guitar-clutching wannabes. The fact that Converse had failed to keep pace with modern marketing or design initiatives only endeared it to these rebels. Discovering that Nike had bought Converse was 'like hearing Elvis Costello had started writing jingles for Microsoft', wrote Rob Walker of online magazine *Slate*. But, with low-tech retro styles back in fashion, Nike had made a typically deft move, buying itself a slice of history. 'Converse really does have an authentic heritage, and the company is smart to make that a selling point,' Walker admitted. ('What's up, Chucks?', **www.slate.msn.com**, 15 September 2003.)

A few months after the purchase, Converse released an advertising campaign narrated by the rapper Mos Def. The shoes were seen on famous feet, and fashion editors began to write about how they'd been wearing Converse for years. In the background, those in the know could hear the roar of a marketing machine getting into high gear. Before long, the shoes were every-where again.

Nike owns other brands, too, including Nike Golf, Bauer Nike Hockey and, most surprisingly of all, smart formal-shoe brand Cole Haan, which it acquired more than 15 years ago.

In December 2004, Nike founder Phil Knight stepped down as head of the company after 32 years, although he remains chairman. Under Knight's watch, the humble sports-shoe market had been transformed into a global multi-billion-dollar industry combining elements of sport, entertainment and fashion. 'He created an entire industry [of sports merchandizing] basi-cally on his own,' commented Marc Ganis, president of Sportscorp Ltd, a Chicago consulting firm, in *The Washington Post*. 'By and large he's made athletes richer, he's made athletic footwear and athletic clothing a luxury item, and he has turned a small company in Oregon... into an international goliath.' ('Father of Nike, marketing guru, gives up post', 19 November 2004.)

Expect a gadget

Take a look at the following comment from a Nike spokesman: 'Because of what they stand for... products can sometimes become iconic. For example, the Dunk made its debut in 1986... The Dunk was designed specifically with the awe-inspiring basketball move after which it is named [in mind]. It features a unique low-profile sidewall that reduces weight to enable players to focus on their game. The concentric-circle-patterned forefoot with flex grooves incorporates maximum traction for better grip, flexibility and ease of rotation during pivoting. The Dunk... went on to inspire other product developments in sports outside basketball, like skateboarding.'

The key to the comment lies in the language: 'Concentric-circle-patterned forefoot with flex grooves incorporates maximum traction for better grip, flexibility and ease of rotation.' It's a typical example of the techno-speak that sportswear brands, particularly Nike, use to seduce consumers. Even though we're only going to wear our sports shoes to the supermarket, we could, if we wanted, make a leap for that cereal packet on the top shelf.

According to Tom Vanderbilt, 'Athletic shoes are to other shoes as sports utility vehicles are to other cars: large, loaded with impressive but rarely-used options, a statement less of need than of desire.' Phil Knight's oft-quoted comment that 'the design elements and functional characteristics of the product itself are just a part of the overall marketing process,' originally made to *The Harvard Business Review* in 1992, clearly still holds sway.

The rise of digital has given sportswear marketers a further opportunity to stress the 'technical' and 'performance' elements of their brands. Nike +, for example, is an app that allows you to monitor your performance, set personal goals, get coaching advice, set and memorize routes and share this information with friends via social networks. It's essentially a sensor embedded in or attached to your shoe that communicates either with a band on your wrist or your mobile device. In effect, though, it's a mine of marketing data.

'By combining a dead-simple way to amass data with tools to use and share it, Nike has attracted the largest community of runners ever assembled – more than 1.2 million runners who have collectively tracked more than 130 million miles and burned more than 13 billion calories... With such a huge group, Nike is learning things we've never known before. In the winter, people in the US run more often than those in Europe and Africa, but for shorter distances. The average duration of a run worldwide is 35 minutes and the most popular Nike+ Powersong, which runners can set to give them extra motivation, is "Pump It" by the Black Eyed Peas...'. ('The Nike Experiment: How the shoes giant unleashed the power of personal metrics', *Wired*, 22 June 2009.)

Other sports shoe brands have followed in Nike's wake. In 2011, to promote its ZigTech sports shoe (its unique design was said to propel runners forward with every step) Reebok unveiled the Promise Keeper. The app was designed to encourage runners to take the most difficult step of all – the one out of their front door. Every run they promised to make on their online calendar was automatically posted on the social network of their choice and spread to all their friends. After all, it's easier to break a promise to yourself than to everyone you know. Reebok's sports stars posted videos reminding people to stick to their promise or commenting on their performance. The campaign was praised by the advertising community and gave the ZigTech a higher profile among a creative consumer group.

Retailers have been getting in on the act too. Foot Locker's Sneakerpedia is a sports shoe wiki where sneaker collectors ('sneakerheads') can upload pictures of their most cherished shoes and the story behind them. After a short period in beta, the project was launched in May 2011 with an online video announcing 'the greatest sneaker archiving project'. This was followed by a hip New York launch party featuring 'legendary sneaker collectors' D J Kool Bob Love and D J Clark Kent. The mix of social, urban and sneaker geek culture melded perfectly into an online success, giving Foot Locker a new layer of credibility.

Stars and streets

Two trends that were prominent in the late 1980s and early 1990s – sports shoes without laces and oversized jeans worn so low that the wearer's underwear waistband is visible – have something in common. They were both started by criminals. When you're flung in jail, you're forced to hand over your belt and your shoelaces, in case you feel like committing suicide in your cell, or maybe strangling one of your cell-mates. Since a spell in the joint was considered mandatory by many rappers, the style became a sign of fellowship.

This kind of cool, hard, urban imagery was useful to sports-shoe companies – but at the same time they couldn't be seen to be placing too much emphasis on it. Tom Vanderbilt writes, 'As companies targeted the urban market, they were also reaching out to certain segments of the suburban market that, in a twist on the aspirational brand theory, often emulated the tough, urban culture beamed by satellite to the most pastoral settings. For the shoe companies it was a tightrope... The shoes had to be "black", but not "too black".'

Sports companies sent 'cool hunters' into the grimmest districts of US cities to find out how their latest shoe designs were being received. Other executives were encouraged to distribute free shoes to influential youth groups. But the urban audience and their heroes had already made up their own minds. Free of white establishment associations but imbued with status, kicks were an established hip-hop accessory, a trend underlined in 1986 by the Run-DMC song 'My Adidas'. The band was later repaid for its unofficial promotional work by being invited to sign a sponsorship deal with Adidas. In 1989, a pair of white Air Jordans played a key role in Spike Lee's slice of urban cinematic poetry, 'Do the Right Thing'.

By the end of the decade, the association of sports shoes with street culture was getting out of hand, with media reports of urban teenagers being slain for their expensive branded shoes. Along with claims that, in Asia, children were being paid peanuts to make sportswear, the stories contributed to a brief downturn in the sector's fortunes.

Today, though, trainers are back on top – and the urban market remains crucially important. Generally, sports-shoe brands have found that the most effective approach is to target icons, and then let the influence trickle down. Adidas, for instance, has established relationships with personalities as varied as David Beckham, Derrick Rose and Katie Perry. But the brand is equally skilled at more oblique approaches. It has a 'global entertainment and trend marketing department' that is responsible for non-traditional branding. An article in *The Independent* explained: '[The department's] educational, permissive approach to communicating the brand and its heritage takes many forms, ranging from localized ambient campaigns, such as the step-risers outside the South Bank that immortalized the Olympic medallists around the Sydney Games of 2000, to shop window displays at Savile Row's Oki-Noki on the evolution of the Predator football boot. The aim... is to assist discovery of details about the brand, rather than to directly coerce consumers into parting with their cash.' ('Stars in stripes', 13 December 2004.)

In the same article Gary Aspden, the brand's global head of entertainment promotions, said that the idea was to 'look at ways to communicate the brand to a more fashion-minded, design-oriented consumer'. Considered a guru of street fashion, Aspden cropped up again in 2011, when the BBC explained that 'the reason why so many of today's so-called "grime" artists are hooked on the brand is that Gary spotted them when they were still playing small clubs and gave them free stuff. Now they're having hit records, they're promoting Adidas as a credible brand to a new generation of kids'. ('How superbrands create our designer desires', 23 May 2011, bbc.co.uk.)

Fashion, in theory much disliked by the sports brands, has been the saving grace of Adidas's traditional arch-enemy, Puma. Although the brand's earnings, at €3 billion, are a fraction of those of its competitors, Puma has an enviably cool image. 'One of our greatest successes was to take sports shoes and apparel out of the gym and get them, at the same time, on to the streets,' the brand's then CEO, Jochen Zeitz, told French magazine *Le Point* ('Puma: le fauve en forme', 2 September 2004). He added, 'Today, the sports shoe... is an indispensable fashion accessory.'

It even has a chimerical name for the strategy: sportlifestyle. When Zeitz took command of the company, at the age of 30, back in 1993, the brand had changed its leadership four times in two years. After he had radically overhauled the enterprise – closing several factories and slashing staff numbers by as much as 36 per cent – the operation went into profit the very next year, for the first time since 1986. Puma managed to differentiate itself from its competitors by charging higher prices, creating regular limited editions, and pulling models off shelves before they become too widespread. It also rolled out a global chain of concept stores. Similar thinking lay behind its decision to develop strong links with the world of motor sport, a sector that had remained under-exploited by sports-shoe brands.

But more than anything, Puma unhesitatingly pushed the fashion button. For both its clothing and footwear, it collaborated with designers such as Jil Sander, Neil Barrett – formerly of Gucci and Prada – and Philippe Starck. It launched a line of yoga wear, Nuala, in association with the supermodel Christy Turlington. A range of urban wear, 96 Hours, designed by Barrett, combined sporty ruggedness with pan-European chic. Puma, the David of sports-shoe brands, challenged its Goliath-like competitors by adopting some of the characteristics of a designer label: elitism, iconoclasm and artistry.

This expansion left the company vulnerable, however, as its profits failed to match its sales growth. By 2006 its profits had plummeted 26 per cent to €32.8 million. Seeing an opportunity, a fashion company, France's PPR – the owner of the Gucci group – swept in to acquire a 27 per cent stake, which later rose to a 62 per cent stake (although Puma remains independent).

In 2010 Puma launched a new strategy, 'back on the attack', in which it strengthened both the sports and lifestyle elements of the brand. On the sporting front, it poured sponsorship cash into soccer, extended its sponsorship deal with sprinter Usain Bolt and patted itself on the back for backing Sebastien Vettel, crowned the youngest ever Formula 1 champion, through its sponsorship of the Red Bull racing team. At the same time, its advertising clearly reflected the lifestyle positioning, with the slogan 'Here's to the after-hours athlete' acknowledging the fact that the end result of most sports sponsorship is a trendy shoe worn on the neon streets of a city after dark.

Virtually dressed

17

It's a fashion magazine where you can click to buy the things you like. What could be more fun than that?

It does not seem so very long since the heady days of the dotcom boom, when swathes of young internet entrepreneurs were transformed overnight into the new yuppies, drunk on venture capital and conspicuous consumption. Drunk on vodka and Red Bull, too, at the parties I went to in London while covering the scene for a media magazine. It was the first time I'd met company directors who were younger than me – and more decadent. One article described the sector as driven by 'three Cs: caviar, champagne and Concorde'. Then it suggested throwing cocaine into the mix, too.

Like all great times, it couldn't last forever. I'm probably not the only one for whom the collapse of Boo.com was the definitive sign that the party was over. Although I'd only observed it from a distance, Boo seemed to be the ultimate dotcom. It was run by a bunch of good-looking young people who appeared on the covers of magazines, it sold urban fashion, and it had millions of dollars' worth of backing.

There wasn't quite enough backing, though. Boo collapsed through lack of funds just six months after it had launched. According to reports at the time, 'Boo fell apart after investors failed to stump up an additional US$30 million' ('Top web retailer collapses', bbc.co.uk, 18 May 2000). This was pretty shocking, given that the company had already managed to burn through some US$120 million from investors such as Bernard Arnault of LVMH, Benetton, and the investment banks J P Morgan and Goldman Sachs.

Boo's failings were many, but they can be summed up as 'over-ambition'. With offices in London, Stockholm, Paris and Munich, it aimed to be a global brand from day one. It spent a fortune marketing Miss Boo, the online character who would help customers navigate the site and choose their clothing. The distribution and tax issues that came with trying to dispatch items across the globe tied the company's management in knots for months. Even more crucially, although the site itself looked great, it was too advanced for the technology that most of its target customers were using. The company wasn't doing nearly enough trade to cover the cash it was spending. In addition, like many start-ups of the era, Boo had become 'as famous for its sybaritic lifestyle as for its... attempts to sell urban sportswear over the web' ('From Boo to bust and back again', *The Observer*, 26 August 2001).

According to the same article, Boo's liquidators sold its technology for about £170,000, and its brand name for roughly the same sum. Its founders, Ernst Malmsten and Kajsa Leander, became consultants and regular public speakers, having recovered from their virtual rollercoaster ride.

The success story

Malmsten and Leander were, quite simply, ahead of their time. Fashion addicts now regularly buy clothing over the web, via sites such as ASOS, Yoox, My-wardobe, Gilt Groupe and online shops created by the brands themselves. In the UK, the bargain-hunting site eBay, once considered a handy source of vintage finds, has grouped clothing into a dedicated 'fashion outlet' that behaves like a fully-fledged discount fashion retailer, through partnerships with 30 different outlet stores. In the United States, its fashion department is spiced up with 'style stories': profiles of well-dressed guests who talk about their personal style while directing users to bargains on the site.

These innovations are interesting, but they're nothing new. In fact they can be traced back to the influence of one site. It's called Net-A-Porter, and despite its virtual status, the British Fashion Council once voted it the best shop in the country. It has blossomed into a global brand and extended its offering into menswear, via Mr Porter, and discounted items, through The Outnet. In 2010 the site was bought by Richemont, the owner of Cartier. Surprisingly, it was launched around the same time as boo.com.

Net-A-Porter's founder is Natalie Massenet, an American fashion journalist. She was West Coast editor of *Women's Wear Daily* before moving to London in 1986, when she joined *Tatler*. She recalls that, foreshadowing later events, 'when I wrote an article telling people to buy something, I always wondered how many of them actually went out and bought it'. Now she knows, because her website, deliberately designed to look like an online fashion magazine, has a turner of over £230 million a year. Massenet says the spark of inspiration that led to Net-A-Porter came when she left *Tatler* in 1998 to go freelance:

'I went online for the first time, to research a piece, and it was a revelation – I was instantly hooked. Being a girl, I wondered whether there was anything I could buy. I was surprised to discover that it wasn't really possible. There were a few American brands online, but they weren't shipping outside the States. And the design of the sites wasn't so great.' At that point, says Massenet, 'the online community was largely male. Now fashion is one of the largest categories in online retail, and there are more women than men online.'

With the seed of an idea growing in her head, Massenet had lunch with several key people in the fashion business to sound them out about the potential of an upmarket internet retail site. 'Plenty of those I spoke to told me I was absolutely crazy, but because I like to prove a point, I thought, "Right, I'm going to do it anyway." I picked up a brochure called "Are You an Entrepreneur?" from Barclays Bank and ticked all the boxes.'

Choosing a name proved surprisingly difficult. '[The site] was originally going to be called "What's New Pussycat?". But my lawyers naturally advised against it. I went to the *Women's Wear Daily* site and in the dictionary of fashion terms I found prêt-à-porter. A light went off, but for days I thought it was too good to be true. I kept turning the idea around in my mind. And then I woke up one morning thinking, "What am I doing? Of course it's got to be Net-A-Porter!"'

Once the brand name was in place, the look of the site came into focus. 'It was such a great, classy brand name that I felt we had something to live up to. The site should deserve the brand. So it would be upmarket, global, black rather than pink, simple but elegant. I was convinced it would work, because we were just beginning to see the globalization of fashion: women in New York and Hong Kong wanted the same jeans from Chloé and the same bag from Dior.'

Around the same period – by now we're in 1999 – Massenet picked up a copy of the *Financial Times* and read about the launch of something called Boo.com. Her heart sank, just for a moment. And then she thought, 'Well, you know, there's more than one store in a city.'

The site was launched in June 2000 by five women with no experience in retailing – although they did know about finance, technology and fashion. The initial investment was £190,000 from a selection of family and friends. At launch, the site offered 35 of the hottest fashion brands.

'As we were all women, we based the service on what we'd want it to be. We were our target customers. That's why we designed the site to look like a fashion magazine. We didn't see why we had to make it more complicated than that, when it was a format that our customers loved. Even today, we've stuck to editorial iconography. It's a fashion magazine where you can click to buy the things you like. What could be more fun than that?'

One criticism of fashion on the web is that it robs designer brands of one of their key selling points – the brand experience. When you're not buying your expensive shirt in a sleek retail hub attended by gorgeous staff, is it worth the same amount? Massenet says, 'We took care of that by providing our own brand experience, which is the service. In a way it's quite revolutionary, because the internet tends to be associated with discounting and no-frills. But this is a luxury service, offering not last season's fashions, but next season's fashions. And you should see the gorgeous packaging it arrives in. Today, the one true luxury is time. And we save you time by enabling you to shop 24 hours a day.'

When the site was being conceived, Massenet and her colleagues would sit around for long evenings, discussing the details of the offering. 'We'd be shrieking and saying, "Wouldn't you just *die* if...", or, "Wouldn't that just make you *cry*...". Basically, there was a lot of shrieking and dying and crying. We launched the business in a frenzy of happiness, and I think a lot of that communicated itself to the consumer.'

Interestingly, Massenet says the site sells more clothes than accessories. But what about the size issue – surely that presents problems? Massenet says, 'If something doesn't fit, Net-A-Porter will come and pick it up from you, at our expense. Of course we realize people want to try things on. The difference here is that you get to try it on at home.'

The fact that Net-A-Porter is thriving long after the collapse of Boo.com, the interloper that gave Massenet such a fright back in 1999, justifies her simple, understated approach to the web. 'I think Boo would still be here today if they'd had a smaller team and less money at the beginning. They were under a lot pressure to go public in six months, and there was a lot of hype. We've only started getting media attention in the last 18 months.'

With the Boo case study now losing its relevance in the face of success stories such as Net-A-Porter, traditional fashion retailers are facing up to competition from the web. 'They're building huge flagship stores in cities all over the world, a strategy that costs them billions of dollars,' says Massenet. 'We're saying you only need one store, and you can get people from all over the world to come to you – a much more efficient way of doing it. Think about it: what would an alien think if you explained the concept of a fashion store to him? "You have to get dressed, drive somewhere in your car, get undressed in front of a bunch of strangers, try something on, then get undressed again...". Our way is much less stressful.'

Interactive fashion

Natalie Massenet once noted that the internet was far more efficient at keeping pace with fashion trends than glossy magazines, with their three- to four-month lead times. She predicted that the glossies would evolve into 'big, beautiful coffee-table books', prestige items full of gorgeous pictures, while the cutting edge of fashion migrated online.

To a certain extent, she was right. But fashion magazines have survived. They've also benefited from the arrival of the iPhone and the iPad, and the apps that go with them. At the time of writing, print media were rushing to create app versions of their publications. These ranged in quality from glorified PDF downloads to interactive editions with video content.

Marie Claire in the UK, for example, came up with at least two different responses to the app opportunity. Publishing director Janine Southall says: 'The first app we launched was Marie Claire Beauty Genius for iPhone. At first readers had to pay for it, but now it's free thanks to sponsors such as Estée Lauder, Bobbi Brown and Clinique.'

Beauty Genius offers readers tips on how to achieve certain looks: 'smoky eye', for example. Once they've watched the 'how to' video, readers are directed to a sponsor's e-commerce site, where they can buy the products that will enable them to get the look.

A second app, this time for iPad, was launched in early 2012 alongside spin-off catwalk magazine *Marie Claire Runway*. It cost £2.99 from iTunes and did not carry any advertising. 'It's a paid-for model, but it won't necessarily stay that way. We decided to launch without advertising because a lot of the relevant brands did not have the correct material or could not make it in time for our deadline. But the door is open.'

Around the same time, French *Vogue* was preparing to launch its iPad application. It did so with characteristic hauteur. 'We're not going to follow the approach of a traditional magazine and sell advertising based on the numbers,' Condé Nast France president Xavier Romatet told me. 'This is a partnership. We're looking for 10 sponsors. We will offer them a price and they will accept it or not. In a way we've copied the business model of luxury brands: we're not offering our customers cold, rational arguments for buying our product. We're offering them a world, a prestigious environment they want to be part of.'

Ironically, the high-end fashion brands have struggled with the digital world. Net-A-Porter proved beyond all debate that luxury shoppers were spending online, yet still they hesitated, feeling that the internet was somehow too mass for their product. They struggled to replicate online not only the opulent store environment, but also the artificial dream world of their print advertising.

And there's no doubt that digital offers many opportunities for failure. Apps are expensive to develop and then sit, unused, on users' phones, crowded out by yet more apps. Facebook and Twitter offer a means of engaging in a dialogue with consumers: but do luxury brands really need that kind of proximity, when distance creates desire? In addition, a new digital platform seems to emerge every week. 'The ground keeps shifting under your feet,' as one luxury brand marketer told me. A cartoon I found on the web – on Facebook, actually – seemed to sum up the situation. It showed two advertising types staring at an open laptop. One of them is saying: 'So we poured our budget into a Foursquare strategy, which we abandoned to pursue an Instagram strategy, which we dropped to pursue a Pinterest strategy. I'm starting to think what we really need is a strategy strategy.'

Quite right. As a friend of mine who works in advertising says: 'Don't follow trends, be a brand.' Digital is part of the marketing toolkit. Don't just pick tools at random – use the right ones for the job. If you know what kind of story you want to tell consumers about your brand, the tools for telling it in the best possible way will present themselves.

Louis Vuitton has been one of the more ambitious converts to digital. In 2007 it appointed the advertising agency Ogilvy & Mather to inject some new life into its travel heritage – which had, as mentioned earlier, been obscured by images of models with handbags – and, more importantly, to pep up its internet strategy. The initial result of Ogilvy's appointment was a trio of print ads featuring very different personalities – Mikhail Gorbachev, Catherine Deneuve and the golden couple Andre Agassi and Steffi Graf – on their 'personal voyages'. Seeing Gorbachev cuddled up to a Vuitton bag was a little surprising, but other than that the ads seemed perfectly banal – even a touch retrograde, although they were immaculately shot by Annie Leibovitz.

The online element was far more unusual. A series of microsites could be accessed from the main Louis Vuitton homepage. Through a beguiling blend of photography, video, narration and music, each personality featured in the advertising campaign shared their personal vision of a favourite city, transporting the user on a magical voyage with them. Thanks to Ogilvy, Vuitton had finally found a way of transferring its high-end brand values onto the web.

Since then, the brand has continued its 'Voyages' series, but broadened its digital strategy into other areas. For example, in 2008 – as China geared up for the Olympics in Beijing – it launched the Louis Vuitton 'Soundwalks'. These were downloadable audio guides that allowed the user to be shown around three Chinese cities by local celebrities: Gong Li in Beijing, Shu Qi in Hong Kong and Joan Chen in Shanghai. Cannily, Vuitton invited a clutch of the world's best-known bloggers to Hong Kong to test the product, with the resulting free publicity.

As the 'soundwalks' reached a dead end in China, without being exported to other markets, their success was presumably limited. One initiative that *has* been repeated is an online video competition, The Journeys Awards. This was originally launched in 2009. Young filmmakers were invited to share their notion of a journey via a short film, based on a script from a previous Louis Vuitton advertisement. An official jury led by director Wong Kar Wai selected 15 films to be shown online. Two would win a US$25,000 prize – one picked by the jury, the other voted for by online viewers. The winners were Sho Tsukikawa of Japan and James Cogels of Belgium. (See them on **www.journeysawards.com** and, if you wish, enter the awards.)

While most luxury brands now include some form of retail on their sites, they feel more at home sharing their universes with potential customers via 'fashion videos' – overlong commercials diffused via their websites, YouTube and, increasingly, Twitter feeds and Facebook fan pages. If Twitter proved a little discomfiting for some brands – after all, it required them to tell rather than show – fashion videos were an easier leap. They could simply shoot moving fashion spreads, using the same photographers they'd always used: Mario Testino, Steven Meisel, Nick Knight *et al*. Most fashion videos studiously avoid anything resembling a story arc. They are fragile and diaphanous. But they can be injected into a magazine app almost as easily as a conventional print ad.

Talking of Nick Knight, he's done more than most to revolutionize online fashion. His genre-bending SHOWstudio launched in November 2000 as an online space enabling creatives to present interactive and mixed-media work. It developed into 'the home of fashion film', an online fashion channel whose archive of videos, interviews, films and art house experimentation could keep anyone with even the vaguest interest in fashion amused for days. True to its philosophy of opening up the sometimes opaque world of high fashion to a wider public, it has pioneered the live streaming of runway shows. Based in Mayfair, it also has a gallery and a shop selling art and designer items.

In 2009, during London fashion week, it staged a retrospective exhibition, 'SHOWstudio: Fashion Revolution' at Somerset House. It incorporated a temporary photography studio, so visitors could watch Knight and other collaborators at work. Knight told British *Vogue*: 'We are in the midst of a revolution in fashion imagery. Moving away from illustration and stills photography, we are now entering the restless world of interactive, self-created, digital-imaging: accessible, downloadable and constantly changing.' ('Fashion revolution', 12 June 2009.)

Knight is no doubt correct, but the upper end of the fashion business remains surprisingly conservative and risk-averse. It speaks volumes that SHOWstudio has little in the way of competitors. Ten years after its launch, it remains the fashion medium of the future.

Rise of the bloggers

18

I'm hacking fashion, I suppose.

Every April, in the verdant grounds of an angular Art Deco villa not far from Saint Tropez, the French fashion pack gathers to determine the future of the industry. The focus of the event is a series of catwalk shows – held in a tent down on the beach – featuring the work of young designers from fashion schools around the world. In between shows, the hopefuls install themselves in makeshift ateliers and share their vision with buyers, reporters and, most importantly, a judging panel that will later award the festival Grand Prix. Alongside the fashion competition is a parallel category for photographers. The event also embraces seminars, networking – and some pretty fabulous parties.

The Hyères International Festival of Fashion and Photography used to be a rarefied, exclusive event, attended only by the happy few who worked in the industry, wrote for the right magazines, or knew the right people. In recent years, though, a new tribe has been spotted stalking across the villa's immaculately barbered lawns, staking out the best places at the shows and helping themselves to finger food and champagne. They are the fashion bloggers, and they are assailing the elitist world of glossy magazines.

One of them is British blogger Susanna Lau, whose blog Style Bubble attracts around 35,000 visitors a day. A minor celebrity among UK fashion fans, Lau occasionally gets spotted when she's out shopping. This popularity with everyday consumers is what makes blogs increasingly attractive to brands – and subsequently gains bloggers access to fashion events.

Not that it was Lau's goal when she started out. She's always considered fashion a hobby, and although she did 'a bit of styling for student magazines' at university, she actually studied history. Now, however, she finds herself being approached by fashion brands for styling and consultancy advice. Not bad for somebody who only started blogging in March 2006. 'I was partly inspired by leading fashion blogs like Fashionologie and A Shaded View on Fashion [by Paris-based commentator Diane Pernet],' she explains. 'And I was always chatting with other fashion fanatics on forums like Fashion Spot. I wanted to express myself, and I thought a blog would be a much easier platform than a website. My idea was to get back to the basics of blogging, which is to express a personal viewpoint. Some blogs have begun to approach fashion in a rather cold way, with newsy posts about dresses you can't afford. But I want to raise issues and provoke debate.'

Their provocative, often irreverent, approach to fashion is exactly what made blogs seem daunting to big brands, which were used to the criticism-free environment of the glossies. But readers quickly realized that blogs were an alternative, refreshing source of news and opinion. And smaller designers saw a promotional opportunity: after all, you can't dismiss 35,000 visitors a day. 'As we all know, glossy magazines devote an extremely limited amount of space to designers that don't have an advertising budget,' says Lau. 'On the other hand, I'll enthusiastically support and promote a designer whose work I find interesting.'

In addition, hyperactive bloggers are arguably more in sync with the changeable spirit of fashion than the traditional glossies. Fashion magazines are planned up to three months in advance – a blogger can report on a show 10 minutes after the designer has left the runway.

Blogs and the press

The organizers of catwalk shows in London, New York, Paris and Milan are now used to dealing with an ever-expanding community of bloggers. But their gradual acceptance by the fashion community has also eaten into the bloggers' independent status. Well-known fashion bloggers are now sent gifts, invited to launch parties and taken on press junkets just like glossy magazine journalists.

Some have crossed to the other side on a more professional basis. Lau is a freelance fashion journalist for *Elle* UK, *Pop*, *Dazed & Confused* and *The Observer*. Another popular blogger, The Sartorialist – Scott Schuman, who wowed the fashion crowd with his razor-sharp street photography and pithy commentaries – was given his own column in the US edition of *GQ*, after stints taking photographs for the Condé Nast website Style.com (a spot later filled by the influential blogger Tommy Ton of Jak & Jil). 'I could see from the statistics on the site that they were watching me for a while,' says Schuman, who started his photo-blog in September 2005. 'I think what they noticed was consistency: I wasn't shooting someone with good taste one day and bad taste the next. They also noticed an eye for detail.'

Schuman had an advantage in that he'd already worked in the fashion business for 15 years, including running a showroom for designers. The blog sprang out of his observation that a certain kind of well-dressed male was not represented in men's fashion magazines. 'I'd be out on the streets of New York and I'd see these ordinary guys who nonetheless had a very distinct sense of style. Some of them were quirky; others were wearing beautiful Italian suits. I thought other guys would be inspired by them, but you never saw pictures of them anywhere.'

He initially toyed with the idea of setting up a website, but it seemed overly complicated, as well as requiring a whole team of people. 'It was only when I found out about blogging that the whole thing clicked. This was a platform that was easy to set up, virtually free, and enabled me to express my ideas.' Less than a year after his blog had gone online, Scott got a call from Style.com, which dispatched him to Milan to take pictures of the guys attending, or merely hanging around, the men's fashion shows. That's when the media really began to notice him, he says. 'I was dressed stylishly, so I didn't look like just another photographer. I didn't blend in. I looked more like a fashion editor with a camera. Before long, people asked me what I was up to, and we got talking. Then one time I was at a Prada show and [*GQ* editor] Jim Nelson called me over.'

As the site evolved, The Sartorialist began to take photos of women as well as men. This broad appeal – combined with media coverage – drove his site's figures up to 45,000 visitors a day. With Condé Nast handling his ad sales, he began to reap genuine income from the blog. He also signed a book deal with Phaidon, and the James Danziger gallery in New York staged an exhibition of his work. Schuman admits that his rapid ascent has left him slightly breathless. 'I could never have imagined that things would move this fast. To use an English expression, I'm chuffed.'

But he doesn't believe that blogs will replace magazines as the most influential fashion media. 'It's a totally different thing. My photos are a slice of life, while a magazine makes you daydream in another way. But I do think blogs are a great source of talent for the mainstream media. And at the same time, the people who run blogs have a certain amount of power. A blogger who is recruited by a newspaper can maybe negotiate a better contract because they have an audience of thousands of people that they're bringing with them.' The bloggers who have been adopted by the mainstream fashion press did not ape it, or fantasize about being part of it, but set out to express their own unique visions. Fashion has a vampire-like lust for novelty.

This new collusion between the outlying world of the blogs and the fashion establishment is generally perceived as a good thing – injecting a much needed breath of fresh air into the industry. In New York, it helps harassed PRs ensure that fashion shows will be packed out, despite an over-supply of shows and an over-stretched press corps. But it can also create some abrasive moments. In early 2007, media news website Mediabistro reported on a fashion show encounter between blogger Julie Fredrickson – of the site Coutorture – and *Vogue* supremo Anna Wintour. Spotting Wintour 'minding her own front-row business', Fredrickson gamely began to interview the powerful editor. Much to her credit, Wintour politely began to answer the questions – until her publicist appeared and sent the blogger packing. ('Bloggers in tents: fashion warms to new media', 6 February 2007.)

In February 2012, professional stylist Mary Fellowes took exception to the caravan of bloggers that now follows the fashion pack from city to city. On a blog, ironically – thegoodwebguide.co.uk – she wrote: 'The "bloggerazzi" have turned fashion week into an ugly circus of attention seeking wannabes, feeding and fuelling the egos of its subjects with flashbulbs for sustenance... An army of apparent nobodies has swelled in numbers, taking over the front line, making entering into a show like running the gauntlet. More often than not clad in outlandish and forced looking outfits, they have adopted the customs of the paparazzi but sadly they have none of the clout.'

For readers – and, of course, for the bloggers themselves – this new media is another stage in the democratization of the fashion industry, enabling them to pierce the façade of a notoriously elitist business. Even the backstage of catwalk shows is no longer out of bounds to the general public, thanks to blogs like the one begun by Anina, a model. Using her mobile phone, she started snapping backstage scenes, parties and images from her travels and posting them on her blog with breezy commentaries. She went on to create 360 Fashion, a network of blogs from around the fashion industry.

'I blog using my mobile about a hundred times a day because, in my work, I'm absolutely not anywhere near a computer,' she told *Wired* magazine. 'Fashion is a mystery to many people. Now, like voyeurs, they can see what's happening in the industry.' Hardly conforming to the clichéd image of the fashion model, Anina learned how to write computer code at school.

'I like to see how systems work... I'm hacking fashion, I suppose.' ('Le chic shall inherit les blogs', 6 December 2005.)

Inevitably, the rise of blogs inspired mainstream media to start their own. Among the most respected establishment bloggers is Cathy Horyn of *The New York Times*. Horyn noted the rising power of blogs back in 2005, when she wrote: 'Although fashion, like politics, is still an insider's game, with its own addicts and agenda-setting editors, nothing, it seems, can compete with the authentic judgement of bloggers and web viewers.' ('The Paris 6', 28 April 2005.)

Forget 'authentic': a positive judgement is what brands are hoping for when they dispatch a freebie to a blogger – or summon them to an exclusive launch event. Some bloggers are easily seduced. Others, though, are determined to remain outspoken and untarnished. 'I still think my first duty is to my readers,' says Susanna Lau of Style Bubble. 'I was recently invited on a trip to Paris by Chanel, to cover the launch of their latest advertising campaign, but in my posts I was absolutely transparent about what the deal was. I certainly won't accept money from brands for posts, which I know some bloggers do. And although I receive at least 30 e-mails a day asking me to promote some product or another, that's not what I'm here for.'

Not all bloggers – or advertisers – share her view. While it's difficult to unearth concrete figures, anecdotal evidence suggests that a handful of bloggers are making a great deal of money out of advertising. Others have used their blogs to supercharge their careers. Bloggers like Schuman and his partner Garance Doré, whose eponymous blog is one of the most popular on the web, have evolved into brands in their own right, hiring themselves out for advertising shoots and consulting. Their success has made them role models for a new generation.

Blogging as a business

'I decided from the start that I didn't want advertising on my blog,' says James Bort, a French blogger and photographer who has worked on a freelance basis for a number of prestigious brands, 'so if I wanted to earn a living through it, I had to find another economic model. The solution was to turn it into a portfolio for my work.'

A former art student, Bort had also worked in advertising before launching his blog. Every blog needs an angle, and his would explore the backstage of luxury: the ateliers and workshops where premium products are created;

or the creative chaos behind the scenes of runway shows. After that, it was a case of calling the brands and asking permission. Many accepted. Occasional photography assignments for *Madame Figaro* provided further access. He was also aided by the brands themselves. 'They'd send me press releases or advertising proposals, and I'd call them up and say: "I'm not interested in that, but what if I came and photographed your atelier, or the backstage of your show, and placed the images exclusively on my site?"'

These days, brands approach Bort for paid projects. He's worked with Baccarat, Lanvin, Patek Philippe, Van Cleef and Arpels, Christian Dior and Jean-Paul Gaultier, among others. The relationship with Gaultier is a good illustration of the advantages of a blog. 'I was invited with a group of other bloggers to an event organized by the brand, and I took a quick picture of Jean-Paul Gaultier, which I posted on the site. The brand liked it so much they contacted me and bought the rights to use it internationally.'

Similarly, Bort met Lanvin designer Alber Elbaz during a shoot for *Madame Figaro*, and has since been hired as a photographer by the brand on numerous occasions. Since then, he's progressed to making short films for Baccarat and even the telecoms brand Orange. 'The brands give me room to experiment because working with me has certain advantages. For a start, I'm much cheaper than a conventional advertising agency. But there's also the fact that I'm more than just a photographer or a director. When the project is done I distribute the content via social networks and the blog. So I'm a creator, a producer and a distributor, in one affordable package.'

Other bloggers have professionalized by becoming part of branded networks run by web media companies. These online magazines don't create, they curate. Typical of these is Glam Media, whose network of sites is led by Glam.com, an aggregation of fashion, beauty and lifestyle blogs. Officially launched during New York fashion week in September 2006, just over a year later its staff had swelled from 25 to 100. By the beginning of the next decade the San Francisco-based Glam Media employed around 500 people worldwide, not to mention 4,000 authors. Together with its male-oriented site Brash.com and its health and beauty arm Bliss.com, it claims an audience of 88 million viewers every month in the United States alone, based on figures from ComScore. It acquired the social networking site Ning in 2011, giving it an additional distribution platform as well as extra content, and advertising and subscription revenue.

Glam.com founder Samir Arora noted that many bloggers were evolving into independent publishers: their blogs had become full-time occupations. And yet they were unable to make a decent living out of their work. Glam allows them to do this by placing their blogs on its network and splitting advertising revenue 50/50, based on page impressions. It also works with the bloggers to create microsites and promotional content for brands. All this has changed the lives of many of the site's 'indie publishers'.

'Arora says that three of Glam's content curators have earned over $1 million in residuals this year – a good year for a writer or editor in any medium. With its focus on women aged 18–49, Glam has forged what Arora called a "very deep connection between the content and the advertiser". Ads appear in context from the 1,000 brands from Gucci to Prada to Neiman Marcus throughout its network.' ('Glam Media forges a global empire based on women', 7x7.com, 13 December 2011.)

The first millionaire bloggers have arrived.

The faking game

19

> *The biggest factory of fakes in the world.*

There are two good reasons to visit the Temple Street night market in Hong Kong. The first is the steamed prawns with garlic sauce and fried noodles at the Tak Kee Seafood Restaurant. The second is to marvel at the vast array of counterfeit branded goods on sale (without actually buying any of them, of course). Bags bearing the Louis Vuitton monogram and the Burberry check are everywhere: lined up in neat rows on aircraft carrier-sized trestle tables, or hanging from hooks on fences of wire mesh. There's plenty of Dior, too; not to mention Gucci, Fendi and Coach. When I finger some 'Omega' watches on one stall, a young man hands me a ring-binder full of photographs – a catalogue of fake luxury timepieces.

There are other markets like this in Hong Kong – and, indeed, in other major Chinese cities – where Western visitors snap up copies of luxury goods, half-hoping that they might pass muster back home. They see it as a bit of fun, one of the obligatory tourist experiences. In the past, I doubt that the sight of all these fakes would have bothered me. The trouble is that, just a few hours earlier, I'd been listening to some of the leading names in the luxury market debating how to stamp out counterfeiting.

The global counterfeit goods market is worth US$600 billion a year, according to the International Chamber of Commerce. US Customs and Border Protection cites China as the number one source of counterfeit and pirated goods and adds that apparel, footwear, handbags, wallets and jewellery are in the top 10 categories of products seized.

At the *International Herald Tribune*'s luxury branding conference in Hong Kong in 2004, LVMH boss Bernard Arnault confirmed that crushing the counterfeiters was one of his group's biggest challenges. Louis Vuitton has its own anti-counterfeiting squad. Arnault stated, 'Counterfeit goods now represent 10 per cent of world trade. Such fakers live off the hard work and creativity of others. As well as working with the police to stop counterfeiting at its source, we are calling on [the media] to send out the message that when you buy a counterfeit product, you are funding crime, misery and hardship.'

As the traditional home of luxury goods, France has long been a victim of the counterfeit trade. Associations such as the Union des Fabricants, established way back in 1877, and the more recent Comité Colbert, founded in 1954 (its glittering list of members runs from Baccarat through to Yves Saint Laurent), have battled to raise international awareness of the problem.

It seems ironic that China, the country that luxury brands so dearly want to seduce, is causing them such a headache. But in developing countries, high import taxes encourage the production of fake luxury goods. And by marketing their products to consumers who can't afford them, the brands themselves may be exacerbating the problem. A familiar conspiracy theory suggests that, while brands are forced to tackle counterfeiting, they are secretly aware that it has certain advantages: it means that their logo carries a cachet, and the fakes act as moving billboards, all the while provoking a desire for the real thing. This comment is only ever whispered.

During the conference, Tan Loke-Khoon, international partner at the legal firm of Baker & McKenzie – which helps brands combat the theft of intellectual property – said, 'Counterfeiting can tarnish the image of a brand for ever. Companies need to factor the cost of fighting fakes into their businesses. They also need a strong long-term strategy.' He described China as 'the biggest factory of fakes in the world'. Counterfeiting had not been a small-scale business for some time, he added. Sometimes, the same factories that produced legitimate branded goods during the day would pump out copies after hours. This rise in expertise has led to the 'super fake', an item almost identical in quality to the real thing. He went on to say that investigators frequently went missing.

Apart from the tourists in places like Temple Street, who's buying all these fakes? Not all the purchasers live in developing markets. When a writer named Osman Ahmed strolled through the market in East London's Walthamstow, he noted 'an impressive array of fashion's most coveted it-bags: oversized Mulberry Alexa's, Hermes's signature orange Birkin bags, even the lesser-known Proenza Schouler's PS1 satchels and Alexander Wang's studded "Coco" holdalls.' ('Counterfeit fashion', 28 June 2011, nowfashion.com.)

The United States has a big problem with counterfeit goods. According to the International Anti-Counterfeiting Coalition in Washington, DC, fakes cost the country's businesses US$350 billion in annual sales. There have been frequent raids on New York's Canal Street, which resembles a black-market bazaar. Yet any visitor to the city will see fake Burberry scarves and Prada bags spread across the sidewalk on blankets, which are swiftly bundled up and whisked away when a cop appears. Such scenes normally take place just a few blocks away from Barney's or Bergdorf Goodman. Councilwoman Margaret Chin, who is in charge of the Chinatown district, has pushed for a law that would threaten the purchasers of counterfeit goods with a fine. But one woman retorted: 'I'll take a risk and sacrifice to look good and pay less.' ('A Canal Street knockoff could cost you a $1,000 fine', 26 April 2011, nyracked.com.) Elsewhere 'purse parties' have replaced Tupperware parties as a leisure pursuit, with women buying counterfeit bags from dealers and selling them in suburban homes at a profit.

Interpol says counterfeiting is generally perceived by society as a victimless crime. And it's true that buyers of fakes are often proud of their acquisitions, having got one over on Big Brand. They see it as a form of bargain-hunting. Interpol would disagree, as it says professional counterfeiters belong to criminal organizations that are involved in drugs and prostitution, and may be funding terrorist groups.

The internet has been a boon for fakers and their customers. As well as sites aimed at those who are looking specifically for fakes, goods are traded over e-commerce and auction sites. In 2008, LVMH successfully argued in a French court that 90 per cent of the Louis Vuitton bags and Dior perfumes sold online were fakes. ('eBay ordered to pay US$61 million in sale of counterfeit goods', 1 July 2008, *The New York Times*.)

Fearing that it would become demonized as a marketplace for fakes and eventually lose the trust of consumers, eBay put a system in place to filter out copies. 'It combats fakes aggressively, in part through a program which gives brands or other intellectual property rights owners special tools to report listings. When brands flag a listing as inauthentic, it is removed within hours... eBay also independently scans its millions of listings for fake products. In a statement, eBay's Dan Dougherty, associate general counsel, intellectual property, said, "In the rare cases when a counterfeit item appears on the site, buyers are covered for eligible purchases through our Buyer Protection programs." The programs enable buyers to return an item if it wasn't what the seller promised.' ('Fashion fakes get more sophisticated', 30 June 2011, WSJ.com.)

eBay has also teamed up with The Council of Fashion Designers in America for an awareness campaign. Since 2011 it has collaborated with well-known designers, who create customized tote bags bearing the slogan 'You Can't Fake Fashion', which are then sold through the site. Proceeds go to the CDFA Foundation, which raises funds for charitable initiatives concerning, among other things, breast cancer and HIV/AIDS.

Digital technology is also giving fashion companies an opportunity to strike back. For instance, a QR code printed on the inside of a bag might include the model number, the date of production and a destination code. Consumers would then only have to scan the code with an app on their phone to assure themselves that their product is genuine. ('The issue of counterfeiting in the digital age', 20 December 2011, fashionscollective.com.)

What all this highlights, of course, is the pervasiveness of branding in fashion. Heavily logo-ed items, such as bags from Coach, Gucci, Burberry and Louis Vuitton, seem to be begging to be copied. Louis Vuitton claims that it seeks to stay ahead of the fakers through constant product innovation, but only a customer with the highest degree of loyalty could keep track of every single model it releases.

The prevalence of fakes is nudging some consumers away from logos. They prize the logo-free basics produced by Japanese brands such as Uniqlo or Muji; or perhaps the more subtle branding of Maison Martin Margiela, where the provenance of a sweater is proclaimed only by the signature white thread securing the inside label. Rather than making any Naomi Klein-inspired gesture, the self-proclaimed stylish are eschewing heavily branded products simply because they are afraid of looking cheap.

Trendy toddlers

20

Babies mean business.

There are moments in life when you become suddenly, acutely aware that you are an ideal target for marketers. One of them is when you get married. Diamond rings, dresses, suits for hire or purchase, classic cars for hire, reception venues, Champagne by the crate, honeymoon destinations... as if by magic, and with no apparent effort on your part, your mailboxes both real and virtual fill with opportunities to spend money.

Another is when you become a parent. It was when the paediatrician appeared with an Evian-branded tape measure around his neck that I began to suspect the presence of baby marketing. After that, a glance around the room at the Parisian clinic where my wife was staying for a few days – after giving birth to our son two floors down – convinced me: if there was another diaper brand than Pampers, you certainly wouldn't know it from the evidence on offer here. 'Maybe it's because they're actually the best,' I offered, clearly addled after a sleepless night. My wife looked at me scornfully: 'I bet this clinic has never paid for a single diaper – just so people like you think Pampers are the best. Chérie, babies mean business.'

When we returned from the clinic, I immediately went out and bought a giant packet of Pampers, as if brainwashed. Then I went to the pharmacy and bought some powdered milk, a bottle and various cleansing products. The bill came to €80. For a person who measured only 52 centimetres, my son appeared to have expensive tastes. His pyjamas, by the way, came from Petit Bateau and his daywear from Gap.

Truth be told, my little one has fairly modest demands, leaning towards affordable French chic and US urban wear, spiced with occasional 'vintage' pieces from friends and relatives. Other tots are far more exigent. Baby Dior, Boss Kids, Junior Gaultier, Paul Smith Junior, Sonia Rykiel Enfant; 'mini' Gucci, Fendi, Prada, Stella McCartney, Burberry and Armani – the list of designer brands making clothes for children grows longer every month. As

The New York Times puts it: 'Business-wise, it makes a lot of sense: kids' garments take a beating and their owners grow out of them fast, meaning that as long as there are children, there will always be a need for more children's clothing. And parents with money can be persuaded to spend it on high-quality clothing for their children.' ('Designer labels go pint sized', 18 October 2010.)

This is proof positive that common sense often goes out of the window when it comes to children. Designer clothes are rarely a good investment at the best of times, but spending a fortune on a designer item that you know *beyond a shadow of a doubt* will be useless in a couple of months is particularly reckless. At the time of writing, Datamonitor estimates that the children's clothing market is worth about US$186 billion worldwide.

A taste of *Milk*

To find out more about clothing for kids, I toddled on down to the Paris headquarters of *Milk*, a high-end fashion magazine aimed at trendy children; or rather, at their parents. *Milk* was founded in 2003 by Isis Colombe-Combréas, a former TV presenter and producer (of interior design and children's shows) and her art director partner Karel Balas.

Its editor-in-chief is Aude Bunetel, an entirely professional and unassuming journalist who I meet in the midst of *Milk*'s bustling offices, where her own young daughter is also hanging out during school vacation, adding a touch of authenticity to proceedings. 'When *Milk* first started there were four or five staffers and two issues a year,' she tells me. 'It could have been considered something of a risk, but Isis and Karel were convinced of the potential of the premium market for children's fashion. Having said that, although the image and the quality of the magazine are high-end, we don't talk exclusively about designer clothing. We also like to feature small brands that are just starting out.'

This is sensible, as there are only two children's wear collections per year, and the magazine must find other subjects to write about and photograph in the meantime. It now comes out four times a year and has a circulation of 50,000, about 15,000 outside France. 'We've grown with the market,' says Bunetel. 'Children's fashion is a small world, and we help each other. It sounds a bit of a cliché, but it's actually quite a family atmosphere.' She adds, however, that the family has expanded considerably. 'When we first started, I had the impression that there were only about 150 brands.

Now there are 700, perhaps more. This is not some kind of cute dreamland. While it can't compete with womenswear, it's a lucrative part of the fashion industry.'

The question is – why? What has made the market for designer clothes for kids explode since 2003? 'I think it's a combination of two factors, marketing and socio-cultural, working in tandem. In terms of marketing, in the 1990s a number of fashion brands began to source cheap labour in Asia and spend the resulting cost savings on advertising. At the same time, they realized that they could target not just adults and teenagers, but pre-teens. They were in magazines, they were on MTV, they were in the school yards. I'd say brands like Calvin Klein, Gap and Nike were pioneers in the field. Gap and Chevignon were particularly skilled at selling clothing that bore the name of the brand, transforming kids into advertisements.'

But the strategy worked, she says, because the role of children had changed. 'They had moved to the centre of the family. They were no longer a secondary consideration when it came to shopping – fashion-conscious adults wanted their children to look stylish. It went hand in hand with the more prominent place of children in their lives. Even babies are seen out with adults at night these days, in restaurants, so there's a sense that their appearance should reflect the attitude and the social status of their parents.'

But doesn't this attitude create spoiled, entitled children? 'That may have been a tendency at first – the little emperor syndrome. But I think we're through it now. We're finding a balance.'

It has also liberated adults. A new generation of parents are not obliged to let go of their youth just because they've had children – they feel it's possible to look 'cool' (or at the very least, stylish) even with a baby in tow. Hence, multi-terrain strollers with chunky rubber wheels and kids dressed in Gap. Or, depending on your wealth and the way you wish to express it, Armani.

'You might be shocked that parents spend a lot of money on their clothing, but what's the alternative? In the past, children were shoved into formless dress-like garments – whether they were a boy or a girl – while their parents were free to express their personalities as they wished. I'm not sure it was altogether a healthier state of affairs.'

'Children are the new accessory,' goes the theory. And even if designer toddler ranges cater to a fraction of the market, the new status of children has two advantages for brands: sales to parents right now, and future customers to win over. How else do you explain partnerships like that of high-end designer Diane Von Furstenberg with Gap Kids?

Bunetel is convinced that, just as brands send free clothing and accessories to influential celebrities, they also shower gifts on popular and influential children. Not convinced? Look at the influence of blogger Tavi Gevinson, born in April 1996, who began her blog Style Rookie at the age of 11 and was a special guest of the New York Fashion Week at 13. Meanwhile, young actresses make their glossy magazine debuts ever earlier: Hailee Steinfeld and Elle Fanning were appearing in ads for Miu Miu and Marc Jacobs while barely into their early teens, and were respectively 14 and 13 when invited to a dinner at Chanel's boutique in Los Angeles. Chloe Moretz broke into the big time at the age of 12 via the film *Kick-Ass* (2010) and rapidly began appearing in magazines as a fashion icon. Of course there have always been child stars, but never have they been so quickly sucked into the celebrity fashion marketing machine. It is no coincidence that, thanks in part to social networks, young girls quickly learn the vocabulary of fame and gossip.

A few commentators have cringed at the frank sexiness of some of the clothes on offer, with the word 'prostitots' being bandied around. 'I can't bear advertising on children,' British designer Rachel Riley, who makes smock dresses and other clothes that actually look like they're designed for kids, told Cathy Horyn of *The New York Times*. 'And why would a child need to have anything remotely sexy? To me, it's unethical.' ('That dress is so preschool', 25 April 2012.)

The subject certainly makes for indignant headlines that play to parental instincts. But does that mean magazines like *Milk* don't have the right to exist? Its editor-in-chief is well aware of the controversy. 'For me, it's a family magazine about the world of childhood,' says Bunetel. 'Parents and children have a right to express themselves through clothing and interior design. We keep things light and playful. Caring about the way your children look is one thing, but I don't believe in taking it too far.'

Maybe we shouldn't be so surprised. Fashion has always been obsessed by youth. It was only a matter of time before the brands turned their attention to the youngest consumers of all.

Style goes back to the future

21

Giving clothes a second life.

This is a secret, so don't go around telling everyone. You know that little tweed jacket you picked up the other day from a leading chain store? You could have bought an even cheaper but much higher quality one in a cramped shop on a side street near the Pompidou Centre in Paris. The only disadvantage is that you may not have been the first to wear it.

'I've had them all in here,' says Aldo, manager of the vintage-clothing emporium Vertiges, on Rue Saint Martin. 'Designers from H&M, Gap, Zara ... and bigger names still. Sometimes they tell me what they're after. Other times they come incognito, but I can tell what they're up to from the way they handle the clothes and take notes, and from what they buy.'

What they are looking for is the rare, ephemeral thing that Vertiges has in spades: inspiration. The narrow, musty, under-lit store, which makes no concessions to brand experiences or even rudimentary interior design (the general ambience is somewhere between cavern and attic) is a treasure-trove of second-hand finds. Aldo himself is a walking advertisement for the place. On the day I interview him, he is wearing an army-issue green parka with fur collar over a US university sweater and tartan trousers. Pointed shoes in patent leather complete the ensemble.

'The first piece of clothing I ever bought was second-hand,' says Aldo. 'In those days, mind you, I didn't have the choice. But it became a habit and after a while I didn't see the point of changing. This way, you get something that's original *and* cheap. Where's the problem?'

Students and nonconformists have been sifting through racks of old clothes for years. The terminology changes – in the hands of fashion editors, 'second-hand' became 'retro', which then became 'vintage' – but the pleasure of unearthing a treasure for a song remains the same. (Technically, I'm told, 'vintage' refers to pre-war clothing, although the term has come to mean garments made between the 1920s and the 1980s – anything before that is 'antique'.)

Long before they became acceptable fashion wear, second-hand clothes were simply the dress of the poor. In the 18th and 19th centuries, clothing markets like London's Petticoat Lane sold cast-off items to the needy. These were often bought for the fabric – considered far more precious than the garments themselves – which was reworked into 'new' clothes for husbands and children. 'Rag and bone men', those dealers in second-hand clothes and bric-a-brac who now seem like mythological figures, would travel from street to street scavenging for unwanted items. Jumble sales, car boot sales, charity shops and the vintage market did away with the need for such middle-men.

Today, used clothes that aren't resold in Europe and the United States often make it to developing countries in the form of donations. Others are sold in bulk to the 'flocking' industry and shredded to be turned into filler for insulation and furniture padding. Reclaimed wool can be mixed with new fibres to make low-cost fabrics. The UK's Textile Recycling Association, however, says that approximately 50 per cent are worn again. It adds that 'if everyone in the UK (60 million people) bought one reclaimed woollen garment each year, it would save an average of 1,686 million litres of water and 480 tonnes of chemical dyestuffs'. Vintage is not only stylish – it's good for the planet.

Aldo says, 'In Europe, the business first began to thrive between the wars. Rich Americans who'd been waiting out the Prohibition in Paris started going home, and a lot of them would sell half their clothes to reduce the weight of their luggage. Then, after the war, there was army surplus.'

In the 1950s, European teenagers wanted to get their hands on original US jeans. Over the years, this evolved into an obsession with retro Americana which, in Italy, would inspire a young man named Renzo Rosso to start a company called Diesel. Aldo says that the pop music and film industries, with their constant recycling of styles and frequent recourse to nostalgia, have always helped the second-hand market along. 'In the 1980s, everybody was after collectible American jeans, especially Levi's. Then the Japanese started making new jeans that looked second-hand, using advanced manu-facturing techniques. It was really excellent work – sometimes even I couldn't tell the difference.' But the innovation also killed off the second-hand jeans market. 'In any case, most of the American stuff gets sold straight to Japan now, either in bulk or on the web. We don't get a sniff at it. That isn't a problem, because the latest vintage trend is about old European designer clothing: while we used to go to the States to look for authentic American jeans, now they come here to look for original Chanel jackets.'

From thrift to vintage

Back in the days of Petticoat Lane, a wealthy person would never have dreamt of wearing second-hand clothing and, of course, wearing a new garment that *looked* as if it were old would have been the ultimate in foolishness. Until the late 20th century, fashions were passed down from rich to poor. Today, though, fashions can move in the opposite direction, with disaffected urban youth often sparking trends that are reinterpreted by designers and sold to wealthier, more privileged customers. This shift may partially explain the fascination with 'vintage', previously the domain of the imaginative underpaid.

The Brits have always had an edgy, eccentric, faintly grungy sense of style that makes them expert 'thrifters'. The concept is much newer in other parts of Europe, as Aldo confirms: 'Until recently, an Italian wouldn't have been seen dead in a piece of second-hand clothing. Even the French were snooty about it. But now they've all joined in the game.'

The popularity or otherwise of vintage clothing inevitably reflects the state of the economy. The years of recession that followed 9/11 made even the wealthiest consumers a little more cost-conscious. Sarah Gray Miller, who launched a magazine called *Budget Living* in 2002, said, 'There is something vaguely obscene – and not a little dumb – about spending hundreds of pounds on a designer handbag that everybody thinks is a fake from your local street market anyway. The word "luxury" has become so overused it has become completely meaningless. For the intelligent consumer it simply means overpriced and over-hyped. The new trend towards thrifty shopping is as much about being ahead of the curve as it is about saving money.' ('The drift to thrift', *The Observer*, 13 October 2002.)

What started out as an attempt to save pennies became a statement of intelligence and personal taste. At the vanguard of that change was Cameron Silver, founder of the Decades store in Los Angeles. Silver specializes in what might be termed 'designer vintage', for stars in search of unusual pieces to wear on the red carpet and film companies in search of authentic items. He started out as a cabaret singer, and it was during his tours that he began buying second-hand pieces. Pretty soon he had a wardrobe full of vintage items. When the touring life began to pall, he decided to open a store. This was discovered by Richard Buckley, editor of *Vogue Hommes International*, who spread the word. It was a fortuitous meeting, but it also showed that Silver had a keen eye. One of the most appealing aspects of vintage for fashion snobs is that not everyone has a talent for spotting decent pieces.

The Parisian equivalent of Decades is a vintage item in its own right. Every fashionista worth her salt has heard of vintage pioneer Didier Ludot, who founded the home of vintage haute couture in 1975 and has two stores in the elegant gardens of the Palais Royal. When Ludot talks 'vintage' he means it in the same way that wine lovers refer to a great year. He stocks immaculately preserved items from the golden age of haute couture – 50s Dior and Balenciaga, for example – alongside standout pieces from the likes of Gaultier and Viktor & Rolf.

A few doors down from Monsieur Ludot's original store is that of Gabrielle Geppert. Quite a character, our Gabrielle: a chatty German-born blonde who says she was 'anti-capitalist' in her youth and could never settle down to a career until she discovered a talent for 'giving clothes a second life'. With a superb eye for merchandizing and colour matching, Gabrielle focuses on vintage accessories from Dior, Chanel, Gucci and others.

When a slump deepened into a recession and further descended into a crisis in 2008, consumers began looking around once again for ways to look good on a budget. The new generation of 'fast fashion' stores were certainly a possibility, but vintage allows for greater individuality. Plus, the scrapbook culture of Tumblr and Pinterest, combined with the success of TV shows like *Mad Men* and *Downton Abbey* have given nostalgia a sheen of hipness. When one of the most popular iPhone apps is Instagram – whose filters give photos freshly snapped on your phone a retro look – you have to acknowledge that consumers are disenchanted with the present.

This time around, consumers are more alert to the subtleties of vintage, searching for specific eras and examining clothes for signs that they are truly period pieces and not just 'vintage' pieces from the early 2000s. In addition, the more organized and sophisticated approach to selling second-hand items by the likes of Asos Marketplace and eBay has made old-style thrifting – the rummage around charity stores and flea markets – seem hopelessly random. Digital culture has turned consumers into traders, too, buying and selling vintage online. Competition is pushing up prices, with the result that some vintage vendors feel the category is edging towards luxury.

'Successful rummages for vintage clothes seem to be few and far between these days. Charity shop rails are full of old St Michael, C&A and shoulder-padded sequinned pieces, all priced higher than non-clothing cast-offs,' writes Jo-ann Fortune, who runs the website vintagebrighton.com. She notes that Judy Berger, who has been running Judy's Affordable Vintage Fair since 2005, 'has recently noted a "surge" in buyers from the Far East and the Netherlands, where vintage is scarce, coming to Britain to buy in bulk. This, she predicts, will push prices up even further.' ('Is vintage clothing passé?', 27 January 2012, Guardian.co.uk.)

So who's going to profit from the new vintage boom? Online vintage boutique owner Lynnette Peck Bateman told Jo-ann Fortune: 'You need to know exactly who your customer is rather than selling random pieces from different eras at lots of different prices… My customers follow trends and want vintage that looks current and has an edge, so you won't see long white gloves from the 1920s or aprons from the 1950s that no one will wear.'

But the current hunger for all things retro in television and film is resurrecting smarter styles that would have seemed hopelessly stuffy a few years ago. Could it be that we are entering a new era of elegance? Is grace under pressure fashionable again? Perhaps the secret is simply to keep one eye on the TV.

22

Behind the seams

There's always a nagging worry that you might not be seeing the full picture.

The possibility that their factories in developing markets might be knocking out fakes on the side should be of minor concern to the fashion brands, in the light of a more serious problem. When I told a friend that I was going to write a book about fashion, he asked, 'So what's the angle – gorgeous models; or underpaid women in sweatshops?'

Although the labour issue has been discussed ad infinitum, it is one that no writer on fashion can afford to ignore. Those who have gone before me have done a good job; brands are so worried about the PR repercussions of the word 'sweatshop' that they now have extensive 'codes of conduct', designed to reassure their customers that they are closely monitoring the situation.

The reality is far from edifying. Back in 2004, a report from Oxfam called 'Play Fair at the Olympics' stated that, 'if labour exploitation were an Olympic Sport, the sportswear giants would be well represented among the medal winners. Whilst the industry can boast its commitment to some impressive principles, enshrined in codes of conduct, its business practices generate the market pressures that are in reality leading to exploitative labour conditions.' The full report can still be seen on Oxfam's site, **http://www.oxfam.org/en/policy/olymp-report**.

Eight years on, in London's Olympic year, one might have hoped that matters would have improved. Not a bit of it, according to a 2012 report from the International Garment and Leather Workers' Federation (ITGWLF). Adidas, Converse, Dunlop, Slazenger, Speedo, Nike, Puma and Reebok were just some of the brands sourcing from the 83 factories in Sri Lanka, Indonesia and the Philippines covered by the organization's research. Others included Banana Republic, DKNY, Marks & Spencer, Ralph Lauren and Tommy Hilfiger.

The report's conclusion was damning: 'Workers in the sportswear and leisure industries work long hours, under huge pressure, to meet production targets. Yet it is often impossible for these workers to provide even the basics for themselves and their families... The widespread use of forced and non-remunerated overtime points to a failure by brands to ensure that the volume and the price of goods agreed by their supplier can be delivered within legal boundaries.'

As with the counterfeiting problem, the labour controversy has been caused by the brands' own marketing strategies. The voracious, constantly changing nature of fashion means that it does not lend itself to heavy mechanization, because the costs involved in updating the machinery would be untenable. What fashion boils down to, then, is lines of women at sewing machines: lots of them. 'Collectively the 83 factories employed over 100,000 workers, the majority of whom were females under the age of 35.'

The report also clearly states that 'not one of the 83 factories covered by our research paid a living wage to workers. In fact many of the factories employed workers on less than the legal minimum wage'. In addition, workers were often lured with promises of a permanent position when a large order came in, then fired after a three-month probationary period, during which they would not have been paid minimum wage.

In one factory in the Philippines, workers were forced to pay a monthly levy to management if they wanted access to drinking water. An incident in Indonesia involved 40 workers who had failed to reach production targets being locked in an unventilated room without access to toilet facilities, water and food for over three hours.

These stories can be dismissed as anecdotal, but they have a ring of truth. At the head of the supply chain are a handful of global, marketing-led fashion brands under pressure from their shareholders to increase sales. The brands have in turn educated consumers to expect a fast turnaround of high-fashion, low-priced garments. With fashion cycles shortening and the demand for new items rising, the brands put pressure on their suppliers to deliver to increasingly tight deadlines. The exigencies of the clients are pushed back down the chain to the workers.

The falling cost of sea and air transport has made it practical for retail brands to delocalize production to Asia. In turn, Asian governments have lured foreign investors with promises of tax exemptions, investment allowances and union-free workforces. Advances such as the internet and barcode-driven stock control have drastically improved communications and efficiency. As the Oxfam report explained, 'When consumer purchases are tracked by barcodes, retailers can automatically re-order just enough products, just in time for restocking their shelves... With this just-in-time response comes the pressure on producers to deliver smaller orders, in less time, and according to tightly planned shipping schedules – or face fines for delays.'

Oxfam added that, in their quest for the cheapest and most efficient suppliers, and their desire for flexibility, brands tended to keep contracts short. Thus there was no sense of partnership or evidence of commitment. This encouraged factory bosses to cut corners by insisting on unrealistic overtime, or by subcontracting work to other, less reputable suppliers.

Even with the best will in the world, codes of conduct are tough to enforce. Suppliers, in their desperation to win and keep contracts frequently conceal the true nature of their operations from visiting inspectors. Bosses bribe workers to lie about conditions, keep double payrolls, falsify timesheets and generally carry out a superficial clean-up of their factories before visits.

Finding and monitoring 'clean' factories in Asia for Western firms is becoming a métier in itself. A source at Zara told me, 'Suppliers are monitored very closely, with regular inspections to ensure that they conform to our standards. But there's always a nagging worry that you might not be seeing the full picture.' Zara produces half of its clothes at its own Spanish factories, but it sources basic items from external suppliers. It hires auditors to ensure that its factories comply with its code of conduct. They visit each factory and its facilities, closely question managers, and hold private interviews with employees. If breaches are detected, contracts are suspended.

H&M also employs a 'sustainability team' of more than 80 people who monitor suppliers' compliance with its code of conduct. Among other things, they ensure that supplier factories do not use child labour and pay 'at least the relevant minimum wages'. H&M drew up its code in 1997, basing it on the UN Convention on the Rights of the Child, as well as on International Labour Organization (ILO) conventions. The brand's website describes 'under age' as up to 15 years old, 'or the lawful age for working in the country in question (but not lower than 14 years)' (about.hm.com).

Most Western fashion and sportswear companies are not apparel manufacturers, but apparel marketers. Behind the familiar brand names are lesser-known supply-chain management companies such as Li & Fung (Hong Kong) and Makalot Industrial Co Ltd (Taiwan), which coordinate the production of garments and footwear for their more famous clients. In order to arrive at the cheapest solution, these companies often dissect the manufacturing process, so that one item may pass through a number of different factories, and even several countries. To quote Oxfam, 'The company may, for example, source fibre from Korea, dye and weave it in Taiwan, buy zips from China, and send it all to Thailand for assembly.'

Today, if you're wearing a global brand, it may be just that.

Ateliers versus factories

Bernard Arnault of LVMH has a low opinion of mass production; or, at least, of fashion brands that use mass production techniques but take on 'designer' airs. At the *International Herald Tribune*'s conference in Hong Kong, he said, 'We can see several companies trying to mix an image of luxury with a mass-market approach. In order to be able to sell a product at a relatively high price, you have to offer the craftsmanship and quality that goes along with it. There's an increase in products that have approximately the same look [as luxury brands] while providing a much lower standard. It's not counterfeiting, but it is misleading.'

Louis Vuitton occasionally invites journalists to its historic 'ateliers' in Asnières, just outside Paris, where special-order goods are handmade by artisans. But this is hardly the whole story. In 2010, the Advertising Standards Authority in the UK banned as misleading a series of print ads showing workers lovingly handcrafting bags, shoes and wallets. The brand argued that the campaign paid 'homage to the craftsmanship carried out every day by Louis Vuitton artisans' – yet it was forced to admit that sewing machines were used for some aspects of the items.

Louis Vuitton has also been known to speed up its production techniques to serve increased customer demand. Vuitton's marketing strategy, as we know, has been to introduce the shorter cycles of fashion into the previously static and timeless luxury sector. 'A year ago, it took 20 to 30 craftsmen to put together each Louis Vuitton "Reade" tote bag. Over the course of about eight days, separate workers would sew together leather panels, glue in linings and attach handles. Then... the venerable French luxury-goods house discovered efficiency. Today, clusters of six to 12 workers, each of them performing several tasks, can assemble the $680 shiny, LV-logo bags in a single day. The factory-floor changes are part of a sweeping effort by Louis Vuitton to serve customers better by keeping its boutiques fully stocked with popular merchandise – to operate, in other words, more like a successful modern retailer.' ('Louis Vuitton tries modern methods on factory lines', 9 October 2006, *The Wall Street Journal*.)

Until 1977, the atelier in Asnières was the only one the brand possessed. Now it has 12 sites in France, two in Spain for smaller leather goods, one in Italy for shoes and another in Switzerland for watches. Inside the French factories, the monogrammed canvas is cut by laser. Patrick Vuitton, who represents the fifth generation of the family and heads the special-orders division of the Asnières atelier, told French newspaper *Les Echos*: 'Machines have replaced the repetitive gestures. But 60 to 70 per cent of the work remains manual... You know, hand crafting is not the best guarantee of quality, as humans are fallible.' ('LVMH veut des magasins encore plus luxueux', 7 February 2011.)

Hermès has also suffered from over-demand for its products by luxury-hungry consumers. With sales surpassing €2.8 billion in 2011 – an 18 per cent increase on the previous year – it admitted to *L'Express* magazine that stocks in its stores were dangerously low. Naturally, CEO Patrick Thomas protested that 'the quality of the object' was more important than the size of the company, while at the same time confirming that production would 'increase considerably' with two new sites in France, each employing between 200 and 300 people. A sensible move considering that the brand was about to open three more stores in China. Hermès has around 40 sites in France and Switzerland. ('Hermès vers de nouveau sommets en 2012', 9 February 2012.)

Hermès loves to give the impression that all its products are painstakingly made by craftsmen in dusty ateliers. But when you can build three stores in China at the drop of a hat – to add to your existing network of more than 300 stores around the world – you begin to look a little like a chain store retailer with pretensions.

If Vuitton and Hermès are to be believed, they are among the few globally renowned brands providing desirable objects without exploiting underpaid workers. But they pass on this 'craftsmanship' to their customers in the form of high prices. Does this mean that political correctness is the preserve of the wealthy, and the rest of us have to swallow our pride in order to clothe ourselves?

Ethical fashion

Edun, Misericordia, People Tree, Veja: brands that promise ethical working conditions, fair trade or the use of organic materials are becoming more prevalent, nibbling at the market share of retail giants whose clothes are made by workers in developing markets. And the self-proclaimed capital of fashion has also become the location for the world's largest event devoted entirely to eco and fair trade clothing. The number of exhibitors at the Ethical Fashion Show in Paris every October has grown from 24 designers in 2004 to well over 100 today, showing at separate spring–summer and autumn–winter events.

The show was created by designer Isabelle Quéhé, who was inspired by a movie shot in Niger by her cameraman husband. '[It] featured a catwalk show by an African designer. I thought, well, Paris is supposed to be the capital de la mode, but we don't support anything like this, and we should.' ('Chic without the suffering: fashion displays its ethical face', *The Guardian*, 12 October 2007.)

In a press release to support the 2011 edition, the event's organizers pointed out: 'The fashion industry... is a huge market and an economic power generating wealth and employment... the textile sector is the second market of consumption after the food industry with 3 billion dollars of sales turnover and 26.5 million people working on all the textile chain of supply. But fashion is also one of the most polluting industries.'

The cotton needed to make just one shirt slurps up 2,500 litres of the world's most precious substance – water (waterfootprint.org). The Aral Sea – once the fourth largest lake in the world – shrunk to one fifth of its volume in a couple of decades as its two main tributaries were diverted to irrigate the cotton fields of Uzbekistan. Now, former fishing villages find themselves living on the edge of a dustbowl, strafed by regular sandstorms laced with chemical pollutants.

But consumer awareness is growing fast; and mainstream names are popularizing ethical fashion. Pop singer Bono was ahead of the curve when he started Edun with his wife Ali Hewson and the designer Rogan Gregory in 2005. The fair trade clothes are made in locally-run factories in Africa, South America and India. A year later, Gap and Armani had signed up for Bono's Project Red collaboration, which encouraged brands to donate a percentage of their profits to helping women and children affected by HIV/AIDS in Africa.

Other leading fashion brands have added an ethical twist to their acts. Diesel pledged to cut down on the chemicals it uses to wash its jeans; and embarked on a company-wide drive to encourage its staff to save energy. Levi's added 100 per cent organic cotton jeans to its product line. The jeans had coconut shell buttons and their indigo finish was created by potato starch, mimosa flowers and Marseille soap. They were created in a separate section of the Levi's factory in Hungary, on machinery that complied with environmental regulations.

H&M is the latest to get in on the act. In April 2012 it launched the Conscious Collection, with pieces made from 'eco-fibres' including organic cotton, recycled plastic and a plant cellulose derivative called Tencel. Apparently with a straight face, the brand's head of sustainability, Helena Helmersson, told writer Lucy Siegle (author of the excellent *To Die For: Is fashion wearing out the world?*): 'My dream is to be perceived as a company who can offer all people in the world – even those without much money – the possibility to dress really well and sustainably. That's how I want people to perceive us, not as a brand connected to mass consumption.' ('Is H&M the new home of ethical fashion?' *The Guardian*, 7 April 2012.)

But it's almost impossible to be mass and sustainable too. Retailers are addicted to growth and under pressure to post bigger sales figures every year. Where does this growth come from if not more clothing, more bags, more sports shoes? The other sticking point is the foggy interpretation by brands of the terms 'ethical', 'eco' and 'sustainable' fashion. As there's no strict definition – and no global code controlling their use – they are essentially meaningless.

The best way to consume fashion ethically is simply to buy less of it.

Conclusion

> *The best marketing in the world comes down to a person standing in front of a mirror.*

The words 'fashion' and 'marketing' are virtually interchangeable. Yet a fashion brand cannot expect to thrive on marketing alone. Consumers, happily, just aren't that dumb. Jean-Jacques Picart, the Parisian fashion consultant, told me, 'Over the years I've advised many brands, and if there is one thing that I am absolutely sure of, it's that you can't lie. You can bluff, you can rearrange the truth, but you can't cheat. Marketing can persuade a customer to push open the door of a shop, but if the clothes they find inside it are ugly, they will leave. Today, a product at any level must achieve the correct balance between price, quality, creativity and wearability. If one of these factors is below par, the customer will not be fooled. The best marketing in the world comes down to a person standing in front of a mirror.'

Marketers often talk about the need to 'educate' consumers. The word they are actually searching for is 'persuade' – or, perhaps, 'convince' – but the process of education sounds less intrusive. None the less, consumers are educated. In interview after interview, advertising executives have told me that consumers are highly sophisticated; that they can decode marketing so swiftly and effectively that if the message is not presented in a subtle and elegant manner, it actually damages the brand. Fashion consumers, I would argue, are the most sophisticated of the lot. Fashion already relies on a complex array of barely perceptible signs and symbols – the width of a lapel, the height of a boot – so the imagery behind it cannot afford to be primitive. Today's best fashion advertising barely resembles advertising at all. The most effective marketing campaigns are carried out under the radar, their targets unaware of the ruse until it is too late – or so appreciative of its shrewdness that they agree to accept the come-on.

Consumers have become wise, and they've become demanding. If fashion was ever a great swindle – with clothes sold for four times their value just because of a label – that is less and less the case. Every shopper has become a fashion professional. They are beginning to resemble those who work in the industry. Throughout my interviews with the people who package fashion, one thing struck me: none of them were particularly fashionable. They were often stylish, but there was never the slightest hint of the victim about them. They wore discreetly elegant clothes, or T-shirts and jeans. They understood the system so perfectly that they refused to get caught up in it. Increasingly, their target market thinks the same way. The designer Alber Elbaz says, 'I think the expression of a free and democratic beauty will progressively supplant the hegemony of trends.'

I wouldn't have the temerity to claim they are definitive, but below are four developments which, I believe, are having an impact on fashion brands.

Searching for a soul

Over many years of writing about brands, I've come to the conclusion that the only ones that generate fanatical loyalty have something I can only describe as 'a soul'. Sometimes it comes from the vision and conviction of the brand's founder; other times from the loyalty and commitment of its staff; more rarely from the skill and discernment applied to the product. All three would be ideal. In any case, I believe that consumers are becoming increasingly disillusioned with brands that have no soul: low-quality, over-priced labels that are designed to make money fast and which derive their image purely from glossy advertising and a tentacular digital presence.

Despite, or more likely because of, the importance of the internet in their lives, many of today's consumers are looking for smaller, humbler brands with genuine human faces behind them.

Honesty as a policy

This trend is, of course, linked to the one above. It's expressed in a number of different ways: 'authenticity', 'positive provenance', 'brand transparency'. But it all adds up to being straight with consumers. Not cutting corners on production. Stating on the label exactly where a garment is made. Offering genuine value for money. Replacing slogans with sincerity.

I'll cheat a bit here and recycle a few sentences from one of my own articles, a piece I wrote for the UK website Stylus.com in 2011. In it I quoted

Lee Clow, the global chief creative officer of the advertising agency TBWA, which counts Adidas among its clients. He said: 'The internet has exaggerated the speed at which an insincere brand is unmasked. There is an online community that takes a recreational delight in auditing brands... If a brand's behaviour does not reflect the culture it communicates through its marketing, it will quickly be called out by consumers.'

Clow recalled growing up surfing in California. 'I was obsessed by a brand called Jacobs, which made my boards. When there were no waves I'd spend the day hanging out at the Jacobs surf shop talking to the shapers. They were totally passionate about what they did.' That, says Clow, is brand authenticity: telling the consumer what you are because it happens to be true.

In the same piece, I turned to Bill Taylor, co-founder and founding editor of *Fast Company* magazine, who spoke about the dangers of a disconnect between a company's external image and its true culture. 'It's no use behaving one way in the marketplace and another way inside the organization. In that context, hiring, training and the way you treat your employees becomes vitally important.' A well-paid, committed and motivated staff member is a cheerful and helpful one. Taylor pointed out that the online footwear retailer Zappos.com offers its new hires US$3,000 to quit at the end of the training period if they have any doubts about working for the company. Only the truly committed remain.

Peter Walshe, global brand director at Millward Brown, noted that simple online tools like price comparison were forcing brands to become more transparent. 'These days, consumers know not only the price of everything, but the value of it too.'

Brands often try to convince consumers of their humanity by aligning with charitable causes. After the 2011 earthquake and tsunami in Japan, many companies publicized the fact that they were making donations. Louis Vuitton was actually criticized for not contributing. The problem was – it had. 'We just chose not to shout about it,' said an insider. 'It's one of those situations where you're damned if you do and damned if you don't.' In other words, companies suspected of opportunistically handing out charity cash face accusations of what might be termed 'kindwashing'. Lee Clow commented, 'It's ok for Nike and Adidas to support grassroots youth sports, because that's part of their established brand behaviour. But if you jump on the latest earthquake or tornado, it feels more like politics.'

One thing is certain: marketing is no longer 360°, but 365 days a year, 24 hours a day. No wonder companies are hiring social media experts to monitor their digital reputations, as well as contributing to the buzz with their own Twitter feeds and Facebook fan pages. But engaging in a 'dialogue' with consumers won't help if your company fails to deliver on integrity, service and value for money.

The cachet of culture

Fashion is not art – it's business. While clothes and accessories sometimes have artistic merit, most of the time they are not destined to become museum exhibits or to be displayed on white walls. They are created to be sold, to be worn, to spend a great deal of their lifespan in dark wardrobes and eventually to be thrown out.

This reality has never prevented fashion brands from adopting a sheen of culture by linking with the art world. Schiaparelli was inspired by the Surrealists back in the 1920s. Far more recently, Louis Vuitton has collaborated with a number of artists, including Stephen Sprouse and Takashi Murakami, on lines of bags. Dior embarked on a similar partnership with German artist Anselm Reyle. For a long period, Maison Martin Margiela behaved more like a contemporary art laboratory than a fashion brand. Brands from Diesel and Levi's to Polo Ralph Lauren have given over chunks of their stores to art exhibitions or created programmes supporting young artists.

The long love affair between fashion brands and culture will not only continue, but grow in intensity, partly thanks to social media. Social networking is less 'look at me' and more 'look at this'; sharing images, films and articles that have bobbed up amid the flood of information that washes over us each day. It's a form of advertising, helpfully carried out by consumers. Brands are aware of this, but they're also aware that they need to create things worth sharing. Some consumers may share pictures of bags and T-shirts, but a subject with more depth – more 'soul' – has a greater chance of attracting attention. Fashion is oddly naked when stripped of its pretensions. It needs additional content to give it legitimacy. We're familiar with the idea of 'branded content': entertainment created by brands. Partnerships with leading figures from the worlds of art and culture will enable fashion brands to enrich that content. Consumers will judge brands not only by the products they make, but by their cultural output.

What could be more creative than content conceived by a genuine artist? Or to put it another way: what's not to 'like'?

'We are all individuals'

In earlier editions of this book I wrote of 'the consumer as stylist'; in other words, the ability to put together a look from a wide range of brands at different levels of the market, without smothering yourself in logo-heavy clothing from a single source. I was thinking of the kind of person who might throw a vintage Chanel jacket together with an H&M T-shirt and Acne jeans. Small 'curated' stores seemed to me to be another expression of the trend.

When I wrote all that, however, there was no Facebook – or at least, not one that was on the radar of the mainstream consumer. Social networks have turned the world upside down: consumers are now brands, constantly honing and tampering with their image to present an idealized version of themselves to their digital audience. This tendency began with 'street style' bloggers, who went out in search of eccentric or individualistic dressers and ended up taking pictures of each other. Social networks exaggerated the situation. Now, we're all dying to present ourselves as charismatic, creative, different. Dressing like everyone else is hardly the best way of doing that.

The 'fast fashion' brands like Zara, H&M and Uniqlo have shown us that we don't need to spend a fortune in order to look good. Fashion is a medium and style is a skill – an ability to put together an outfit in a way that expresses our unique personality. It's a surprisingly democratic movement; but our search for the alternative has made us far less loyal to mainstream brands.

So there you go – as I said, it is not a definitive list. A few of the predictions may be wide of the mark, but as I shamelessly plundered them from some of the leading names in the fashion business, I'm expecting a reasonable degree of accuracy. The main problem, of course, is that this is a book about fashion.

Tomorrow, everything will have changed.

REFERENCES

Books

Agins, Teri (1999) *The End of Fashion*, HarperCollins, New York

Barthes, Roland (2001) *La Bleu Est à la Mode Cette Année*, Institut Français de la Mode, Paris

Baudot, François (1999) *Mode du Siècle*, Assouline, Paris

Erner, Guillaume (2004) *Victimes de la Mode?*, La Découverte, Paris

Frankel, Susannah (2001) *Visionaries*, V&A Publications, London

Gross, Michael (1995) *Model: The ugly business of beautiful women*, Harper Paperbacks, New York

Lannelongue, Marie-Pierre (2004) *La Mode Racontée à Ceux Qui La Portent*, Hachette Littératures, Paris

Morand, Paul (1996) *L'Allure de Chanel*, Hermann, Paris

Siegle, Lucy (2011) *To Die For: Is fashion wearing out the world?*, Fourth Estate, London

Vanderbilt, Tom (1998) *The Sneaker Book*, The New Press, New York

Various, *Repères Mode 2003*, Institut Français de la Mode, Paris

Various (2003) *Cool Brand Leaders*, Superbrands, London

Zola, Emile (1883) *Au Bonheur des Dames*, Folio Classique, Paris

Online resources

Adbrands.net (www.adbrands.net)

Brand Keys (www.brandkeys.com)

Charles Frederick Worth Organization (www.charlesfrederickworth.org)

Dr Martens (www.drmartens.com)

Ermenegildo Zegna (www.zegna.com)

Exposure (www.exposure.net)

Fédération Française de la Couture, du Prêt-à-Porter des Couturiers et des Créateurs de Mode (www.modeaparis.com)

Gucci Group (www.guccigroup.com)

Harvey Nichols Ltd (www.harveynichols.com)

Hint Fashion Magazine (www.hintmag.com)

Nelly Rodi (www.nellyrodi.fr)

Nike (www.nikebiz.com)

The Photographers' Gallery (www.photonet.org)
SHOWstudio (www.showstudio.com)
Slate Magazine (www.slate.com)
Style-Vision (www.style-vision.com)
Victoria & Albert Museum (www.vam.ac.uk)
Vogue (www.vogue.co.uk)
Worth Global Style Network (WGSN.com)

INDEX